Faith, Politics, *and* Belonging

Faith, Politics, *and* Belonging

A Reflection on Identity, Complexity,
Simplicity, and Obsession

IAN GEARY

Foreword by Michael Wear

Afterword by Jon Cruddas

RESOURCE *Publications* · Eugene, Oregon

FAITH, POLITICS, AND BELONGING
A Reflection on Identity, Complexity, Simplicity, and Obsession

Resource Publications
An Imprint of Wipf and Stock Publishers
199 W. 8th Ave., Suite 3
Eugene, OR 97401

www.wipfandstock.com

PAPERBACK ISBN: 978-1-6667-7797-0
HARDCOVER ISBN: 978-1-6667-7798-7
EBOOK ISBN: 978-1-6667-7799-4

07/17/24

'Jeremiah 29 a biblical framework for place', Mary Glen, Fuller Studio, 9 June 2020.

'Welcome to the post-Liberal majority', David Goodhart and Tobias Buck, *The Financial Times*, 11th May 2012.

Crucible (January-March 2014), ‹*Blue Labour and Post-Liberalism—a Lay Christian Perspective.*' Ian Geary, Hymns Ancient and Modern, 2014.

This essay collection is dedicated to the loving memory of:

John S. Geary, 1935–2016:
thanks Dad for always encouraging me and always believing in me.

Rt Hon Bruce T. George, 1942–2020 :
thanks Bruce for giving me the privileged first chance to work and
serve in Labour politics, and for being generous and giving me many
chances thereafter.

"Thus saith the Lord, Stand ye in the ways, and see, and ask for the old paths, where is the good way, and walk therein, and ye shall find rest for your souls."

—Jer 6:16

"Resident aliens are resident where they are alien. It is not a question of whether we engage in common life but how."

—James K. A. Smith

Contents

Section One | Faith

Section Two | Politics

Section Three | Belonging

Foreword

The public does not seem to think highly of politics these days, and when it comes to public issues, many seek to avoid thinking about Christianity at all.

There is good reason for this. Our politics has become a forum for self-aggrandizement. Christianity is all too often leveraged for reactionary purposes, to reject and condemn. These are cynical times.

Thankfully, Ian Geary is no cynic.

Here, you'll find political vision honest enough to express doubt, and political commitment clear-eyed enough to hold tension. Geary leaves behind the tribal fandom of his football team and advances a view of politics, but not as an arena in that we must pick a team and then work up certainty about the rightness of that team—no matter what it does.

Instead, Geary finds his political interest and involvement rooted in his Christian faith and oriented toward the common good. Geary's politics is occupied with the well-being of persons, particularly as they find themselves in relationship with one another. He understands how dehumanizing so many of the structures of modern life can be and understands that our social relations and our sense of identity are influenced by political decisions. He recognizes the challenges of "secular capitalism, environmental degradation and family breakdown," and calls for a "long-term, transformational approach to public life" that "foster(s) institutional life," "allow(s) individuals to flourish and character to form," "honor(s) liberty but eschew(s) extreme liberalism and moral relativism," and "pursue(s) the common good in the family, locality, workplace and society."

As powerfully as Geary can convey his political convictions, what is perhaps most contributive is his model of *how* to carry those convictions. I find that many Christians want to stay away from politics, because they see that so many who claim God has called them to politics seem to find their way to making politics their God. It seems safer, then, to stay away from politics altogether, or to consider politics outside of—and separate from—faith.

In these pages, you will be introduced to a different kind of approach to faith and politics. It is precisely when Geary turns to making his most compelling arguments for his politics, that he acknowledges the imperfections and tensions of politics. So, it is just as Geary is making his case for Blue Labour that he writes this:

> "'I am trying not to impose my opinion but be unguarded and open about the tensions a Christian involved in politics might have to negotiate and also to underline the sense of disappointment and failure that can characterize this path."

He further reflects:

> "As I alluded to earlier, my faith is primary and has an allegiance to the Kingdom of God yet finds an expression politically. Do I get this right all the time? No. Indeed, I find that in these challenging times of flux, the challenge of applying my faith to a certain political position becomes ever more complex."

Geary then proceeds to describe exactly how he would apply his faith to a certain political position. This book is full of a radical earnestness and openness which we desperately need today.

I know we need it in America. We need a Christianity that is not reducible to the short-term interests of a political party or candidate. We need a Christianity that shows itself to be bigger than our politics, not a Christianity that can fit comfortably inside of it. We need hope—real hope. As Geary writes:

> The kind of hope we are talking about leads to involvement in the real stuff of people's lives, bringing love and God's presence to the broken. Engagement in politics can be an expression of this Kingdom activity. Yet, it is only a small part of it and of course is not the domain of one political party or movement. Seeking the common good and connecting with the real issues of people's lives should be what we are about.'

This is what life is about. This is what our politics can be about. Allow Ian Geary to tell you his story of following Jesus into politics. Perhaps this will be the start of your own journey of faith in pursuit of the common good.

Michael Wear is the Founder, President and CEO of the *Center for Christianity and Public Life* (www.ccpubliclife.org). He is the author of *The Spirit of Our Politics: Spiritual Formation and the Renovation of Public Life*, published by Zondervan Books.

Preface

This essay collection has been compiled alongside hope and prayers that its insights and offerings are of service to the Church and also to those Christians who seek to live humbly and faithfully, in a complex and divided world. Furthermore, it is hoped that this collection can contribute to a debate that sees Christians engaged in the public square for justice and righteousness, bearing witness to God's kingdom and, moreover, that this can animate all Christians engaged in politics.

As I write today, it saddens me to witness a culture war in US politics and to some degree in the UK, and across Europe, electorates are faced with an unappealing choice. It is a choice between right-wing populism and now so-called 'Christian Nationalism' on one hand and an out of touch, technocratic, progressive social liberalism on the other. Increasingly it feels like no choice at all. Christians are feeling increasingly 'homeless'[1] in political terms. However, I would submit that these problems are at root are anthropological in nature and Christianity has something to say about them. I finalize this section on Easter Sunday, reminder if one was needed that resurrection is real: there is hope.

It is acknowledged that this essay collection cannot heal those afore-mentioned divisions. Neither can it resolve my own contradictions, nor even begin a vital renewal and revival in all its senses that might offer hope.

As someone who can start an argument in an empty room, I smile to myself for seeing the need for peace, justice and reconciliation in the political realm. We really do need to 'disagree well' and we need to see the good and importance of politics for the sake of the common good. We need

1. A point that has been made by Michael Wear.

a better politics, one that is informed by Biblical insights and not division nor self-interest (or hopes) of a utopia on Earth that is wedded to bland managerialism.

My home politically is the center-left: the UK's Labour Party; the trade unions; Christian Socialism; and latterly the crucial conversation of Blue Labour and postliberalism—both much contested and misunderstood terms. Yet I wish for them to remain my home and to be truly plural—in breadth and depth. This calls for a humble and robust debate and engagement from Christians and people of good faith and a politics that is genuinely plural.

I am grateful to Wipf and Stock for giving me the opportunity to contribute to this conversation and hope and—yes—pray, that it helps others to navigate this important journey.

IAN GEARY
Athens, Greece
March 2024
Jesus Domibus Caesar non est.

Acknowledgments

This essay collection has been written with the help of many people; like any good project. Being in Greece and not the UK for this season means I do not have the opportunity of bumping into friends and sojourners to ask advice or chase them regarding one of my many demanding emails. Thanks to everyone for your generosity and patience.

I am grateful to Matthew Wimer and colleagues at Wipf and Stock for considering the book in the first place and for his patience and advice and thankful to Emily Callihan for advice conveyed promptly in response to my many questions. I thank Professor Luke Bretherton who advised me to try Wipf and Stock and this speculative approach has paid off; further thanks are to be recorded to Rev Matt Bullimore, Danny Aanderud, Michael Wear, Lord Glasman, Jon Cruddas MP, Professor Tom Greggs, Dr Dave Landrum, Andy Flannagan, Mary Glenn, Elizabeth Jewkes, Russ Rook, Andrew Bradstock, Sunder Katwala, Lieutenant-Colonel Dean Pallant, The Salvation Army, Stephen Spencer, Director of The Salvation Army International Heritage Centre. Phillip Blond and Mike Mavrommatis at Respublica, David Goodhart, Toby Buck, Daniel Johnson, Father Aristarchos-Vasileios Gkrekas, Rt Hon Liam Byrne. Professor Adrian Pabst, Rhea Pearson, Lachlan Poulter, Graham and Sheila Taylor, Dave Abney, Jenny Sinclair, Rachel Woodward, Dr John Lloyd, the prayer team; Martin Robinson, Richard Robinson, Louise Davies, Valerie Geary and Becca Henney and Minas Carayannis for driving my beautiful daughter back from 'Annie JR' and buying me precious time! Thanks also to Marietta for all the support she has given to 'our Sam'.

Amanda Geary Pate PhD for her excellent copywriting and Benjamin Kim for invaluable help at the start of the project.

Thanks to all those who contributed generously to make this project possible and thanks to Poppy, Kathy and Julian for helping me reach the target; and thanks also to all those attended the 'Labour and the Common Life' curry discussions at the Shapur, Strand, London on 23 May and 14 November 2018.

Thanks and much love, to my wonderful family: Susan, Joshua, Sammy, Martha and Bella.

Introduction

"Place is much more important in human experience and in the Christian scheme of things than is generally recognised."

—JOHN INGE

"Labour owes more to Methodism than to Marx, more to Moses than Momentum, more to the Apostle Paul than to Progress."

IAN GEARY, TAWNEY DIALOGUE, 2018

To the reader: I invite you on a journey through my attempt to find meaning in the world guided by my Christian faith and political convictions. The journey is still ongoing, you are invited to witness a formative section of the journey.

My name is Ian Geary, I became a Christian aged fourteen, and—perhaps unusually for a teenager—had developed a passionate interest in the politics of the Labour Party. Since then, my life and vocation has—in the main part—entailed working out how these convictions cohere and the endeavor of working through and accepting when they do not.

My aim is to articulate a type of Christian thinking i.e., a contextual theology that reflects a certain disposition. It is a story about my lived experience, of trying to be a faithful evangelical Christian in a complex and changing context—that being the center-left of UK politics. All of this in a world that has been changed in a disorientating manner pushing me to rely ever more on my faith and its related theological wisdom to make sense of things.

I realize that we look for certainty in an uncertain world and that can only be found in Christ. Politics and faith are becoming polarized and the search for certainty in things uncertain can lead people to all kinds of places. So, reflecting on lived experience and the Christian faith are anchors in these stormy seas. I believe that politics—though flawed—is of profound importance and can be a force for good. My conviction as a Christian is that my faith has important correspondence with the world of politics and cannot be shut out from the life of the world.

Furthermore, in a world of labels—political and religious to name a few—saying you are either liberal or conservative does not always fit neatly with most people's lived experience and contemporary priorities. This does not mean labels or signifiers are not important or helpful per se, but rather that they are necessary as they provide a reference point and keep us accountable while they can also be an unhelpful distraction. After all, the term *Christian* was coined by the people of Antioch as a noun bestowed on followers of the way by others.

In my Doctoral studies I am realising that the space I seek to mine is neither postliberal nor illiberal. I am seeking a place to stand, but also while finding a place to pray, work, live and engage and *serve* in this disorientating earthly *polis*.

This collection collates a number of essays that I have written over the past ten years or so. They concern faith and politics—particularly the politics of the common good and how this applies to Labour politics in the United Kingdom.

It was a project birthed during the global COVID-19 pandemic and has a strong theme of identity and place, hence the working title was originally *God, Politics, and West Bromwich Albion*—the latter being my soccer team for whom I am tribally passionate about. When I was a Masters' degree student at the University of Manchester, I remember sitting in the John Rylands Library café and a fellow student from my faculty commented on my simplistic passionate nature. He said to me: "You can sum up your life as God, politics, and West Bromwich Albion," not that he thought I was a deity but it was just I was passionate and obsessive about a few things and wore my heart on my sleeve. I am both simplistic and complicated, but as theologian John Milbank[2] once said: " . . . you have to think paradoxically." Thus, the schema of these essays is organized along the lines of the title, broadly—but not entirely neatly—reflecting on faith, politics, and identity.

2. Glasman, *In the rich man's world*, 2–3.

In admitting there are overlaps I would hope that for an illogical person like me, it contains at least *some* logic and the intersection infers we are all complex and our lives cannot be tidily compartmentalized.

I confess to becoming increasingly nervous about the initial title, especially since I have developed an amateur interest in the great theologian Karl Barth. Though far from agnostic about politics, Barth asserted that humanity is barely in touching distance of the Almighty. Indeed, I have realized via Stanley Hauerwas and—with respect to Barth—that there is an inherent danger in insisting on: "God *and* . . . ."[3]

As I reflect upon the time that has passed since I originally wrote these essays, I have observed how my views have become more nuanced. One should reflect on our own views held in life as objectively as possible, yet my essential dispositions have not changed. I would say that I am now less black-and-white in some opinions, but that is not an endorsement of relativism. In many ways after I re-read them, they represent the journey to the PhD in political theology I am currently undertaking at the University of Aberdeen.

My love of theology as a source of strength and reflection is still growing. As an undergraduate, I had little interest in theology. I loved church history and thought the theology on offer was liberal and I did not want to go near it, perhaps out of fear or more that I did not understand exactly how crucial theology is. Now, as an armchair theologian, I am in a different place. I am more appreciative of the necessity of theology and furthermore my love of theology has even surpassed my love of football and kebabs, but I digress.

Faith, Politics and Belonging is the title and over-arching thematic scheme of this essay collection. Each part unpacks one of these themes, yet exploring each of them in correspondence with other themes and subject matter. Faith should lead to engagement in the wider world and engagement in the wider world should inform our faith and cause us to lean on it for strength and inspiration.

The first part on *Faith*, includes articles I have written that are rooted in my Christian faith, ranging from reflections rooted in the Bible to biblical reflections on the lives of individuals such as Keir Hardie and Alfred Salter, as well as engagement with weighty other matters like euthanasia. When I reflected on my conversational piece *Why I am a Christian on the Left*, I realized that it touched on all the elements of faith, politics, and

---

3. Hauerwas, *Politics of the Church*, Lines 314–15.

identity that constitute this collection. I wrote it mainly to help me clarify my thoughts and the tensions and contradictions that I sought to navigate and thus it serves as a vignette for the broader collection.

Furthermore, and taking a devotional focus, I explore the relationship between prayer, retreats, and political activism. In an article written mainly to challenge my own tendency to be hyperactive, I conclude that prayerlessness and restlessness equal destruction. My own journey in the past fifteen years has led me to go on retreats and I have realized that I am by nature an introvert, and so I try and integrate this discipline into my life cycle. In this interest, I am grateful that my wife is very generous and understanding of this need. I wonder, what would political life and debate look like if prayer and monastic disciplines were more prominent?

I include my Tawney Dialogue contribution from 2018. This was a major privilege for me, a bit like being asked to play at the Hawthorns,[4] and of personal significance as social justice was the reason, I joined the Labour Party in the first place.

Although I have not arranged my essays in chronological order, as I looked again at *Politics: It's Just Stuff* I realized it is of some significance as it indicates something of where I believe my thoughts were heading. As I conclude the essay I write:

> "It may be that the church re-evaluates, over time, its engagement with politics. Not to abandon it but to affirm its value and recognise its limits in a more expansive sense of God's kingdom and perhaps to explore a different way of understanding politics. Politics though important, is not a be all and end all. Indeed, we need more confidence in the kingdom shaped political call of the church and its identity as a *polis*."

If I get the opportunity in the years ahead, this is a question I wish to give some further thought and prayer to.

In the second section, having proved or asserted that I do *do God*, I include some politically focused essays, naturally they are inclusive of faith but they have a distinctly political texture. In seeking to support a postliberal path for Labour Party politics, they correlate to my previous involvement in the Blue Labour movement. Although my involvement has lessened in recent years, I felt when *Blue Labour: Forging a New Politics*[5] was launched that—despite some flotsam and jetsam and a lot of

---

4. The home of the football team I support: West Bromwich Albion.

5. Geary and Pabst, *Blue Labour: a New Politics*.

misunderstanding—at the irreducible core of this narrative is something of beauty i.e., the common good.

Like many of the milestones on my journey Blue Labour has proved an indispensable conversation partner for Christian engagement on the center-left of UK politics. However, there does not appear to be in the near future a chance for this exiled tradition to flourish. Yet as a friend once said to me: " . . . doing the right thing, is the right thing to do." Politics should be about faithfulness to one's convictions rather than grasping at what appears to work for the moment. Pragmatism as a virtue is necessary in politics, yet as a foundation pragmatism leads to despair and the worst kind of compromises.

I have included my (as yet) unpublished essay *At Its Best*, which was withdrawn from *Blue Labour: Forging a New Politics* in order to create space for other contributors due to tight word limits for publication. In this piece I am basically arguing for pluralism in the Labour Party and ergo on the left. An objective you would think decent people would be interested in, even if only to have a broad appeal at a General Election. I was, and still am, skeptical how much breadth and—dare I say it—inclusion, those in the Labour Party really want. Thus, I argue that Labour was at its best when at its broadest.

In an article for *Crucible* (an Anglican Social Ethics periodical), I try and dig a little deeper into how Blue Labour can be an important conversation partner from a Christian perspective. I believe that Blue Labour and postliberalism are potentially of more than a passing interest to Christians. However, I would hesitate to describe them as an opportunity for the church, that smacks of looking at faith through the wrong end of the telescope. Moreover, in the continuum or tension between the churches prophetic social witness and the necessary pragmatism of political engagement it is a phenomenon to be taken seriously. In this contribution I explain why this is the case.[6]

I confess I am a bit of a stuck record at times, there are numerous mentions to Maurice Glasman and to Jon Cruddas, who in this period have been important voices in the Labour Party in my opinion. There are also many references to my favorite football club, West Bromwich Albion. I do however er reflect on a former leader of the Australian Labor Party and include a real email to an Australian Labor Party staffer so I qualify as an internationalist. Read carefully and you will even find a reference to socialism.

---

6. Geary, *Blue Labour and Postliberalism.*

I now reflect: has the Labour Party moved forward since my writing these articles? The failure to accept the European Union membership referendum verdict was a low point and Labour deservedly paid the price at the ballot box. Perhaps there is still hope, if Labour can rewrite its story rooted in meaning? I remain to some degree skeptical.

The bulk of these essays are on faith and politics, hence the earlier sections are more substantive and they intersect with each other—with a streak of *identity* and *place* popping up at points. In this polarized space, a generous and thoughtful examination of issues of identity are crucial for a peaceful and authentic politics of the common good.

In terms of my background, I refer to a speech I gave to the National Club, in London, in March 2016, when I shared the following:

> "Who am I? I am Ian Geary, forty-three years old, I live in southeast London with my wife and three children and worship at an evangelical/charismatic church in Bermondsey. I grew up in Walsall in the Black Country and become a Christian and Labour Party activist at the same time aged fourteen. Apart from my love for West Brom that is all you need to know about me. I have worked for two Labour MPs, a trade union, various lobbying companies and am on the Executive of *Christians on the Left*. Last year I co-edited an essay collection on the theme of Blue Labour—a stimulant on the center-left which advocates the primacy of relationships in politics, family, place the essential centrality of faith and also most importantly asserts the politics of the common good as essential to renewing our civic, political and social life."

In this aforementioned speech, I described myself by referring to family,[7] faith, vocational calling and place. These things are bound up in my narrative, my story. They are of significance to me, so I seek to unpack their meaning. This is why I seek to anchor my case in lived experience, yet lived experience needs to be evaluated in the light of other narratives.

These shorter essays on place and identity were originally gathered under the perhaps, partisan heading: *West Bromwich Albion*, as mentioned this is the soccer team I support and is based in the English Midlands town that my father, grandfather, and great grandfather, all came from. I acknowledge that in many of the essays a reference to West Bromwich Albion may pop up, this was not planned. However, I do feel more sanguine about football than when I was younger—I guess it is tied to my self-identity and

7. I never liked the 'Faith, family and flag' phrase but for some it was a helpful rhetorical device.

attachment to place and, in the context of these essays, it felt like an appropriate title and a metaphor. Nevertheless, the new heading for this part of the collection *Belonging* covers it well. Belonging is an important theme in an age of restlessness and uncertainty, if people do not find their belonging in the Christian faith it will be located elsewhere.

Moving on to the crux of the contributions, I would submit that to understand *identity* and *place* we need *faith*. In fact, I feel *faith* is crucial to reconciling the passions and fissures that contemporary identity politics has occasioned. Furthermore, *place* as a category is emerging within *faith* and it has clear political logic i.e., we vote for MPs for geographical constituencies and as an issue it is an important category in political considerations: planning being one area that springs to mind.

Thus, these essays cover an insight I gleaned at the Catherine Program, a Salvation Army training program I had the privilege of attending in Leiden, the Netherlands, in 2017. In my reflections from this course, I was most inspired by the lecture given by a Welsh Salvation Army Corps Officer, Steve Dutfield, who explained how his background in South Wales had shaped him. This essay is based on those reflections.

I also include my essay reflecting on my acceptance of the Brexit vote in 2016 and why it was important for Labour also to do so. The title *Whatever They Throw At Us, We Will Take*, I would like to think reflects the working class resilience, bitter-sweet in many ways, that has epitomized the character of many working class communities. In hoping to be faithful to a real-time comment I try and situate the essay in the deeper Christian hope, the prism through which all politics must be viewed.

In reviewing Michael Lind's *The New Class War*, I seek to engage with the contemporary impact of class through a biblical lens. I found this a challenge, yet it is a relevant matter, and it fits in with this section fittingly. Faith speaks to lived experience and lived experienced speaks to faith.

In my short reflection on the classic film *It's a Wonderful Life*, the only part where popular culture appears, apart from football, there is a serious ethical theme. If I may be so bold, there is a strong argument to infer this is a Blue Labour film. Frank Capra, the Catholic filmmaker affirmed in his biography who he made *It's a Wonderful Life* for:

> " . . . the downtrodden, the pushed around, the pauper, *Heads up, fella.* . . . A film that expressed its love for the homeless and the loveless; for her whose cross is heavy and him whose touch is

ashes; for the Magdalenes stoned by hypocrites and the afflicted Lazaruses with only dogs to lick their sores."[8]

It is a film that has a compelling story. It is the power of story and narrative that are key to Blue Labour and I would say it forges space where place, identity and other touchstone issues can be allowed full expression without becoming caricatured or being co-opted by toxic narratives. Thus in *Blue Labour—Stories of the Common Good*, I write:

> "Blue Labour offers a social and political narrative that speaks of the primacy of faith and family life: those anchors that give working people meaning and belonging, including also the value and dignity of good and meaningful work. It also honors a sense of place in undergirding the attachment ordinary people have to their local community. A disposition that has been degraded and tested in the modern world but still holds true for many people. It is these stories and traditions which constitute Blue Labour. Blue Labour allows these stories to be articulated and therefore offers a real opportunity for Labour to reconnect with ordinary people. Allowing those stories which secular modernity resists or disowns to be fully expressed implicitly recognizes the importance of the people who can articulate and identify with these stories."

Although I feel Blue Labour needs renewal and refocusing it still holds potential to make an important contribution to national political debate. Perhaps these essays can renew that debate and bring to postliberalism the corrective not to drift into illiberalism and pointless oppositionism?

Please let me know your thoughts. I hope they are of help to the common good, for the common life, and in some way to the glory of God. They are written in the hope that Christians engaged in politics will find them helpful, but I hope they reach a wider audience. I venture to say that politics—despite its critics—is a necessary and good thing. After each section I include questions for discussion and some suggestions for further reading to stimulate further reflection and I trust this is useful.

I offer these essays of my lived experience. My name is Ian Geary, this is my story: it is a story of faith, politics and belonging.

IAN GEARY
September 2023

---

8. Mattingly, *After 70 years*, Lines 36–39.

SECTION ONE

Faith

1

Faith, Elijah, and Obadiah

This essay is a reflection on the story of Elijah and Obadiah in 1 Kings 18 as a paradigm for why Christians should get involved in politics set in a broader context. It was written in the run-up to the 2015 General Election in the United Kingdom.

As the General Election approaches, many churches in the United Kingdom will rightly want to take seriously this important national political moment. Churches will pray for the election and the candidates. They might perhaps hold hustings debates to facilitate a serious discussion of the key issues. A key driver will be a sincere desire to *be salt and light* and an influence for good as the election proceeds.

The Church of England made a positive and welcome contribution to the debate, seeking a " . . . call for the new direction that we believe our political life ought to take." In a letter aptly entitled *Who is My Neighbour?*. the House of Bishops stressed that the key election issues highlighted the need for " . . . a fresh moral vision of the kind of country we want to be."[1] Given the challenges we face, we need more, not less, emphasis on a common good approach to political life.

---

1. House of Bishops, 3.

Of course, engagement and interest may vary, and Christians are not immune from the culture we live in and the attitudes that prevail. As the election draws near, we will be reminded (very swiftly I expect) that we are in the midst of a time of deep disenchantment with politics and politicians. The reasons for this are complex, and this perception will filter down to Christians. In response, the *Show Up* campaign, a positive Christian initiative, is attempting to highlight the positive need for Christian engagement in public life up to the election and beyond. Such endeavors are vitally important, particularly when there will be a lot of anti-political *noise*.

However, my specific concern is this: How do we uphold the good that is done in politics and not lose sight of the central purposes of God's kingdom and the significance of the place that the church occupies? How can we be political and not lose our prophetic edge?

In seeking to unpack this question, I find 1 Kgs 18 and the story of Elijah and Obadiah a helpful starting point. It reminds us of the need to remain faithful to the kingdom and also to be wisely and thoughtfully engaged in politics. This passage suggests a dynamic interaction between Obadiah who works within the *system*, and Elijah—who in his role as a prophet—challenges the *system* and powers. Both are valid, but not equally. I would submit that Elijah is the fulcrum of the story. We see the value of Obadiah's faithfulness, but it is Elijah who confronts Ahab and the pagan prophets.

Through the account of Elijah and Obadiah, we learn that good can be achieved within the political system, that revelation shapes prophetic action, and that the kingdom is the ultimate source of authority and is not subject to temporal powers.

In the passage in question, we see that Obadiah, who faithfully serves King Ahab, has achieved good while in that role. We are told that he protected one hundred prophets from death at the hands of Jezebel and in verses five and six he is sent to see if grass can be found to feed the animals as a famine was besetting Samaria. Crucially we see that he is an active believer, his faith is not nominal, he pleads with Elijah that he has: " . . . worshipped the Lord since my youth."[2] Thus, godly devotion and political service are not incompatible. Discipleship and spiritual formation make for good politics.

Obadiah underlines the fact that good can be achieved in politics, even though any earthly system of governance is flawed. Politics reflects

2. 1 Kgs 18:12.

4

God's rule, albeit in a limited and constrained manner. God by his grace is at work through the gospel message of his incarnated Son who came to redeem all things. God's plan is to "restore everything"[3], and that means he is interested in every human activity and institution. Therefore, politics cannot be immune from the reach of God's amazing love, indescribable grace, and the extension of his kingdom.

It must be possible to appreciate God's plan of ultimate redemption and respect where through political action and struggle justice and righteousness have prevailed. Political action in the United Kingdom has seen health care established, minimum standards in the labor market, the abolition of the transatlantic slave trade, and the foundation of the welfare state following years of destitution in parts of the country. Those who criticize politics in a blanket and cynical way should reflect on their lazy thinking when they overlook these important achievements. Prophetic engagement by the church should not inadvertently endorse this attitude (which feeds populist politics) and in some respect is generated by the parts of the press interested in sensation and excessive negativity. Many politicians in all parties enter the profession with some measure of good motives, however defined. Again, this does not mean that they are perfect, or indeed the system cannot be improved, but our assessment of politics must be clear and balanced. MPs and local councillors work long hours serving their community and constituents, helping people who have no voice and little resources. This is barely mentioned in the national discourse. There are many Obadiahs in the UK serving their local community through politics and achieving good. This might be limited and temporary, but it should be acknowledged.

Of course, the Obadiah analogy is not confined to politics. Good can be realized in all manners of public life and community work such as being a school governor, journalist, businessperson, classroom assistant, or road sweeper. My concern, experience, and reflection are focused on the political realm. If we can appreciate the virtue of pragmatism, then we can understand how Obadiah saved the lives of the prophets and how Wilberforce was single-minded in challenging the slave trade. Obadiah was a pragmatist, he had the ability to get things done.

What we don't know are the things that Obadiah *didn't do*, perhaps the things he did because he had to do but would rather not have wanted to, and things he did that might look dubious to our modern eyes. We don't know. All Christian politicians will need to know that there is a time

---

3. Acts 3:21.

to comply and a time to defy the established political order. This is not a straightforward matter. It calls for discernment and grace.

And now to Elijah. I would submit that if Obadiah signifies legitimate political service as a mission, then perhaps Elijah is representative of the kingdom of God. We see that from verse one it is the word of God, his prophetic revelation, that sets the scene for the activity: ". . .the word of the Lord came to Elijah. . ."[4] Could this be an encouragement and corrective to all of us? We need to seek God's guidance and word in all our activities. Without it, the scene is set by humanistic and secular assumptions and well-meaning liberalism dressed up as Christianity. We are not here to endorse the liberal social, political, and economic order. Engagement with the political culture should not mean we become assimilated to its presuppositions.

We see that Elijah carries God's authority, and Obadiah recognizes this. In verse seven, he bows down at the sight of Elijah and calls him: ". . .my lord. . ."[5] Elijah then instructs Obadiah to tell Ahab that he is here. Elijah is confident, aware of his mission, and unbeholden to the powers. This is why we must never conflate the important but temporary work of politics with the kingdom or see the kingdom and church as somehow marginal. Politics is important and can make a difference, but it is imperfect and imperfectible, limited, and hollow, and it cannot save, transform, or redeem. Of course, much of political discourse acts to mask and conceal this fact. Like Elijah, the church is to know its mission, to be clear of its role, and speak truth to power, and not baptize and sacralize earthly powers. There will be tension, and there should be. I heard the American preacher Louis Giglio preach in 2013[6] that the world thinks that the church is marginal to it when in reality, the world is marginal to the church. This may sound arrogant, but I would submit that it is true. We need to be absolutely clear on this. We cannot do politics without theology. And unless we get our theology right, our politics will be wonky.

Finally, Elijah is simply not beholden to the powers. Obadiah who works within the system fears for his life (the powers, like all empires, rule through fear, and as feeble humans, this will impact us) but Elijah won't have any of it. He must present himself to Ahab. ". . .As the Lord Almighty lives, whom

---

4. 1 Kgs 18:1.

5. 1 Kgs 18:7.

6. I recall this was at the FOCUS event organized by Holy Trinity Brompton in Mablethorpe, Lincolnshire.

I serve, I will surely present myself to Ahab today." See the operative principles: God lives, we serve him, and we must surely do his will. Everything else is commentary. Walter Brueggemann describes Elijah as someone on a " . . . rampage of transformative action, confronting and challenging the power of the throne and creating, beyond royal control, zones of new life that defy any normal explanation."[7]

How can we operate in the communal, political, commercial, and social spheres and create these *zones of new life*? This election is important for many reasons, but there is a bigger, deeper, and richer story of God's politics, his rule, and reign that is life-giving.

The last twenty years have seen a growing appreciation that evangelism and social action are integrated activities. Flowing from this, Christian engagement in politics has taken a fresh, more positive tone within the mainstream. Yet, my sense is that there is much more to do in our engagement and crucially in our theology.

I believe that we need both an affirmation of the legitimacy of political service and a more mature understanding of the political dimensions of the church in an eschatological sense. We also need a wise understanding of the powers. In these endeavors, a reflection on the example of Obadiah and Elijah is a helpful starting point from which to set our compass.

7. Brueggemann, *Truth Speaks to Power,* 84.

2

Keir Hardie—Stirring up Divine Discontent

This article was written after Jeremy Corbyn's first
speech at Labour Party conference as leader. It seeks
to explore the significance of Keir Hardie to the
Labour Party and his faith and anger at injustice.

"I have said, both in writing and from the platform many times, that the
impetus which drove me first into the Labour movement, and the inspiration which has carried me on in it, has been derived more from the
teachings of Jesus of Nazareth than from all other sources combined."

—J. KEIR HARDIE

One hundred years ago last weekend, the Battle of Loos had started
in France, Everton were football league champions, and Keir Hardie,
founder of the Labour Party, passed away.[1] Today, the newly elected Labour
leader, Jeremy Corbyn concluded his wide ranging and powerful speech
with an intentional reference to Keir Hardie. Quoting Hardie, Mr. Corbyn
said: "My work has consisted of trying to stir up divine discontent with

---

1. "100 Years On."

wrong."[2] You would be hard pressed to generate a better strapline for the mission of *Christians on the Left*.

Keir Hardie was born in 1856 in North Lanarkshire. He was the son of a domestic servant, and his stepfather was a ship's carpenter. Hardie began working at the age of seven and by ten, he was sent to work in the mines in the mornings, and in the evenings, his parents taught him to read and write. Hardie was elected to Parliament in 1892 and was integral to the founding of the Labour Representation Committee (the forerunner of the Labour Party) in 1900, later becoming its leader in 1906. His life was a canvas overlaid with the story of the birth of the Labour Party as a movement and its establishment as a Parliamentary force. Hardie's upbringing and life is an amazing story, both sobering and inspiring:

> "While he had some idyllic early memories of growing up in countryside around Lanarkshire, Keir Hardie later wrote that his upbringing was so hard that he never really knew childhood. First the stigma of being child of single mother in a small nineteenth-century village, then adopted by his mother's new husband who would call him a bastard when drunk. When children today would have been in the first years of primary school, he was working in the shipyards where he saw another boy fall to his death. Later, from the age of ten, he worked in the mines, often alone for hours at a time in the dark."[3]

Keir Hardie's life story and key contributions have been wonderfully summarized in the recent series of vignettes introduced by Blair McDougall on the *Labour List* website,[4] which unpacks the multi-faceted outlook of the bearded Scot who forged the Labour Party. The series testifies that Hardie's political outlook was not grounded in materialistic Marxism. Rather, his worldview was " . . . in favor of a humane and popular approach to socialism that comes out of his Christianity and other influences."[5]

Hardie's faith was all about resisting the powers and injustices of the day. As a journalist writing for the *Labour Leader* in January 1899, Hardie once reflected: "I believe in Christ's Gospel of love and brotherhood and service."[6] Yet, his concern in this context was not pious sentimental-

---

2. Jeremy Corbyn, *Labour List*, Lines 36–37.

3. "100 Years On." Lines 1–8.

4. "100 Years On.."

5. "100 Years On." Lines 10–12.

6. "100 Years On." Line 40.

ity but rather to expose the shortcomings of Lord Overtoun, a Christian philanthropist responsible for exploiting his workers at a large chemical works. Hardie's agitation won the day, and thankfully Lord Overtoun saw sense and improved the conditions of the workers.

Please read the words in Hardie's account of the workers' experience: they have a prophetic edge. We should thank God for trade unions and health and safety and remember why they are necessary. We also see Hardie's burning rage against injustice and remember that the creation of the Labour Party was a battle in and of itself. Without people of faith, such as Keir Hardie, George Lansbury, and Arthur Henderson, it would never have been created or even survived.

As Jeremy Corbyn has reminded us, the battles to reform private sector housing, to show humanity to refugees, to protect workers, to work for peace and combat climate change, to cherish the welfare state and the NHS and not denigrate them, are still with us. These are campaigns that require divine discontent with wrong. This is a party in which the light of Christian faith has shone and must continue to shine.

Listening to the leader's speech today, I was reminded of the passion for social justice that I was taught by my family. Yet, as Kenneth Morgan observed, Hardie combined passion with a strategic mind: "Hardie was both our greatest strategist and our greatest prophet and evangelist."[7] As the leadership election proved, managerialism and electoralism alone cannot construct a compelling vision. However, Labour needs to be more than the voice of protest to fellow travelers in the echo chamber of a conference hall. Labour must fuse passion with organization, rebuild a movement, and win elections in both Nuneaton and Nunhead and Hamilton and Hampstead. The party must reach out to the window cleaner and the public servant, connecting with those attached to family, work, place, and faith as the anchors of their lives. We were reminded today of a key element of the Labour story, a rage against injustice and also that from its inception some Labour leaders sought to express their mission in terms of faith. The task is precisely the same today as it was when Hardie passed away one hundred years ago. Our inspiration is also the same as the one that drove Hardie on. Stirring up divine discontent with what is wrong is the task for Christians on the left both in and out of season.

---

7. Morgan, "Labour's Greatest Hero: Keir Hardie," Lines 8–9.

3

Foolishness to Greeks

Blog on the Assisted Dying Bill

This essay, which explores the vexed issue of euthanasia, was
drafted in 2015 when I assisted the campaign to oppose a private members' bill seeking to liberalize the law related to assisted dying. It draws on the Apostle Paul's engagement with the
Athenian intellectuals in Acts 17.

On September 11, a private members bill will be debated in the House
of Commons. This bill, as an attempt to legalize a means of assisted
dying, is of immense significance. Through the heart of this debate run
themes that are shaping public policy in our nation, attempting to normal-
ize pre-suppositions that do not accord with a Christian worldview. We
should approach this debate with prayer, humility, and compassion for
those who suffer to the point of wanting to end their lives. However, we
should not be naive about what this represents. It is an attempt by the 'secular liberal elite' to enshrine into law their individualistic interpretation of
the meaning of life. It really is that grave. We should absolutely empathize
with those who may support this bill through seeing loved ones suffer. But
for the reasons I lay out, I submit that we should oppose this bill and resist
the arguments and contest the movement behind it.

The ethical and intelligible concerns against these proposals have been articulated by charities such as CARE. A few of the numerous practical reasons to query the bill are as follows:

- Most members of the medical and health professions are strongly opposed to the bill

- A good alternative exists, as the UK takes a lead globally in palliative and hospice care

- All the main disability lobby groups[1] oppose a change to the law.

Life and death are weighty matters, and we know that they are at the center of the Christian faith. We believe in a God who is the author of life. God's son conquered death, rising from the dead to transform our lives now and for eternity. Thus, we cannot avoid this debate, it is central and not marginal to what we believe and hold dear.

There are a number of reasons to propose a vision of life which precludes going down this unwelcome road. The first objection is informed by the Bible and theology. In the context of this debate, I believe that Paul's dialogue with Greek philosophers in the Areopagus is instructive both in terms of context and content. He was a witness to the living God, a giver of life to a pagan, intelligent, sophisticated audience. In Acts 17:16–34, Paul testifies that there is a God, Jesus the Godman, who rose from the dead. Our opposition to the bill is rooted in a theistic worldview, and it is far from incidental that we believe in God. Rather, it is fundamental. For our God ". . . he himself gives everyone life and breath and everything else."[2] Indeed, this God oversees the very details of our lives. He is not disinterested in us, for ". . . and he marked out their appointed times in history and the boundaries of their lands."[3]

It was John Stott who outlined that: "we have intrinsic value because God created us in his own image."[4] He highlighted that a clear understanding of a doctrine of God and humanity is requisite in order for right thinking and right practice on such matters. Further, Stott infers that: ". . . the

---

1. Disability Rights UK, Scope, the UK Disabled People's Council and Not Dead Yet.
2. Acts 17:25.
3. Acts 17:26,
4. Stott, *Issues,* 411.

decision to terminate a human life involves an implicit judgement that a particular form of human living is not worthy of ultimate respect."[5]

We see that a biblical worldview has a life-affirming basis. Ethicists such as Stanley Hauerwas argue that our life is a gift from God, and it is not within our wit to determine its limits. "For the Christian the reasons for living begin with the understanding that life is a gift."[6] This is a profound point, and this is why the debate over assisted dying delineates a Christian sense of life as a gift and a liberal assertion of human autonomy and the limitations of life. There is no middle ground on this point. It is a clash of worldviews. Or, as Hauerwas further reflects: "We are not our own creators. Our desire to live should be given shape in the affirmation that we are not the determiners of our life, God is. We Christians are people who must learn to live, as we have learned that life is a gift."[7] A second reason to oppose this bill should be second nature to Christians on the center-left. Altering the law on assisted dying would have a detrimental impact on the most poor and vulnerable in society. If we hold to at least a communitarian perspective that we are relational creatures bound to each other, we must ask, not with doubt but with all sincerity and genuine compassion, why some on the Labour side have supported such measures.

A change in law not only places health professionals in an invidious position, but it also renders the vulnerable more prone to being at the wrong end of the decision to end their life. They would be at the mercy of pushy professionals and wealthy lobbies who see the poor and ill as a burden, a commodity to devalue and reject. This may sound like a stark prognosis, but I submit to you that a change in the law alters the rules against the poor in favor of the powerful.

For these reasons, the assisted dying debate is not an abstract pro-life issue. Rather, it is a social justice issue. For the sake of the common good, we must protect the vulnerable many from the vain projects of the rich couched in the language of rights and compassion. Giles Fraser neatly summed up this danger: "This is the shadow side of liberal freedom. It's a young and healthy person's ideology, suited for the well-off. It amounts to the renunciation of our obligations to each other and to the vulnerable." Fraser further explains that this is the logic of the marketplace: "For by eroding the long-term mutual obligations we have to each other, in sickness

---

5. Stott, *Issues*, 390.

6. Hauerwas, *Memory, Community, and the Reasons for Living*, 585.

7. Hauerwas, *Memory, Community, and the Reasons for Living*, 585.

and in health, we have arrived at the existential equivalent of a zero-hours contract with life, a contract that can be terminated at will."[8]

This concern also has a class component. In a world ever more conforming to the morality of the dystopian fantasy *The Hunger Games*, the working class and poor—too often mocked, pilloried, and abused by the liberal elite who really run this country—will be ever more vulnerable to the wishes of the powerful. It must be resisted, and this makes it a Labour cause. Our call is to organize the powerless vis-à-vis the self-interest of the powerful.

Thirdly, the rationale behind the bill needs to be challenged. The Assisted Dying Bill and the arguments it reflects is instructive to some of the most important values debates operative in UK public policy. An argument to end life rooted in a *right to die* plays to the spirit of the age. Yet, it is straight from the enlightenment play book, seeing man's autonomy as sovereign. This is utterly at odds with a Christian worldview, as articulated thoughtfully by Hauerwas, which depicts human life as dependent on a creator God.

The language and sophisticated lobbying of the pro-euthanasia camp will be clever and appealing to the zeitgeist of our era as if we were the *masters of our destiny* and the *masters of our fate*. However, the Bible does not allow us to subscribe to such a view of ultimate human autonomy. John Stott makes this clear, stating: "Human freedom is not unlimited. We find our freedom only in living according to our God-given nature, not in rebellion against it. The notion of total human autonomy is a myth.[9] Paul reminds us we are to: ". . .demolish arguments and every pretension that sets itself up against the knowledge of God. . ."[10] The right to die is not just one opinion among many, it is a pretension that sets itself up against the knowledge of God.

Finally, a persuasive reason to oppose this bill is informed by the evidence from nation-states that have followed a comparable path. Studies have shown where a liberalization of the law has been pursued, disturbing outcomes have been witnessed. For example, in the state of Oregon in the United States, patients have been refused life-saving drugs and offered suicide instead. Patients with a history of serious depression have been offered

---

8. Fraser, "Assisted Dying is the equivalent of a zero- hours contract with life," Lines 56–58.

9. Stott, *Issues Facing Christians Today*, 414.

10. 2 Cor 10: 5.

lethal drugs. In Belgium and the Netherlands, changes in the law have been followed by further calls for the law to go further. The call for further liberalization would not end if the law was amended.

Our God is the giver of life. He is close to those who are suffering and has suffered in Christ. As we pray and reflect on this central truth, we can see the Assisted Dying Bill in a full and biblical light. Hard cases make bad laws, and the Private Members Bill on Assisted Dying would open the door to bad laws and bad practices. Christians must strongly oppose this bill, the worldview which fosters it, and its unintended consequences for the vulnerable and powerless in our society. Certainly, we should not condemn those who support it through genuine desperation and compassion. But we should resolutely oppose any moves to bring in a law on assisted dying, for its very existence is a feature of a society that has given up on God, the common life, and ordinary people. It is the last throw of the dice of a self-interested and nihilistic clique who want to bend public policy toward their perversions. "It is therefore not surprising, but indeed a correlative of liberal political theory, that one should have the *right* to commit suicide. We must ask ourselves whether in accepting that right we have unwittingly affirmed a society that no longer wishes to provide the conditions for the miracle of trust and community."[11]

---

11. Hauerwas, *Memory, Community, and the Reasons for Living,* 592.

4

Preparing our Hearts
and Lifting Up Our Hands

This reflection posits the importance of prayer
and contemplation for the political activist.

"Yet if you devote your heart to him and stretch out your hands to
him, if you put away the sin that is in your hand and allow no evil to
dwell in your tent, then, free of fault, you will lift up your face; you will
stand firm and without fear. You will surely forget your trouble, recalling it only as waters gone by. Life will be brighter than noonday, and
darkness will become like morning. You will be secure, because there is
hope; you will look about you and take your rest in safety. You will lie
down, with no one to make you afraid, and many will court your favor.
But the eyes of the wicked will fail, and escape will elude them; their
hope will become a dying gasp.,"

JOB 11:13–20

"There is a pervasive form of contemporary violence to which the
idealist most easily succumbs: activism and overwork. The rush
and pressure of modern life are a form, perhaps the most common
form, of its innate violence. To allow oneself to be carried away by a

multitude of conflicting concerns, to surrender to too many demands, to commit oneself to too many projects, to want to help everyone in everything, is to succumb to violence. The frenzy of our activism neutralizes our work for peace. It destroys our own inner capacity for peace. It destroys the fruitfulness of our own work, because it kills the root of inner wisdom which makes work fruitful."

THOMAS MERTON

The year—2016—saw sweeping and unexpected changes. The world has become more uncertain and more frightening, it seems. In our disorientation, we may keenly want to do something, though we may not know what to do. But do we need to do *something* I ask provocatively. *What* are we as Christians called to the public square to do? Well, there is much to do, and the missional imperative is one of action. Yet to some, prayer and contemplation is a good place to start and a good place to remain. Does that sound complacent and other-worldly? I submit that some time away on retreat might be more fruitful than going to the Fabian New Year's conference, or a visit to a monastery might be a better place to start than a fifty-two-week subscription to the *New Statesman* with *Aunt Ethel's* Christmas money. Campaigning is good, even a form of discipleship (potentially), but what if it is actually an empty act, or even an act of "violence"[1] as Thomas Merton, the spiritual writer of the last century, so starkly warns if we become subsumed by activism and overwork?

Political activity is not a bad thing. In fact, it is a positively biblical thing. Yet, if it is part of an over-active approach to life, sundered from rest and reflection, we could be fruitless and burned out. Thus, we find in Job 11 an instruction that might speak into our modern predicament. We are exhorted to prepare our hearts and pray. In fact, it is the *only* thing Job is asked to do, although I am stretching the meaning of the word *only*. We see in this passage the tremendous transformation and altering of perspective that is rooted in a life of prayer. For without this focus, the activist may become oppressed by the here and now, the urgent, the needs of the hour, and their troubles and lose sight of what is of true and eternal importance.

As 2017 begins, let us "devote our hearts and stretch out our hands. . ."[2] Let's not get sucked into political hyperactivity. If you are called into politics,

1. Merton, *Bystander*, 73.
2. Based on Job 11v14.

then your action should flow from prayer. You are political, you won't be able to help yourself getting worked up, formulating thoughts, giving money to causes, campaigning and chewing the fat over contemporary issues. If that is the ". . .rock from which you were cut. . ."[3] it will pretty much happen with some effort or application. Some outworking of your political vocation is likely. Of course, others need to be challenged, encouraged, and equipped. But for those in the political space—to whom I am addressing these thoughts—that is rarely the problem. Yet, if political activity is all we do, we are not in the right rhythm. Pay close attention to these verses in Job and orientate your life on a different track. Attend to your heart and prayer life. Align with the Lord's priorities. Take a radically different view of what it means to be political, which is to pray, know your neighbors, attend to the local environment, and spend time with your children. These are some of the *most* political things you can do. To be political is to serve your local church because God's politics is located in his *polis*. Everything else is marginal or commentary.

The Prime Minister Tony Blair was fond of saying: "Doing nothing is not an option."[4] However in in some instances doing nothing—for a season—is an option! Let's camp out a little on that scandalous Thomas Merton quote that describes a certain form of activism as violence. Really? Yes. It may seem like he was trivializing violence, but he warned that activism can reduce our peace. Again, Merton is not criticizing activism per se but a certain approach to activism—this is a man who wrote a book entitled *Contemplation in a World of Action*. The worst critique of the monastic lifestyle is to see it as passive and other-worldly. Slowly, many in the contemporary church are rediscovering the riches that can be gleaned from monastic life. These forms of church and disciplines and practices will become ever more important in our uncertain future. We face a capitalism without virtue, a consumerism that colonizes our being, a disenchanted secularism, a pagan popular culture, and a hyper-busy world. We need to learn to survive, rest, and resist. As F. B. Meyer once wrote:

> "We must be still before God. The life around us, in this age, is pre-eminently one of rush and effort. It is the age of the express-train and electric telegraph. Years are crowded into months, and weeks into days. This feverish haste threatens the religious life. The

3. Isa 51:1.

4. Blair, "Speech by UK Prime Minister at meeting of the NATO-Russia Council," Line 22.

stream has already entered our churches and stirred their quiet pools. Meetings crowd on meetings. The same energetic souls are found at them all and engaged in many good works beside. But we must beware that we do not substitute the active for the contemplative, the valley for the mountain-top. . . . We must make time to be alone with God. The closet and the shut door are indispensable. Be still and know that God is within thee and around! In the hush of the soul the unseen becomes visible, and the eternal real. . . . Let no day pass without its season of silent waiting before God."[5]

Where I live, near Bermondsey, you can visit the site of the town's former abbey. Little is left of the structure that closed after its destructive dissolution ordered by Henry VIII. Just a street named Abbey Street and a section of the wall in a restaurant remain. This monastery was inhabited by Cluniac Monks who came to the area and settled and died there. They were committed to prayer and place, they weren't mobile. Instead, they stayed and prayed.

As Alasdair Macintyre indicates at the close of his signature work *After Virtue*, we may be in the midst now of a new ". . .dark ages. . .[6]." And it was a figure such as Saint Benedict who started movements that overcame the last dark ages. It is time to take monasticism more seriously. As much as I would love the monasteries to be rebuilt, I am alluding to a monasticism of mind and heart. It was the twentieth-century theological giant Dietrich Bonhoeffer who prophetically pointed to the essential vitality of a life formed by new monastic practices:

> "The restoration of the church will surely come only from a new type of monasticism. a life lived in accordance with the Sermon on the Mount in the discipleship of Christ. I think it is time to gather people to do this."[7]

Silence and solitude don't happen naturally in our culture. Yet, they are essential spiritual disciplines. Let's pray and be contemplative and not be involved in forty-seven ways to change the world via the click of a mouse or a blog that only reiterates what twelve other people have said anyway. Let's also listen rather than foist our opinion on others as a mark of our politics. A false binary such as the 52 percent versus 48 percent outcome of the EU referendum should cause us to actively listen to those with whom

5. Meyer, *Secret of Guidance*, Chapter IV.

6. Macintyre, *Virtue*, 263

7. 29 Hans Goedeking, *Bonhoeffer*, 284–5.

we disagree. Listening should proceed talking and action. Prayer should precede and follow our listening. The discipline of silence can be a fruitful posture. As A. W. Tozer wrote: "More spiritual progress can be made in one short moment of speechless silence in the awesome presence of God than in years of mere study."[8] The verses in Job 11 focus on getting our heart and devotion right and lifting up our hands in prayer. The point about the heart is fundamental. Our heart, the seat of our being, needs to be orientated to a holy goal, a *telos*, or it will find another goal. James K. A. Smith points out we are "affective beings" who are lovers more than cognitive rationalists, and that our heart is centered on what we love:

> "Because our hearts are orientated primarily by desire, by what we love, and because these desires are shaped and molded by the habit-forming practices in which we participate, it is the rituals and practices of the mall—the mall and market—that shape our imaginations and how we orientate ourselves to the world. . . . liturgies—whether 'sacred' or 'secular'—shape and constitute our identities by forming our most fundamental desires and our most basic attunement to the world. In short, liturgies make us certain kinds of people, and what defines us is what we *love*."[9]

Good habits of the heart of worship, prayer, and solitude are to be encouraged and cultivated. The alternative is that secular liturgies will act to shape our desires, be it the market, media, or sporting passions. We will find a liturgy, the question is which one will it be? Our lives will orientate around practices and towards ultimate love. Which one will it be? Let us prepare our hearts.

These few verses in Job admonish us to pray and repent. They also contain promises, visible manifestations of transformation that are granted to the one who prays and repents. Verse 14 stresses repentance. We must be serious about leaving behind the past and its sin. We must be accountable and in the arena of public life and *walk the walk*. This is not about moral, legalistic perfectionism. It is about integrity. It is quite rightly about narrowing the gap between policy and lifestyle. We will fall short of this, yet we must hold it up as a value and discipline. To pray is to repent, to turn from our normal activity, confess our weakness and brokenness, and orientate towards God. This is not some legalistic turning over thirty-seven thousand sins we may have committed in thirty-six hours but to be aligned with God.

8. Quoted by Nicky Gumbel in 'Bible in One Year', November 15, 2016.
9. Smith, *Desiring the Kingdom*, 25.

It is an essential part of prayer, for to pray is to change. Definitions of the root of repentance allude to a complete change of heart and mind.

In praying we will know release from circumstances of misery and gain a transformed perspective. We see in Job 15–19 a new perspective. This is a critical link between our prayer life and our politics. For without this, we slip into the mode of the world and are oppressed by drudgery. If we are involved in politics we will be surrounded by imminent concerns and, to an extent, these concerns will grip us. We need a space to be un-gripped, not to be bound to the temporal concerns that can overwhelm us and to pray so we might have a different perspective on our woes, "You will surely forget your trouble, recalling it only as waters gone by."[10] as the writer promises in Therefore you don't need to be bound to the imminent, i.e., local, government cuts, the economy, the state of the Labour Party, Brexit, Syria, Iraq, or the election of Donald Trump. These are rightly so all things we should care about. But without an encounter with God in prayer and devotion, these things can cripple us. Looking to this section of scripture, transformation is promised. The misery will not last, but it will be forgotten. The heart has been prepared and hands have been lifted up in prayer.

I am encouraged and intrigued by this final promise[11]: We see that there will be an external and not just a personal blessing in this path of formation. This is where the politics come in. Too often, I run around seeking the counsel and presence of others. We all need good advice, but must we always hurry to others? To this meeting or that think tank? Instead, let's hurry to the presence of God, the secret place of prayer and, on some occasions, let others look for us. For in this unsettled world, perhaps a community of prayer that dwells in the political world can be a place where others seek counsel and advice. When people come to us for help, we can be better equipped to help if we are rooted in the secret place. So, we are about being practical, as were the monks and monasteries, yet it all comes from an intentional spirituality.

There is a final encouragement and warning. This path of prayer and promise is clearly not just *nice to have*. It is the only path, as for the alternative path is destruction. The wicked face grim prospects. Prayerlessness and restlessness equal destruction.

My concern is not to call people to passivity or to devalue the worth-while and critical involvement of Christians in political activity but to offer

10. Job 11:16
11. Job 11:19.

a corrective to activity and engagement without prayer and reflection. For believers, the gospel is the primary driver and activity of our lives, and this means action. However, our action will bear fruit if it attends to the heartbeat of the Father. Jesus only did what the Father ordained. Jesus explained: "...Very truly I tell you, the Son can do nothing by himself; he can do only what he sees his Father doing, because whatever the Father does the Son also does."[12]

As the New Year is upon us, whatever we are resolved to do, let's be devoted to God and lift up our hands. Be prepared to find silence and solitude and ask: *what is the Father doing?* You may be surprised.

12. John 5:19.

5

Bring Back the Three R's

Relationships, Reaching Out, and Redemption

This article, written in Autumn 2017, explores my work at the
main political party conferences. I highlight the missional importance of this work and even squeeze in a reference to West
Bromwich Albion.

In my job with the Salvation Army, I have the immense privilege of attending three party conferences and connecting with the key Christian
groups in each party. Attending the Labour Party conference in Brighton is
a particular joy for me. I am a Labour Party member, and a Christian on the
Left member, and I love Brighton. Brighton even has a football team called
Albion, but not the *real* one of course (I am a West Brom fan!).

On a serious note, this year's conference leads me to reflect on the following
thoughts. Conference is a time for reconnection and putting relationships
back into the center of politics. Sadly, I only meet some people each autumn at the Labour Party conference. However, in citing the importance
of a relational orientation to politics, I mean something richer than my
erratic networking. It is good to reconnect and more important to rebuild
our relationships As the recent Christians on the Left video[1] prophetically

1. Christians on the Left, *Relationships.*

reminds us, it is a relational approach to politics that is required. God is a relational god and rooting our approach in a wholesome and graceful relational approach would avoid some of the barbarity that seems to define contemporary discourse. In fact, while in Brighton I happened to be interviewed by the BBC asking if I would ever be friends with a Conservative. My answer suggested that not to do so would be *un-Labour-like* and *unneighborly*, and I hoped it contained seeds of the gospel. Party Conference is a time of reaching out in mission because politics is mission. I like much, but not all, of Rod Dreher's book *The Benedict Option,* that highlights the changing context for Christians in the West, yet, despite this important insight, now is not a time to retreat from certain forms of cultural engagement. Now is a time to pray and to reach out all the more in mission and not retreat to our caves. With my employer—the Salvation Army—and along with colleagues in the Methodist Church, United Reformed Church, Baptist Union and Quakers, we spent much time talking to NGOs and Labour MPs. We discussed issues that concerned us but looked to lift up the vocation of political service and offer prayer. We reached out in this manner not just at conference but at the Liberal Democrat, Conservative, and SNP conferences too.

We need to be reaching out and engaging all the more in a time of division, impoverishment of vision and empty discourse: the need is to be involved and not to withdraw. Hudson Taylor prayed to God to send fellow workers missionaries to China and Mongolia (incidentally while on Brighton Beach). I am not a numbers chap but let's pray for more fellow workers to penetrate the world of politics, media, enterprise, the arts, and the world of work. If the Reformation taught us one thing, it is that all work can glorify God.

It was a time of, dare I say it, repentance. The only fringe Tom Watson MP spoke at was on gambling and the epidemic this nation faces. The Labour Deputy Leader seemed determined to clean up the mess left by the last Labour Government in an act of turbo-charged liberalization. I believe he means business. Certainly, we should encourage more politicians trying to redeem past mistakes. In this oh-so-toxic age, we need redemption alongside justice, politicians, and political structures, are fallen and fallible. We have needed a little reminder of this over the last several deeply depressing weeks.

To be of any lasting meaning and truly impact the renewal of relationships, the power to reach out and the gift of redemption can only come from one source: Christ. The outgoing director of *Christians on the Left*, Andy Flannagan, reminded us at the annual Labour Party Conference church service of a political vision shaped more by the eternal vision of the *new Jerusalem*[2] than by pulling away at Labour's roots in search of elusive progress. This simply leaves in its wake an unhealthy utopian air. For politics to get to a better place, across the spectrum, we need a renewal of the values that drove the early Christian pioneers of Labour. Dispositions of love, fellowship, and mutual respect. Now, that is a revival I can pray for.

2. A phrase appropriated by the Labour Party to describe their aspirations for social reform, particularly in the post-war era. See Clement Attlee's speech to the Labour Party conference 1951.

6

Equality, Opportunity
and Social Mobility

Can We Make Britain a Society that Works for All?
(Tawney Dialogue, March 14, 2018)

In March 2018, I had the immense privilege of speaking at the Tawney Dialogue, an annual debate organized by *Christians on the Left* (the [English] FA Cup Final for Christian Socialists), speaking to the title *Equality, Opportunity and Social Mobility: Can we make Britain a society that works for all?* I gave the following talk and was announced as a *theologian*! The other speaker was Rt. Hon. Angela Rayner MP who was very warm, down to earth and human.

As I was preparing for a presentation for an interview, I phoned a friend, saying : "I have an interview and have to give a presentation. It is only ten minutes." To which he replied: "It is enough time to make a fool of yourself." So, one prayer this evening is that I don't make a fool of myself.

Thank you *Christians on the Left*, for the amazing privilege of speaking at the Tawney Dialogue.

We live in an affluent, innovative nation, blessed with a rich history. And in many ways, it is a charitable society with a strong civic ethic. However, we are a fragmented and divided nation. Inequality is rife. Levels of child poverty are now at alarming levels, with some constituencies have more than half the children there, growing up in poverty.

The use of foodbanks has skyrocketed in recent years. From April 2016 to March 2017, the Trussell Trust gave three-day emergency food supplies to 1,182,954 people in crisis.

A Shelter commission into social housing launched in January with the following insight: "Almost half (48 percent) of families in social housing who reported issues around poor or unsafe conditions felt ignored or were refused help. Problems included fire safety, gas leaks, electrical hazards, mold and pest problems, among others."[1] The Grenfell Tower incident, tragic in ways many of us here probably cannot relate to, reveals a nation where the poor are ignored by the *tin ear* of the powerful and the result was scandalous (*The Hunger Games* is perhaps not just a story).

It would be too easy to pin the blame for these problems at the door of the current government. Now, they don't help in many of these matters, but the roots of the problem go much deeper. Britain as a society simply does not work for all. We are grossly unequal. Opportunity, in many ways, knocks spots off previous generations' experiences, but it is still limited and social mobility, whatever that means, is stuck.

In this short talk, I wish to outline some brief themes that might help us reflect on this critical question in a distinct way. Thus I seek to talk about worldview, the world economic system, and the world of work, not as systemic answers but some pointers to stimulate debate.

Worldview

I read a blog called *Experimental Theology* by Richard Beck, an American (he is like Andy Flannagan meets a psychology professorship). Last February he wrote: "In *After Virtue*, Alasdair MacIntyre makes the argument that because modernity lost its story, to use the words of Robert Jenson, we lack a coherent moral vision of our common life together. What we have, instead, are bits and pieces of a variety of incomplete and rival ethical systems. We have lots of different ways of defining "the good" but no clear way to adjudicate between these goods when they come into conflict."[2]

How do we begin to navigate these challenges? My concern is if we don't have a robust, biblical, and generous worldview, we jettison God's story and imbibe the world's narratives. I hold that the Bible is true and is sufficient in all matters.

1. "Shelter launches new social housing commission," Lines 19–21.
2. Beck, "Democracy and the Demonization of the Good," Lines 3–11.

The title of today's talk, which has a deeply Christian concern, we might see how we can easily get blown off course. Because modernity has lost its story, we can't begin to build a Britain that works for all because we have lost the means to posit what the *good* really is.

The concept of equality has deeply biblical roots. Yet, in modern parlance, it has been secularized and fought over by rival ethical systems[3], as Beck indicates. Equality is good and is a Christian concept. The New Testament both affirms gender and racial equality in Gal 3:28. Also in Philippians, we see Jesus saw equality with God as a selfless, giving thing. Indeed, it was R. H. Tawney himself who said: "The essence of all morality is this: to believe that every human being is of infinite importance, and therefore that no consideration of expediency can justify oppression of one by another. But to believe that is necessarily to believe in God."[4] Belief in God was to Tawney a pre-condition of equality. However, equality, defined apart from Christianity can lose its meaning.

And what of *social mobility*? I am not sure this is a concept that coheres with Christianity. It sounds like the dream of the self-maximizing liberal, free floating individual. Socially mobile to where? Why? And who is left behind? Is it a middle class, professional presumption that everyone should be like them and climb? What happens when our path is blocked? When there is failure and disappointment? Seriously, we do need to make Britain work for all. And equality is a good thing, and indeed opportunity and social mobility are too. However, without a rich and expansive Christian vision of human flourishing. they could be meaningless words, echoing the dominant narrative of progress.

To root equality, opportunity and social mobility in a thicker concept, I think that we need to camp out on the notion of human flourishing. Anthony Bradley, a US commentator has said: "An emphasis on human flourishing, ours and others, becomes important because it is characterized by a holistic concern for the spiritual, moral, physical, economic, material, political, psychological, and social context necessary for human beings to live according to their design."[5] Our worldview needs to be explicitly Christian and cultivated or the *acids of modernity* will eat us up.

---

3. Beck, "Democracy and the Demonization of the Good," Experimental Theology, Line 9.

4. Tawney, *Commonplace Book*, in *The British Political Tradition*, 449.

5. Bradley, "The new legalism.," in Welchel, Flourishing, Institute for Faith, Work and Economics, Lines 6–10.

World Economic System

A Christian Socialist agenda needs to have a biblically rounded understanding of how the global and national economy works. It is abundantly clear, it works largely for the benefit of the rich and to the marginalization of the poor. According to Oxfam, 82 percent of all wealth created in the last year went to the top 1 percent, and nothing went to the bottom 50 percent.[6]

While there is no alternative to capitalism, capitalism is no alternative. It may generate prosperity, yet it commodifies, divides society, creating inequality on a vast scale, generates destructive consumerism and has despoiled the natural environment. Where the unjust ordering of the economy dehumanizes, causes economic inequality, lack of economic opportunity, we have to speak out.

The face of this dominant ideology in our communities is austerity, and what we have seen in the last ten years was by choice and the poor have borne the brunt of it. When it comes to social security cuts, the same people have been paying the price time and time again: the bedroom tax; the benefit cap; freezing on benefits uprating are just a few examples. So, Britain is not working for all. The economic model we have been running for forty years is well and truly broken. There can be little equality and social mobility in this system.

World of Work

It is in the world of work where we see many of the current inequality manifest, yet an alternative Christian agenda can begin to help. Work gives not just an income but vocation and meaning, to name just a few challenges, the contemporary labor market has the following deleterious features to name just a few:

- Insecure jobs such as zero hours contracts
- An imbalance of power at work and lack of employee voice
- Inexplicable gender pay gaps.

An agenda rooted in the common good and human flourishing might start to unlock some of these problems. Where do we begin? An agenda that may help is as follows:

6. Oxfam, "Richest 1% bagged 82% of the wealth created last year"

- Workers on the boards of companies

- A drive for the Living Wage

- A vocational system rooted in school and connected to the workplace, on a Germanic model

- A renewed trade union movement, particularly in the private sector with collective bargaining restored

- Tougher action on the gender pay gap.

These changes, a few ideas, with others will not make the world perfect, but they are a Labour agenda and they, along with other measures, could turn the tide on inequality and lack of opportunity.

The Christian vision of human flourishing honors all of our dignity and our undeniable personhood. It is not the self-maximizing liberal bourgeois fantasy of *social mobility*. It places people and their sense of place at the heart of policy. Neither is it a society where all human existence is ordered to the reification of the money God.

Labour, the party defined by work, the party of the common life must embrace a Christian inspired vision of flourishing in the workplace. This would transcend any flat sense of equality and social mobility where my success is your success, where we love and care for our fellow neighbor and that is all our aspiration.

Yes, let's celebrate achievement and aspiration and the fulfillment of potential. But let's also honor and love those who fail and are not *socially mobile* but are valued and can make a valuable contribution to the common weal. Our message is one of hope and abundant life: ". . .I have come that they may have life, and have it to the full."[7] It is about human flourishing rooted in the gospel of Jesus Christ.

I work for The Salvation Army, and I find the figure of its founder, William Booth, inspiring and challenging. He was no utopian, and he was no political radical. Yet, his movement achieved amazing feats. Roy Hattersley's biography, a warts-and-all account, impressively reflects on what Booth achieved in his life: "The Salvation Army which William Booth founded—although sometimes derided as an essentially nineteenth-century organization—can take pride in having helped ease Britain out of its nineteenth-century attitude to sin and poverty."[8] And yet it was also Booth

---

7. John 10:10
8. Hattersley, *Blood and Fire*, 441.

who warned one of the chief dangers of last century would be "politics without God."[9]. For no theology leads to dead ideology.

In order to have a Britain that works for all, we need a Labour Party that works for all. And, Labour, this party, was founded by Christians. It is our party: when we look back at Keir Hardie's faith, Arthur Henderson MP, a tee-total Methodist and peacemaker, the endearing High Anglicanism of George Lansbury, when we consider the contribution of the Roman Catholic Scot, John Wheatley, pioneering municipal housing for the working class through the Housing Act 1924—all these Labour pioneers fought for a different society driven by faith.

In Methodist Central Hall, we are reminded that Labour truly does owe more to Methodism than it does to Marx. It owes more to Moses than it does to momentum, more to the Apostle Paul than it does to progress. So, in these challenging times, let's remind ourselves that without a robust Christian presence, Labour is bereft. This is our party. Let us fight and fight and fight again to save the party we love. And let us pray and pray and pray again for it. Then with a powerful vision of human flourishing—maybe, just maybe—we may see a Britain that works for all, and all the glory will belong to God alone.

9. Booth, New York World, 8–9.

7

Politics—It's Just Stuff

Unintentionally, I continue a theme based on the 2018 party conferences. I try and position politics' relative insignificance within the context of the greatness of God, perhaps as a corrective to my own idolatry of politics. It is, after all, just stuff.

"Who has measured the waters in the hollow of his hand, or with the breadth of his hand marked off the heavens?"

"Who has held the dust of the earth in a basket, or weighed the mountains on the scales and the hills in a balance?"

"Who can fathom the Spirit of the Lord, or instruct the Lord as his counselor? Whom did the Lord consult to enlighten him, and who taught him the right way? Who was it that taught him knowledge, or showed him the path of understanding?"

"Surely the nations are like a drop in a bucket; they are regarded as dust on the scales; he weighs the islands as though they were fine dust."

"Lebanon is not sufficient for altar fires nor its animals enough for burnt offerings."

"Before him all the nations are as nothing; they are regarded by him as worthless and less than nothing."[1]

"LORD, our Lord, how majestic is your name in all the earth! You have set your glory in the heavens. Through the praise of

---

1. Isa 40:12–17.

children and infants you have established a stronghold against your enemies, to silence the foe and the avenger."

"When I consider your heavens, the work of your fingers, the moon and the stars, which you have set in place, what is mankind that you are mindful of them, human beings that you care for them?"

"You have made them a little lower than the angels and crowned them with glory and honor. You made them rulers over the works of your hands; you put everything under their feet: all flocks and herds, and the animals of the wild, the birds in the sky, and the fish in the sea, all that swim the paths of the seas."

"LORD, our Lord, how majestic is your name in all the earth!"[2]

What do Liverpool, Birmingham, and Brighton, have in common? Only two of these locations have a Premiership football team. But more importantly, they were the focus of the recent party conference season.

Through my employment with the Salvation Army, I was able to attend three conferences. My focus was very much on my work, so I am not really qualified to give you a definitive account of all that went on, although that doesn't usually stop me. I do, however, offer my reflections.

Sometimes these conferences are known for the bold headlines, huge egos, and sometimes comical events that take place. However, they set the scene for the important application of Christian witness. After all, it was Desmond Tutu who famously quipped: "When people say that the Bible and politics don't mix, I ask them which Bible they are reading."[3]

Thus, each year, the Salvation Army along with colleagues from other churches—the Methodist Church, Baptist Union, Quakers in Britain, and United Reformed Churches—make a beeline for the Conservative, Labour, Liberal Democrat, and SNP party conferences. Our work is, in many ways, relationship-building. We can share our experiences as churches and learn from each other. Fundamentally, it is underpinned by the recognition that there is a need for Christian witness at the conferences as we work with politicians in the work of reconciliation and committing to the common good. At a time when political debate can be polarized or even toxic, this model of engagement should not be underestimated. In addition, the Salvation Army runs fringe meetings each year. These are focused events seeking to highlight a specific policy concern, build our profile, and make an

---

2. Ps 8.

3. Attributed to Desmond Tutu—https://quotepark.com/quotes/1771720-desmond-tutu-when-people-say-that-the-bible-and-politics-dont/.

impact. This year at the Labour Party conference in Liverpool, we focused on employability, and at the Conservative Party conference our campaign on adult social care.

Our ecumenical work has a commonality at all three conferences: connections with the main prayer breakfasts—organized by the respective Christian fellowship associated with the particular political party—a series of meetings with MPs; and organizing fringe meetings.

My aim is not to bore you with the details of my comings and goings but to reflect on some deeper themes that emerged from these areas of mission.

Prophetic and Pastoral

I attended an event in the summer promoted by Sojourners. They reflected on work that the US churches had done to protect the poor when the Obama administration came under severe budgetary pressure. This campaign that transcended the US culture wars was called "The circle of protection,"[4] a protective encircling of the poor by churches and their prophetic campaigning. Crucially this work had a pastoral and a prophetic dimension. To some degree, our work in politics is to embrace a prophetic and pastoral orientation, i.e., holding all systems up to the reality of God's kingdom and loving the people whom we engage with and are advocating for. It would be unfair to oversimplify this, but one tends toward a right love of truth and one towards a right love and acceptance of people. Together they personify the multi-faceted majesty and grace of Christ.

In the same register, when I witnessed the launch of *Christians on the Left's* latest campaign, *Love your CLP*, I felt something prophetic stirring. Labour does not need civil war, it needs civility. It needs some love. The prophetic and pastoral embraced in one campaign.

Prayerful

Our engagement at Party conference sees prayer as an essential part of the political process. When too much of the policy world is rooted in enlightenment wisdom and the technique of modernity, we could lose our distinctiveness. We should be careful not to abandon our fundamental practices

4. Wallis, "What is the circle of protection?"

and try and ape the world and its desire for influence, positioning, and success. We can't always do this, and we don't always need to. In my view, prayer breakfasts should be more about prayer than breakfasts. Of great encouragement, our conference meetings with MPs offer prayer. It is refreshing to see it being received. When the Reverend Michaela Youngson from the Methodist Church spoke at the *Christians on the Left* prayer breakfast about *prayer as a revolutionary act*, you could clearly see the need for us to raise our voices and raise our sights. What if each party conference had one day in the week devoted to prayer? Bono once said: "Dream up the kind of world you want to live in. Dream out aloud."[5]

Perspectives on poverty

The Conservative Christian Fellowship prayer breakfast reflected on the interaction between loneliness and poverty. We heard about the dangers of isolation in an increasingly fragmented and isolated world. As Christians, I believe we need to care about material and relational poverty. Again, the very fact that the Conservative Christian Fellowship even put on such an event is prophetic and pastoral. Who would have thought that loneliness would become a political issue? Well, there has been a cross-party campaign on this issue, but to their credit the Conservative Government has pioneered a strategy on this issue and appointed a Minister to oversee it too. Maurice Glasman once reflected that: "There is no love in the system."[6] If we could bring a bit of love, befriending, and decency into politics, we might see some amazing changes. To some this will sound *twee*. Yet, friendship can be prophetic.

Our perspective on any issue cannot simply be the same as the world's view. That is why I quote Isa 40 and Ps 8 at the start of this article. So much about politics is rooted in human priorities not God's perspective, let alone his kingdom. Let's strive to start from his perspective and we shall end up in a good place.

5. Bono, Quotemaster.
6. Glasman, "Labour Pains," Third Way, March 2012, Line 260.

Paradox (Embracing)

During the Liberal Democrat Party Conference in Brighton, we attended the Liberal Democrat Christian Forum prayer breakfast—the main Christian body associated with the Liberal Democrat Party. Tim Farron MP, Liberal Democrat, Westmorland and Lonsdale, spoke about the power of total forgiveness.

The political world is harsh and unforgiving. Some might say that the media—or rather social media—has a lot to blame for this but the companies running them don't bear the whole responsibility. It is hardly surprising if the system is at times dysfunctional if MPs are berated for every mistake they make or every nuance that is misinterpreted. Fed by a shallow social media culture we are creating a vortex of spite. We need to pray for a forgiving spirit to permeate national life.

The current Liberal Democrat *Christian Forum* magazine refers to the "power of listening," again this message of forgiveness and listening is a prophetic and pastoral statement as it runs counter to the modus operandi of contemporary politics.

Christian engagement in politics should seek the paradoxical as a prophetic statement. Forgiveness, listening, love and friendship—all alien to certain political creeds—if embedded in the political system could be transformational.

Positive yet perpetually counter-cultural

Christian involvement in politics need not be throwing rocks all the time at politicians, in the main and in my experience the vast majority of politicians, left, right and center enter the vocation for noble reasons. Yet, we are not meant to be genuflecting to liberal democratic culture either. We are not the prayer wing of *Progress* or *Bright Blue*[7]. We are to be as Stanley Hauerwas said: "resident aliens."[8]

There is a crucial point to be made that a Christian perspective is not just a lovely, healthier contribution—although it is—it is vital. For example, the below quote which reflects on a theological perspective on the global refugee crisis leaves us in no doubt, that it is impossible to reflect on human life—apart from the mystery of God. So, politics without God —something

---

7. Progress and Bright Blue are UK based think-tanks.

8. Hauerwas and Willimon *Resident Aliens.*

William Booth warned about—is a real danger and a dangerous reality. We need theology in our politics, it's not just a *nice to have* the alternative is a culture of death.

> "In the book of Genesis we are introduced to a central truth that human beings are created in the image and likeness of God. (Gen 1:26–27; 5:1–3; 9:6; 1 Cor 11:7; Jas 3:9) This is not just another label but a way of speaking profoundly about human nature. Defining all human beings in terms of "imago Dei" provides a very different starting point for the discourse on migration and creates a very different trajectory for the discussion. Imago Dei names the personal and relational nature of human existence and the mystery that human life cannot be understood apart from of the mystery of God."[9]

So, let's be positive and affirming but please God always counter-cultural. There is a very important reason why this is the case. The incarnation was THE political event not the 1997 election, the repeal of the corn laws, Suez, Brexit or the fall of the Berlin Wall.

> ". . . the vibrant certainty that history has been invaded by God in Christ in such a way that nothing can stay as it was, and all terms of human community and conduct have been altered at the deepest of levels."[10]

A prelude to the Polis

Inevitably party conference season ends. The hustle and bustle of political life resumes and the ongoing debate about Brexit once again dominates the headlines. However, while party conferences are soon forgotten—even with dancing Prime Ministers—yet, from our vantage point, all those attending, in my work sphere, felt it was a highly worthwhile thing to do.

I see clearly that churches have both a prophetic and pastoral role in brokering a space where serious and civil conversation can take place on the issues that we care about. Party conferences provide a space to undertake this work and crucially to bring the churches concerns to the attention of policy makers.

9. Groody,"Crossing the Divide:Foundations of a Theology of Migration and Refugees," 644.

10. Bentley Hart, *The New Testament, XXIX*.

Yet, there is a bigger story. It may be that the church re-evaluates, over time, its engagement with politics. Not to abandon it but to affirm its value and recognize its limits in a more expansive sense of God's kingdom and perhaps to explore a different way of understanding politics. Politics though important, is not a be all and end all. Indeed, we need more confidence in the kingdom shaped political call of the church and its identity as a *polis*. By this I mean a perspective advocated by Stanley Hauerwas. A reviewer of his work reflects:

> "We need not deny Hauerwas oft-repeated claim that the church is a social ethic or the claim of this volume that we need a 'theological politics' that understands the church as an alternative to every other polis or civitas."[11]

We may need as much emphasis upon a sort of new monasticism as predicted by Bonhoeffer and more recently in the *Benedict Option*, embracing what C. S. Lewis termed *deep church*.[12] We are being slowly consumed by capitalism and technology and a very shallow but pervasive variant of liberalism. We should relinquish our fantasies and love of power and seek our calling at the margins of empire. It is time to dig deep and think again about political engagement. Paradoxically, the aforementioned Christian practices can renew the church, society and therefore renew politics.

For the world thinks that the church is marginal to it but the world is marginal to the world. I am all for getting involved in politics, I have spent a lot of my life doing this very thing and it is a good thing, yet it is a drop in the ocean and if we take it too seriously we idolize it. As John Wimber once said about another phenomenon "it is just stuff" and life starts and ends with God.

". . .we can only understand how God is knowable from the way He actually gives himself to be known."[13]

---

11. Meilaender *Keeping Company* Lines 199–202.

12. Walker and Parry, *Deep Church*, 11–16.

13. Barth 'Church Dogmatics', "The Doctrine of God," Editors Preface.

8

Why I am a Christian on the Left

This wide ranging magnus opus, was an answer to a question that lingered with me and so it proved for me to have a cathartic purpose. It was written around the time I was doing voluntary work with the Christian Socialist movement, in the summer of 2010. I am grateful to Andy Flannagan for that opportunity at a difficult time.

This article has taken me a long time to produce. I confess, I somewhat struggled with the title. Does it need to be written? Some Christians are political, and some are not. Some are on the left, in the center, and on the right. Does it matter? Aren't *left* and *right* notions and legacies from the modernist/enlightenment era anyway? Indeed, if we reflect on John Milbank's analysis, traditional references to left and right are pretty much redundant or even deceptive as he has said:

> "We're now at a crossroads. Politics has become a shadow play. In reality, economic and cultural liberalism go together and increase together. The left has won the cultural war, and the right has won the economic war. But of course, they are really both on the same side."[1]

Bertrand Russell wrote a famous essay *Why I am Not a Christian,*[2] and more recently, William Connolly has written an article entitled *Why I am*

1. Suriano, *Three Questions*, Lines 175–177.
2. Russell, "Why I am not a Christian"

Not a Secularist[3]. So, I will attempt to explain why I am a Christian and on the left and, more pertinently, how that shapes my politics.

So, let us begin the journey. I became a Christian when I was fourteen, not too long after I had become politically aware. Essentially, my Christian and political journeys occurred during the same period. The faith element has always been my primary passion, yet my politics—flowing out from this commitment—was also something I have felt strongly about over the past twenty-four-years that I have lived and explored the Christian life while being involved and active in center-left politics. On the basis of the past twenty-four-years, I expect to be on this journey for the rest of my natural life. Sometimes, the connection between my faith and politics feels natural, sometimes there are tensions. I hope it does not contain contradictions, but it does embrace paradox.

First Principles

I believe Christianity is true, it has solid intellectual foundations and is experientially dynamic and vital. I believe in the loving God of the Bible who has revealed himself through his son Jesus Christ. I believe that believers are to seek the kingdom and build the church. We are to "seek first the Kingdom of God and his righteousness." (Matt 6:33) That is where our true heart and passion is, moreover, this is to precede any other allegiance, political tribe, football team, career, or even family. Thus, as a Christian, I should seek to view the world—and political sphere—through a biblical and theological lens and not to view Christianity through a worldly or secular lens.

Pledge our allegiance to the Kingdom of God

Bob Ekblad, a U.S. Christian activist, wrote a book called *Pledging our Allegiance to the Kingdom of God: A New Christian Manifesto*,[4] which is not about procedural politics—although one might argue its core message is political—,but I find the title challenging. It helps me to focus on where my heart should be, and I try and pray that I will pledge my allegiance to the Kingdom of God. This is because in politics, ideologies and world

3. Connolly, "Why I am not a Secularist"
4. Ekblad, *Pledging Allegiance*

views can—no matter how notionally attractive—prove to be idolatrous or ultimately worse.

This allegiance does not infer withdrawal from the world. Our commitment to Christ and his church is realized and lived out in a broken world, fatally loaded against fairness and justice. Man has wrecked social relationships and the environment. We see in scripture that: God's heart is for the poor[5] Isa 61, even to the point of *Bias*[6]—as David Sheppard said.

The Poverty and Justice Bible affirms that more than two-thousand biblical verses relate to matters of justice and poverty. This is central to the gospel and not a *bolt-on* or after thought. Tim Keller has explained clearly, simply and beautifully that God is a God of "generous justice."[7] Justification of sinners leads to seeking justice in God's world. They are linked and not separate.

So, we are not bystanders, God has revealed his passion and agenda and our commitment is to the King and his Kingdom. This Kingdom and the Christology it is rooted in has a particular character or set of distinctives: Jesus showed compassion for the broken, God is passionate about justice and stands against injustice.[8] In Acts 2 we see the early church practicing an authentic and radical form of community. Resources are shared and met in a profoundly counter-cultural manner. We catch a glimpse of the common life that a society founded on humanistic principles might be able to mirror but not match.

This insight of being on the side of the poor, and seeking justice are important to me as a Christian. I am wholly imperfect in what I have actually done based on this disposition, but I would say to a degree they inform my political worldview. They are in my DNA.

The Beauty of Paradox

Despite laying out my starting point and perspectives a number of questions are generated. Does being a Christian and valuing justice and caring for the poor make one left-wing? Does this mean we judge others who attach themselves to different political traditions? Clearly it does not.

---

5. See Isa 61.

6. Sheppard, *Bias*, 10.

7. Keller, *Justice*, 40.

8. See Isa 58.

The problem is life is not so simple. Are all on the left caring and compassionate? Are all on the right indifferent to injustice and the poor? Clearly not, I cannot help but admire what Iain Duncan-Smith (IDS) has done to restore the Conservative case for standing up for the poor. His work in establishing the Centre for Social Justice has, I believe, provided a challenge to the Labour Party on matters of social justice. A cause that it seemed to believe was its domain. In doing so, IDS stands in a long and noble tradition of compassionate Conservatism including such luminaries as William Wilberforce and Lord Shaftesbury.

I would, however, critique the noble one-nation[9] Conservative tradition. It is one strand within the broader Conservative tradition, other elements of Toryism I find slightly unsavory and alien.

So, I acknowledge these facts, tensions and paradoxes. Yet, I am still a Christian who is drawn to the left side of politics. Yet, this statement is made when perhaps we are seeing slight but certain changes in the assumptions that underpin UK politics. As Phillip Blond recently wrote:

> "Perhaps for the first time in thirty years politics is changing. The old orthodoxies of left and right are still dominant, but they are no longer hegemonic. Beneath the surface the tectonic plates are shifting, boundaries are blurring, and ideologies are returning to first principles, creating a new terrain that is slowly beginning to emerge."[10]

So, I acknowledge these facts, tensions and sense of paradox that rightfully counsels against some of the points I am making. Yet, I am still happy to describe myself as a Christian drawn to the left-side of the political spectrum.

I will continue to explore and explain this journey, please bear with me.

What is means to be a Christian and involved in politics has been something that I have been reflecting upon much more in the past five years. Initially, I took the view that being involved in the political realm was important as an act of citizenship. I still think this is the case. Although my initial articulation of this was a little superficial.

The following quote from Theodore Roosevelt reminded me of the importance of being involved in politics. It contains a warning not to merely observe and perhaps being judgmental from the sidelines.

9. 'One Nation' refers to the more socially and economically moderate wing of the Conservative Party in the United Kingdom.

10. Blond, *Changing the debate*, 1.

"It is not the critic who counts: not the man who points out how the strong man stumbles or where the doer of deeds could have done better. The credit belongs to the man who is actually in the arena, whose face is marred by dust and sweat and blood, who strives valiantly, who errs and comes up short again and again, because there is no effort without error or shortcoming, but who knows the great enthusiasms, the great devotions, who spends himself for a worthy cause; who, at the best, knows, in the end, the triumph of high achievement, and who, at the worst, if he fails, at least he fails while daring greatly, so that his place shall never be with those cold and timid souls who knew neither victory nor defeat."[11]

There is something in Roosevelt's wise words and perhaps I am importing them into a different context, but I have found this helpful. Of course, it is not the last word in Christian analysis. For example, a prophetic voice might be seen as critical. Thus, at one level we should not endorse a view that says we must have no truck with criticism where it is rooted in the right motives and expressed in a loving spirit. Christians are at times called to take a critical or rather prophetic stance, this might take place *inside* or *outside* the system.

Christian Socialism

The home for many Christians on the left has been the Christian Socialist Movement (CSM). Earlier this year CSM celebrated its fiftieth anniversary.

Through the work of R.H. Tawney and Donald Soper and many other pioneers there is a tradition of Christian Socialism that is recognized within the Labour movement. I am now happy to say I am a Christian Socialist, in that order as well.

For me it is Christian Socialism that needs to be further defined in this era. For it holds within its tradition's treasures and perspectives that Labour sorely needs. The need for values, the championing of the common good, a response to commodification of relationships, secular capitalism and consumerism are all urgently required. The affirmation of the role of faith in public life, the politics of relationships and the primacy of family life must form the bedrock of a Christian Socialist contribution to Labour's necessary renewal.

11. Roosevelt, "Citizenship in a Republic," Lines 114–123

This tradition is distinct from progressivism and liberalism that seem to be dominant in important sections of Labour's architecture. I will expand on what I mean later.

The Common Good or Progress?

The notion of the Common Good is deeply associated with the Christian Socialist tradition and the phrase has become more familiar across the political piece. Rooted within Catholic social teaching—a vital resource for the Christian left—it talks of a form of politics that eschews individualism and notions of the self-detached autonomous person from our true humanity.

The common good posits a notion of human flourishing rooted in our commitments to the wellbeing of others. It speaks of the question of establishing a political settlement that is more profound than a society orientated around *my needs* and *my rights*. To use a contemporary example, did the closure of Roman Catholic adoption agencies due to their *failure* to conform with particular notions of equality achieve the common good? The closure of many of these agencies and the loss of loving support for vulnerable children suggests to me that this decision was not in accord with the politics of the common good. I chose a controversial example, but it was the first one to pop into my mind.

It would seem that the common good does not accord with certain forms of liberalism which is rooted in individualism and an enlightenment conception of the self. Neither does it accord with the narrative of progress which seeks commitment to certain nostrums in the hope of a perfect future, yet can have unhelpful impacts on ordinary people. In general—while the environment is fundamentally important—environmentalism appears, inadvertently, to produce policies that fall disproportionately on the working class. This need not be the case.

Thus the espousal of Christian Socialism and the politics of the common good are a helpful and historically fecund starting point. This tradition needs to be strengthened because the alternative narrative on the left-liberal progressivism is problematic for a number of reasons.

I need to be careful here. I am not liberal and not progressive. I understand what people mean when they use these words as they are nearly always well-intentioned. Crucially, critiquing liberalism does not mean I am adopting a conservative tradition as conventionally or historically understood. Alasdair MacIntyre accurately describes the position I am attempting to articulate.

> "This critique of Liberalism should not be interpreted as a sign of any sympathy on my part for contemporary Conservatism. That Conservatism is in too many ways a mirror image of the liberalism that it professedly opposes. Its commitment to a way of life structured by free market economy is a commitment to an individualism as corrosive as that of liberalism. And, where Liberalism by permissive legal enactments has tried to use the power of the modern state to transform social relationships, conservatism by prohibitive legal enactments now tries to use that same power for its own coercive purposes."[12]

Yet we must critique liberalism, as its hegemony is almost unquestioned. It has become synonymous with being *good* without requiring much more reflection. I would say liberalism now has reached its limits and has *morphed* into something distinct from original post-English Civil War liberalism with which I have sympathy. In contrast, progressivism has less of a heritage, is shallow and taken to its logical conclusion actually dangerous and anti-Christian.

It is understandable how these phrases become the *lingua franca* of the center left. Understandable but not always helpful. To my mind when the Labour Party became less certain of the relevance of socialism or democratic socialism, the use of the term *progressive* crept in. It was an attempt to define someone who is on the left and not conservative. The problem is that even now some conservatives of a liberal bent might call themselves *progressive*, so it is a kind of complex matter, as complex as some of the points I alluded to earlier. As I said, one needs to be compassionate and not shrill about this discourse. For, it should be a good thing that one looks to the future with hope and seeks to move things forward. Christianity is a message of hope and faith and redemption. The problem is that very few people can define what it means to be *progressive*, it is also problematic from a Christian perspective. I don't believe we are progressing towards a perfect, humanistic utopia in this life. In fact, attempts to do so are potentially disastrous. I sense that much of the *liberal progressive* agenda is rooted in a secular humanist view of the world. So, the scope for a Christian engagement with this phenomenon is limited. Hence, I feel a far healthier

---

12. MacIntyre, *After Virtue,xiii.*

path lies in contextualizing Christian Socialism for the challenges of today and defining what we mean by the common good.

Surprised by Hope

My belief is in a hope rooted in God's *inaugurated* kingdom, which was ushered in by the death and resurrection of Jesus Christ. One day this kingdom will be realized forever. That is where history, I believe, is heading. God is concerned in this real hope, found in Christ transforming and shaping people's lives, their families and communities. So true progress can only be linked to an understanding and belief in God's purposes for mankind. We are called not to be gloomy and defeatist but to work with this God of hope that his purposes may be established. Yet, this is different from an abstract ideology looking for secular humanistic solutions to the intractable problems faced by the human race.

Importantly from my perspective, I do not believe I have ever heard the word progressive, or many other words used by the political class used by an actual voter. It talks of a future day that may never come, pursuing long-term idealistic goals whose effect is to cause pain now—unwittingly—and mitigates against the common good and common sense. It is a word that, pushed too far, is anti-Christian and its use reflects the paucity within UK left thinking.

The kind of hope we are talking about leads to involvement in the real stuff of people's lives, bringing love and God's present to the broken. Engagement in politics can be an expression of this Kingdom activity. Yet, it is only a small part of it and of course is not the domain of one political party or movement. Seeking the common good and connecting with the real issues of people's lives should be what we are about. It is about being human abstraction is a distraction. Talking about *things getting better*, raising expectations through vast public expenditure programs that mean little to people and hinting at "jam tomorrow"[13] and what the Tories would cut are no longer an option for Labour. It needs to be straight with the electorate and re-orientate the party in the experience and language of ordinary people. So, are we about the common good or progress? Do we promise *jam tomorrow*? Or do we promote flourishing now and seek community and contentment. For if seems to me rather than the mantra of strident progressivism some things will get better, some things will get worse, and

---

13. Perkins, "Barbara Castle Obituary," Line 76

some will stay the same. My football team finished eleventh in the Premier League last season.[14] Next year might be better, it might be worse—I don't know. We can speak of a world of love, relationships and beauty or condemn people to the disenchanted world of utilitarianism, rationalism and managerialism.

Rooted in Reality

In my teens I used to work with a laboring company run by a chap from my local church. I worked with local men who had experienced unemployment at some point. The vast majority of them were not materialistic or greedy or necessarily aspirational. Of course, they were not perfect but they were decent. Their expectations were not unrealistic or fancy, but were content with a steady job, the ability to take their family out for a pub meal every month and having one or two family holidays a year: not a lot to ask for. Furthermore, I would add to that list of expectations the presence of good healthcare and half-decent local schools and I think you are near what a lot of people are content with. Pretending we can build utopia or that one government is vastly better than another one is not credible. That is not the starting point with some of the blokes I am referring to.

Identity and Place

Being a Christian Socialist also demands that I reflect on who I am and where I am from. Now, here is a paradox. I have largely and still largely believed that as a Christian I am slightly suspicious of national or any other local identity. Indeed, I believe this to be my disposition. I aim to identify with God's kingdom and his worldwide, beautiful and diverse church as a primary attachment. Yes, and the paradox is I am from somewhere, I was born in the English Midlands, I now live in southeast London. One on level, I relate to these identities. Surely, the fact that God became incarnate in Christ, in a real place to some degree reflects God's commitment to people and places. My natural inclination to eschew local identity as parochial is now being challenged. Place is important. Parish churches have names and contexts.

14. I think things got better then worse for West Brom.

For we are not free-floating, rational beings ripped out of context. In the era of rapid globalization and world culture the pace of change threatens traditional identities and sense of rootedness. Identity is important.

I am a Christian, from the Midlands, with an Irish surname and some Scottish blood. Yet, I am English and am intrigued by the reference to the need for the specific Labour tradition in England to be developed. This English tradition of virtue as referred to by Jon Cruddas MP and Maurice Glasman is worthy of an essay on its own. It needs more than an essay, it needs embracing. It is a tradition of liberty, justice and virtue. One of Labour's overlooked and misunderstood leaders, George Lansbury, perhaps embodies this tradition. One of romance rather than rationalism.

> "I believe the significance of George Lansbury was his ordinariness; he was embedded in the common people. That is why he was so loved and adored. Dylan Thomas once said that the Labour movement at its best is both "magical" and "parochial." That perfectly describes Labour's greatest leader, George Lansbury—"good old George"—his humanity is both magical and parochial. It is timeless. Tragically, he gave more to us than *we* gave to him. He deserved so much more."[15]

Labour's forgotten leader, George Lansbury, an English working class leader of Labour deserves to be honored. He was a Christian, Eastender, a champion of the poor and many unfashionable causes. History has been unkind to him. Yet, here was an individual Labour should look to romantic, Christian, principled who lived among the people. The English tradition of virtue will be needed as Labour faces an uncertain future. What matters is not what works—ultimately does anything really work in politics and life? What matters is what is right, virtuous and true. Give me one dreamer over a thousand rationalists any day.

Note Lansbury was a Christian Socialist, the radical English tradition has a strong religious flavor. Tony Benn seemed to understand that the Labour tradition is located within a radical stream that has flowed through English history. From Tyndale giving the Bible to the people and the radical tradition of the Diggers; Levellers; Tolpuddle Martyrs; and Chartists. If we have lost this then we need to revive it.

---

15. Cruddas, "George Lansbury: The unsung Father of Blue Labour," Lines 172–177.

The Primacy of Family Life

I have been married for three years and have two sons. I am enthralled literally every day with the joy, focus and responsibility that fatherhood can bring. In the past year I have felt the profound difference that family has meant to me.

When I was unemployed for five months in 2010 it wasn't the state, my trade union or the Labour Party that helped me, it was my family, friends and my church. Recently, it has been family and the church that have proved immeasurably supportive as our family has expanded.

Families should not be a political football. Yet, they are centrally important to the common good. If politics really is the right ordering of our relational priorities[16] this must mean affirming family life. I find it hard to see how a Christian view of the primacy of the family should not be expressed somehow in public policy.

Yet, for some reason, the left seems to be nervous about the family and marriage. Well, to me there is nothing wrong with expressing the truism that children need to be raised in environments of love, fidelity, security and with two parents. To me families should not necessarily come in all shapes and sizes all of the time, they might well do, but they shouldn't. There is a normative pattern, this is not to be ungenerous or judgmental to those whose experience of family falls short of the ideal. To me it is commonsense, and a liberalized view of the family unit has been corrosive in our society.

When we reflect on the recent riots and we do need to be careful it seems to be issues of family and fatherhood cannot be overlooked in our prognosis. In an article reflecting on the disorder, Jon Kuhrt identifies consumerism, a breakdown in moral authority and the collapse of the family as factors potentially fueling the disturbances.

> "What we are seeing is the massive impact of broken and dysfunctional families. Where are the dads stopping their kids from going out and rioting? Too often it is left to mums struggling alone who cannot physically stop their children. A cocktail of poverty, amoral attitudes, both parents having to work and the loss of any sense of personal responsibility means that the traditional barriers to poor behaviour simply don't exist. We have been too scared to talk

16. Bickley, *Building Jerusalem*,1.

about family breakdown for fear of being judgmental but it is the biggest cause of poverty, exclusion and violence in the UK today."[17]

This is not a dividing line between the right and the left, Labour should be relaxed about affirming family life and marriage. It may well be that the state can do little to promote marriage and family life—the state is not neutral. However, my heart drops when I see the overreaction of Labour colleagues to David Cameron's proposal—as yet unfulfilled—to recognize marriage in the tax system. It strikes me that this policy is not about the extra £3-a-month it is about a positive affirmation of marriage. I welcome that.

Labour cedes the ground of marriage and families to its peril. After all, as John Harris seems to be alluding to, it should be natural territory for the left, a no-brainer.

> "More fundamentally, what about the family? Sometimes, perhaps, it's best to prize apart the words 'liberal' and 'left', and realize that if you claim to base your politics on such ideas as mutual concern, you'd better start with the institution in which most of us first learn what it means—and yes, that entails a long-overdue conversation about the importance of fathers."[18]

Being Unguarded—Being a 'Loser'

I have started to chart my journey thus far and the insights gained. I suggest some themes where I believe the Christian faith speaks into the renewal of Labour.

I am trying not to impose my opinion but be unguarded and open about the tensions a Christian involved in politics might have to negotiate and also to underline the sense of disappointment and failure that can characterize this path.

As I alluded to earlier my faith is primary and has an allegiance to the Kingdom of God yet finds an expression politically. Do I get this right all the time? No. Indeed, I find that in these challenging times of flux, the challenge of applying my faith to a certain political position becomes ever more complex. For example, I like the Red Tory thesis as I support Blue Labour.

17. Kuhrt, "The unpredicted tinderbox—3 factors which fuelled the riots," Lines 55–63.

18. Harris, "These horror stories offer the left home truths," Lines 73–77.

My aim is to be a Christian first and foremost, I have Conservative friends, I feel much in common with some of them, but I am Labour. This is all part of the beauty of life but perhaps in the final analysis perhaps it proves how fragile notional political identities are or have become.

In positing a paradox perhaps there is an element of doubt within the points I am seeking to make. Perhaps, the complexity that I acknowledge makes a mockery of my own title—are not left and right vestiges of a failed and crumbling apparatus? Does the need to ask the question hint at what is problematic in seeking to straddle these worlds? Perhaps the notion of being left has been made so interchangeable with being liberal that this secular turn causes dilemmas for people like me. Hence the article.

In the final analysis as a Christian, I will aim to ". . .seek first his Kingdom. . ."[19] and find my identity there. Yes, indeed one does need to be suspicious of all other competing and even idolatrous identities. Yet, mature faith leads to engagement and love for God's world. Politics is *missional* and can be an element of Christian discipleship.[20] The content and tone of that area of discipleship will vary considerably.

Engaging Secular Capitalism

Having stated my journey, conviction, and apparent paradox, there is one area that I feel is of defining importance. I refer to the sphere where I am perhaps most at home with identifying with a left-sided worldview is on economics or political economy as it is described.

The last four years of credit-crunch, recession, exposure of the financial system and debt-laden economies have clearly asked questions about the architecture and foundations of the economic system—both in the UK and abroad.

We need to ask serious questions about the assumptions and values that the economy has been built upon. Of late I have felt myself moving more to the left on this issue. Why? A personal experience of unemployment left me feeling like a commodity and it was difficult. I am fortunate for all the support and anchors that I alluded to earlier. Please don't tell me that personal experience does not inform political economy. There aren't many Keynesians in Surrey, nor affiliates to the Chicago School, in the Rhondda.

19. Matt 6:33
20. See Reimer, *Missio Politica*.

This experience, I hope, has not made me cynical—not an emotion for the people of hope—but combined with the evidence we all see of the economic dysfunctioning, it begs important questions. Should Christians in the West be more critical of capitalism? Should Labour develop a more strident narrative on globalization and capitalism? I believe the answer to both these questions is *yes*, the answer lies within Christian Socialist traditions of ethically rooted notions, not in secular Marxism. In seeking to explore this possibility and constructive and loving manner R. H. Tawney and others provide a rich seam from which we may mine.

One of the significant elements of the Blue Labour contribution to renewal on the left has been the re-visiting of the work of Karl Polanyi. The Hungarian economist in his "Great Transformation"[21] accounted for the development of the market society in England after the industrial revolution. Land and labor became mere "commodities" at the hands of the market, representing a radical and corrosive break from previous social and economic norms. The "commodification" thesis rings true in the situation in the UK. We witness exploitation and the reach of the market penetrating seemingly every section of the socioeconomic infrastructure. It is the dominant paradigm to the level of idolatry.

Perhaps, now is an opportune time to draw upon Polanyi in understanding the challenge we are presented with.
"It is also important now to re-read carefully Karl Polanyi's The Great Transformation, arguably the most important work of political economy written in the last century."[22]

In the aforementioned interview Milbank even alludes to the tendency of capitalism to be no respecter of the sacred.
"Again Polanyi clearly saw that capitalist 'primary accumulation' is always also an act of desacralization."[23]

This does beg the question, if this analysis is correct, what is our response? Perhaps a response to the pressures of the market—and the state—based on the sacred. Human beings are endowed with a sacred worth and relationships have primacy. These are not to be subordinated to the whim of the market or the agenda of the state.

---

21. Polanyi, *Transformation*.

22. Suriano, "Three Questions on Modern Atheism: An Interview with John Milbank," 5.

23. Suriano, "Three Questions on Modern Atheism: An Interview with John Milbank," 6.

The oft-cited example of London Citizens rightfully points to the power of faith communities working to affirm the dignity of labor. The London Living Wage[24] is a living breathing witness to the fact that relational power can transform capital's interaction with labor. It has recently been adopted as a key campaigning objective by Labour Students. Good for them, because there is much to do in this Labour campaign to drive exploitative wages out of our nation for good. Importantly, the Christian church cannot accept the *God* of the market as a given. It needs to challenge the hegemony and logic of *big business*. I would differentiate here enterprise, which is a good thing, and systemic capitalism, which is not so good.

I appear that there is something deeply secular now about capitalism and that is truly frightening.

Was there once an era when an ethos of trust and virtue, albeit perfect, might for a few generations or more ensured that markets were embedded in some semblance of decency? If such a time did exist, I would now submit that we are no longer enjoying the fruits of such a settlement. Capitalism is secular, nihilistic, and able to do profound damage to many things that Christians hold dear, we need to be prepared to expose it to serious theological critique and where possible resist it.

We need to be biblical, prayerful and rigorous in our analysis. Indeed, how can we suspend our critical faculties and a theological perspective on economic activity?

> "That is why theology is so important—so indispensable, a believer would say . . . It recalls us to the idea that what makes humanity human is completely independent of anyone's judgments of failure or success, profit or loss. It is sheer gift—sheer love, in Christian terms. And if the universe itself is founded on this, there will no sustainable human society for long if this goes unrecognized."[25]

This strikes me that theology and the Christian concept of humanity is at odds with the reality of secular capitalism. They inhabit a profoundly different universe. This also contains a warning about the future of human society.

Indeed, questions about the virtue of capitalism are being asked by thoughtful, mainstream thinkers such as Michael Schluter. In *Is Capitalism*

---

24. See here for a definition of the London Living Wage—https://www.london.gov.uk/programmes-strategies/business-and-economy/london-living-wage.

25. Williams, *Knowing our Limits*, 33–34.

morally bankrupt? Five moral flaws and their social consequences[26] he questions the moral basis of capitalism, suggesting that Christians need to seek a new economic order based on biblical principles.

In unpacking his analysis Schluter specifically suggests that capitalism is "exclusively materialistic"[27] offers "reward without responsibility"[28] and he queries the morality of the principle of "limited liability of shareholders"[29] He infers it disconnects "people from place"[30] This is a Blue Labour argument and it refers to the historic injustice of the enclosure movement. Schluter also criticizes capitalism's "lack of social safeguards"[31] These flaws result in family and community breakdown and the growth both of state and corporate power.

In concluding his paper, Schluter seems to suggest that Christians must face the need to address the destructive inadequacies of capitalism in the name of the gospel.

> "If Corporate Capitalism is contributing significantly to the moral bankruptcy of Western societies, can Christians nevertheless accept it as part of their cultural context and concentrate just on personal evangelism and meeting individual need? The prophets thought it was necessary for God's people to tackle the causes, not just the symptoms, of social breakdown and injustice. So did Jesus himself. How, then, can Christians avoid the urgent call to reform Capitalism radically?"[32]

According to Adrian Pabst Christianity ushered in a peaceful end to the Cold war, and it can also address the failure of secular capitalism: "There is now a unique opportunity to enact a new socioeconomic settlement centered on human relationships, families and communities rather than the binary, secular logic of the individual and the collective."[33]

---

26. Schluter, "Capitalism"
27. Schluter, "Capitalism," 2.
28. Schluter, "Capitalism," 2–3.
29. Schluter. "Capitalism," 3.
30. Schluter, "Capitalism," 3.
31. Schluter, "Capitalism," 3–4.
32. Schluter, *"Capitalism,"* 4.
33. Pabst, "Christianity ended the cold war peacefully," Lines 90–93.

The Primacy of Civil Society

We are witnessing a debate on the *Big Society* agenda and renewal of localism. We are now at a fascinating juncture in British politics and one that could provide for the renewal of the left, yet this is a big *if*.

It is uncertain when we will see Labour re-elected. My sense if Labour might be in for a considerable period of opposition. There are many variables for and against this proposition and I cannot elucidate this possibility here. Yet, whenever a future Labour government does form, it surely must regain the trust of the people on the basis that it will control public spending and not adopt an overt statist posture. For too many people, Labour is seen as the party that ushered in the current economic malaise. Fair or not, the deficit was racked up on Labour's watch, and was seen as too intrusive and too bossy. This applies to Labour's record on religious liberty as well as the criticisms on civil liberties.

A Christian Socialist agenda should be one that is skeptical of the state being the singular default instrument through which Labour achieves its aims. There is much that can be achieved in seeking a renewal of civic society—Big Society or Good Society, I care not—and an ability to propose solutions on a local level. This is not to argue for a minimal state but to seek possibilities for the common good and human flourishing beyond the bureaucracy of the state. It is a matter of political imagination. I have referred earlier to the example of London Citizens working in the civic space, powerfully energized by faith communities. Community organizing needs to develop and the institution of Movement for Change, operating within the Labour Party, is a recognition of that.

My heart would be warmed if in future the Labour Party is identified with a relational politics at a local level, local banks and small businesses and dynamic partnerships with faith communities and for many people that means the Christian church.

In my area of southeast London a Labour MP called Alfred Salter, with a strong religious faith, virtually built the Labour Party on a foundation of ethical good works and municipal socialism. This may have been a different era, but it stands as an inspiration of what Labour can be and once was. It was a real, transformative presence in local people's lives, year-in-year-out, and was associated with an authentic and virtuous local leadership.

Years of hope

Christian involvement in politics, can be a vexed affair. The fear of, disastrous models of engagement and domination abound, co-option and idolatry remain clear and present dangers.

I would never say that Christianity should ever be associated with one party or political philosophy. In fact, Christian engagement can be practiced across a spectrum of modes as Kenneth Leech alludes to[34]. It will manifest slightly differently in each context.

Yet, God is a God of incarnation, involvement, and redemption. He does not want us to stand far off merely chucking rocks at flawed social institutions and our equally flawed political leaders. Some of us will be called to seek the Kingdom of God and find our place in this messy jungle called politics.

I would encourage Christian engagement with all modes of public life and all parties. I humbly submit why I find myself identifying with engaging and agitating within the Labour tradition. In this paper I have tried to explore the rationale for that and hopefully be unguarded about the questions and contradictions it too embraces. I hope too that I have suggested some questions and themes that might inform a renewed Christian Socialist agenda that might renew the Labour Party.

I have tried to be honest about where I am Labour have got it wrong and I expect my journey of paradox to continue. I think Labour faces some profound challenges, electoral and existential. But there is hope, there is always hope.

"There are great times ahead for the Labour Party."[35]

---

34. Leech, *Long Exile*, 214–219

35. Glasman, "My Blue Labour vision can defeat the coalition," Line 151

Faith

Questions for Discussion

In the section on *Faith,* I seek to explicate reflections on politics from an explicitly Christian vantage point, you might find the following questions helpful for reflection or discussion:

1. Why should Christians engage in politics? What are the positive possibilities and what are the potential pitfalls?

2. Can we learn lessons from politicians who had faith but lived in a different era?

3. How does an ethical issue such as euthanasia highlight the limits of a liberal worldview?

4. How does prayer correspond to a life of political activism?

5. Is it possible to be a Christian and *on the left*?

6. What difference would a focus on the common good make to political debate and practice today?

7. Should the left in politics develop a discourse that is not progressive per se?

8. How does the Christian faith correspond to capitalism?

Recommended Reading

Walter Brueggemann, *Truth Speaks to Power: The Countercultural Nature of Scripture,* Kentucky: Westminster John Knox, 2013.

John Stott, *Issues Facing Christians Today*, 4th Edition, Grand Rapids, MI: Zondervan, 2006.

Stanley Hauerwas and William H. Willimon, *Resident Aliens: Life in the Christian Colony* Nashville: Abingdon, 1989.

Tim Keller, *Generous Justice—How God's Grace Makes us Just*, London: Hodder and Stoughton, 2010.

SECTION TWO

Politics

9

At Our Best When at Our Broadest

Why Labour needs to be open to a postsecular,
pro-faith and postliberal narrative
and how Blue Labour might be of help

This essay was my contribution to the Blue Labour[1] essay collection, I withdrew it as we needed to reduce the wordcount to meet the publisher's specification. I am delighted to include it in this essay collection.

"What we did for the Labour Party in the new Clause IV, freeing us from outdated doctrine and practice, we must now do, through reform, for Britain's public services and welfare state. We are at a crossroads: Party, Government, country. Do we take modest though important steps of improvement? Or do we make the great push forward for transformation? I believe we're at our best when at our boldest So far, we've made a good start but we've not been bold enough."

TONY BLAIR

1. Geary and Pabst, *Blue Labour: Forging a New Politics*

Introduction

I live in a corner of southeast London, which was synonymous with the London Docklands. Having moved here, I discovered— in addition to it being a wonderful place—it has a special history and specifically a Labour history. More than eighty years ago, it was represented by an MP called Alfred Salter. We could learn a lot from him. While preceding Blue Labour by many generations, Salter may well have recognized where it came from.

Alfred Salter and his wife, Ada, literally devoted their lives to the local people, building a Labour Party founded upon an ethical creed and evidenced in many practical and meaningful works of service. Their history is an inspiring and enduring one. Salter had a strong and principled faith which must have underpinned his conviction and activity. His approach was ethical, and he exhibited a profound commitment to Bermondsey.

> "Salter took greatest pride not in the growth of the material strength of the Labour movement and its achievements, but in its spirit . . . Bermondsey Socialism had two characteristics: First it was humanistic and idealistic—Salter would have said it was religious and Christian. Its motive was not so much a self-interested desire for better material conditions. . . .as a desire for a society of happiness and fraternity for all."[2]

Having read Salter's story, I remember one of my first conversations when I moved to London. I told my housemate's mother that I was working for a Labour MP. She told me that she had grown up in Bermondsey and that her father, without fail, made sure he paid his Labour Party subs. She mentioned the impact that the Labour Party had in the community and that they owned launderettes and so on. I confess, this meant little to me until I read the Salter story and then realized that Gary's mom was describing the Alfred Salter Labour Party in Bermondsey and its legacy that most definitely meant something to ordinary people.

My sense is that Labour has lost something of this ethical tradition, this is not just nostalgia, something that people cherished has died out and it need not have been the case. Blue Labour offers a route to firmly demonstrate that these practices and traditions are relevant to the needs of the working people. The aim of the movement is not to wallow in some romantic notion of life in the 1920s. Rather it asserts that expressions and attachments that characterize Labour's formation have resonance today.

2. Brockway, *Alfred Salter,* 111.

The Labour Tradition

This tradition that has been exiled within Labour has many expressions and the disconnect can be witnessed on many levels. The day after the General Election of 2005 I remember having a telephone conversation with a friend. I remember sitting in a pub talking to an ex-Labour voter disenchanted with New Labour and appalled at the invasion of Iraq, he like it must be said, many others had voted Liberal Democrat in the belief that they were a left-wing alternative.

I remember desperately trying to prove that Labour really was distinct from the Tories, sincerely but a little bit tenuously stressing there were detailed differences, but they were not always apparent. A few years later I only now see the irony and fragility of my position.

In presenting this vignette, I am not seeking to relive the perhaps sterile debate about the 2005 election—remember the negative Conservative campaign— but one thing sticks in my mind from that brief chat, my friend said: "It's not the Labour Party anymore," that's all he needed to say, that was reason enough for him not to vote or even consider voting Labour.

"It's not the Labour Party anymore," you can just hear the Labour Party spokesperson reciting all the achievements that testify to Labour's social democratic integrity and to a point I would do that myself. However, if people instinctively feel that the Labour Party is not authentically Labour anymore—and many do I sense—that's a real problem that no amount of bludgeoning with technocratic statistics will solve. It is in reshaping the Labour Party away from the dead hand of the machine and bureaucratic approaches to politics that this chapter is about. It seeks to honor a breadth of habits and attachments that would enrich Labour and free it from the narrow dominance of a certain, stale expression of center-left politics that I see as too liberal, too secular and fails to recognize the vitality and moral contribution of faith.

As I draft this in March 2012, it is nearly two years since Labour lost power in Westminster and we saw the formation of the Coalition Government. I feel that Labour might be in for the long haul and be facing a while out of power. There are many reasons for this, and this is not a criticism of the leader whom I voted for and have no regrets about doing so. Rather, I feel that Labour faces a profound crisis of identity. To me, Labour's problem is not primarily electoral, it is existential. To be a party that is elected it needs to properly be a party that knows its values, identity and mission. I am not sure that it does. Worst still I believe that Labour, in its present expression, is too narrow and too unrepresentative of the concerns of ordinary people and desperately needs to be a broad and inclusive party. Labour needs to be truly inclusive and specifically not a pale reflection of the political class and liberal elite whose interests seem now dominant.

There are many variables in UK politics at the moment, we cannot be sure what will happen to the economy, we cannot be sure how the eurozone will fare, we do not know if the Coalition will endure, I suspect it will. Yet, all these profound visible and immediate problems mask the deep structural problems that I feel that Labour itself faces. In the opening quote I cite Tony Blair's reasonably well-known conference speech, charging the troops with " . . . we're at our best when at our boldest."[3] Well, yes, in the right context, I would slightly parody this and say Labour is at its best when it is at its broadest. It is at its best when it is truly plural—by that I mean it should be more accommodating to those who have faith, who do not possess a liberal view of the world and it should not be so rigidly secular. By being broad and inclusive Labour could contribute to the genuine political and civic renewal that the nation craves. Yet, it will be hard, and Labour needs to be honest with itself if it really is serious about being plural and not having a tin ear to the concerns of ordinary voters.

My concern is not instrumental, i.e., that Labour should change purely to accumulate votes. I am longer interested in Labour being some sweeping combine harvester for voters. It is a deeper desire that causes me to pen these words. Rather, the party needs to be a truly representative vehicle to fulfill its historical task. It should seek to be genuinely plural and able to accommodate differing voices that well might find their home within an authentic Labour party. This is why I believe that Blue Labour has a role to play in stimulating a broader debate within the movement. It affirms those conservative traditions of faith, family, relationships and honoring of place that a narrow, liberal, metropolitan outlook unwittingly overlooks.

A snapshot of the social and political terrain in the UK underlines the challenge for Labour. The nation appears too deeply conservative. The political class is largely liberal (economically and socially), the old certainties of left and right are fracturing.

The instincts to which I have referred are dispositions which are aligned with the commonsense perspectives of ordinary people in the UK. It would appear that empirical evidence suggests that the instincts of the

3. Blair, Labour Party Conference Speech, 2002, Line 13.

UK population are increasingly conservative, hence rendering Labour's shallow liberalism even more bizarre:

> "Ipsos MORI data shows that in 1998, one third of people agreed that they wanted Britain "to be like it used to be." Ten years later that figure had risen to 61 percent. The Campaign Company divides voters not by left and right, but by "settlers" who want stability and order and "pioneers" who want change. The former group now makes up a massive proportion of the electorate that is being ignored."[4]

We live in a time of apparently paradoxical dispositions. On one hand the nation appears to be more socially liberal, outward looking and tolerant, however the inference that the settlers'[5] constituency is forming, suggests the conservative aspects of the nation are not in atrophy. Simply characterizing the nation as liberal or pioneering won't do, perhaps people seek a desire for continuity as much, if not more, than they thirst for change and progress. In a social context which is increasingly liberal but paradoxically some people seem to be more conservative than perhaps liberalism has reached its limits? If it has over-extended what does that mean for society, for politics—and crucially—what does it mean for Labour—the people's party?

In contrast to this *dispositional conservatism* amongst the people it would appear that this has not shaped the political class. It does seem that increasingly politics is becoming dominated by a narrow genre of people, both in Parliament, Whitehall, the media and be it through lobbying or the aforementioned estates the professionalization of politics now appears deeply embedded. Over the past generation working class representation in Parliament has noticeably and regrettably declined: "Since 1979 there has been a large decrease in the number of MPs who were formerly manual workers, from around 16 percent of MPs in 1979 to 4 percent in 2010."[6] Interestingly, there has also been a relative decline in MPs over the same period from identifiably professional backgrounds. Noticeably, there has been a rise in MPs who come with a political background. All the leaders of the main UK parties have spent a considerable period of their working lives

---

4. Davis,"Labour needs to rediscover its Conservatism," Lines 27–31.

5. In fact it may well be that the mass (five million) of the votes that Labour lost between 1997–2010 belong to this traditional, socially conservative constituency. See Paul Hunter, *'Labour's Missing Millions'*.

6. McGuinness, "Social Background of MPs"

in what most people would recognize as political roles. This generation of politicians I would contend hold a worldview that I would recognize as liberal and secular.[7]

This divergence between the electorate and their representatives is problematic. To a degree (and it is not straightforward) the less MPs look and sound like the people they purport to represent surely the less able they are to do the job yet equally the less plural politics is. It becomes monochrome and rather depressing. It is particularly a problem for Labour, given its roots, electoral base and claim to be the people's party. Do we wonder why the public feel so alienated from politics?

Blue Labour and Postliberal Politics

The UK political settlement is not entirely static, we can reflect that we might be at a moment when things are changing in UK politics, I cannot be certain that they are changing for the better. It appears that the old vestiges of left and right are still with us, however, there might be an emerging fracture in the traditional configuration of politics. In *A New Political Settlement*, Phillip Blond states that:

> "Perhaps for the first time in thirty years, politics is changing. The old orthodoxies of left and right are still dominant, but they are no longer hegemonic. Beneath the surface the tectonic plates are shifting; boundaries are blurring, and ideologies are returning to first principles, creating a new terrain that is slowly beginning to emerge."[8]

What does this new terrain mean for politics? What are its implications for the Labour Party? Is it an inherently welcome development or potentially *regressive*? Or is too early to tell? If Labour is monochrome and introverted, attached to a secular liberal orthodoxy it might find itself in an odd place. This is the key question and my concern in this chapter. It is a

---

7. The outlook of the current crop of Labour MPs is markedly different to that of 80 years ago. Citing *America's God* by Mark Noll, John Micklethwait and Adrian Wooldridge reflect that "[. . .] only eight of the 249 Labour MPs in the House of Commons in 1929–31 described themselves as atheistic or agnostic." See John Micklethwait and Adrian Wooldridge, *God is Back—How the Global Rise of Faith is Changing the World* (London: Penguin Books, 2010), 47.

8. Blond, *Changing the Debate*, 1

dilemma that I believe Blue Labour can at least begin a conversation to honestly confront some of these uncomfortable and sensitive disconnections.

Other esteemed commentators are noticing this new possible moment of flux. For example, David Goodhart has made some interesting observations on a nascent postliberalism that to paraphrase Blond, is beginning to emerge:

> "The liberalism that has dominated British politics for a generation is looking battered. The financial crash has eroded confidence in economic liberalism, while the shocking inner-city riots have done the same for social liberalism."[9]

The jaded liberalism that Goodhart refers to and is a problem for Labour contains economic and social expressions. Engaging with both these discourses is essential for Labour and offering a distinct alternative. Simply put, they result in an individualism that is potentially corrosive, harmful to the community and what is sacred and is at odds with the logic of Labour's best traditions. As Goodhart writes elsewhere, both forms of liberalism have been de rigueur with the political elites. They have brought benefits, however now they have reached their limits, exemplify the disconnectedness of the political class and left unchecked represents a major problem. By broadening out beyond these exhausted discourses Labour can begin to renew itself and its connection with the people.

> "The two liberalisms—the 1960s (social) and 1980s (economic)—have dominated politics for a generation, with good reason. Postliberalism does not want to go back to corporatist economics nor to reverse the progress towards race and sex equality. Britain is a better place for these changes. But postliberalism does want to attend to the silences, excesses and unintended consequences of economic and social liberalism—exemplified in recent years by, respectively, the financial crash and last August's shocking riots. With their emphasis on freedom from constraint the two liberalisms have had too little to say about our dependence on each another. They have taken for granted the glue that holds society together and have preferred regulations and targets to tending to the institutions that help to shape us. As the philosopher Michael Sandel puts it: "In our public life we are more entangled, but less attached, than ever before."[10]

9. Goodhart, "The next big thing? Blue Labour and Red Tory: the age of post-liberalism," Lines 1–3.

10. Goodhart, "Welcome to the post-Liberal majority," Lines 21–35.

Finally, in this potential situation of flux which I have alluded to, being open to alternative paths to political liberalism is, I would submit, critical. Not that I want a shrill politics of the Daily Mail, rather in a nuanced way Labour needs to understand what its relationship is to the liberal tradition and define a positive expression for the needs of today. Blue Labour is a vital resource for this reconstruction. As James Purnell wrote in 2010:

> "Labour is best placed to govern because the tradition the times need is ours. We have strong roots in the liberal tradition, but we are not a liberal party, our identity is rooted in the interests of working people and an analysis of capital. While there are deep conservative elements in the Labour tradition, and we should honour them—particularly in relation to the ethics of work, loyalty and love of place, family solidarity and a respect for the moral contribution of faith—we do not accept the distribution of assets as they are, we do not accept that inherited mega-wealth is deserved, and we do not accept that our rulers are always other people."[11]

So, Labour is not a liberal party, it may have a debt to the liberal tradition, but its DNA is distinct. Yet, this distinction appears to have been lost. This is vitally important, not only because a plural party has space for people alienated by metropolitan social and economic liberalism. It also is important because we might be entering a postliberal political phase. As Rowenna Davis has suggested:

> "There is an increasing intellectual fascination with 'postliberalism'. Demos, the left wing think tank, is drawn to the work of Jonathan Haidt, who believes that liberals overly focus on fairness at the expense of wider human concerns about sanctity and loyalty ... Oxford University and a tide of progressive academics are chattering. The tide is turning."[12]

Indeed, the form of liberalism that has been associated with the British left is deeply problematic, particularly for ordinary people. However, I feel the fact that Blue Labour is facilitating the challenging of liberal (or illiberal) hegemony gives us all hope.

I am willing to concede that liberal principles, as properly understood, are good and contribute to the good life, but not liberal dominance.

---

11. James Purnell, "Where is the vitality and vision to win?," Lines 122–130.
12. Davis, "Labour needs to rediscover its Conservatism," Lines 33–37.

Furthermore, for some commentators there has been a need to identify that divergent liberalisms have emerged, some more preferable to others:

> " . . . a schism could be detected in liberal ranks long before September 2001. I call the rival camps 'fleshed-out' and 'hollowed-out' liberalism. The former retains a close resemblance to the ideas of the great liberal thinkers, who were optimistic about human nature and envisaged a society made up of free, rational individuals, respecting themselves and others. The latter, by contrast, satisfies no more than the basic requirements of liberal thought. It reduces the concepts of reason and individual fulfilment to the lowest common denominator, identifying them with the pursuit of material self-interest."[13]

Within Labour ranks, there are signs that people are beginning to question the limits of economic and social liberalism—or libertarianism—might now have now been reached. It is nuanced assessments as proffered by David Lammy the Labour MP for Tottenham that hint that the left might be able to think beyond the rigid limitations of this mindset.
"The two revolutions that have shaped modern Britain—the economic liberalism of the 1980s and the cultural individualism that emerged from the 1960s—produce a shrill society unless they are ameliorated or moderated by something else."[14]

It is in exploring the postliberal space that might herald a future for Labour, not a vapid third way but meaningful expressions of the rich heritage that Labour was birthed in. For in the process of critiquing liberalism I am not adopting a Conservative tradition as conventionally understood. Alasdair MacIntyre accurately sums this up this position as follows:

> "This critique of Liberalism should not be interpreted as a sign of any sympathy on my part for contemporary Conservatism. That Conservatism is in too many ways a mirror image of the liberalism that it professedly opposes. Its commitment to a way of life structured by free market economy is a commitment to an individualism as corrosive as that of liberalism. And, where Liberalism by permissive legal enactments has tried to use the power of the modern state to transform social relationships, conservatism by prohibitive legal enactment's now tries to use that same power for its own coercive purposes."[15]

13. Garnett, *Snake*, 8.

14. Lammy, *Ashes*, 155.

15. MacIntyre, *After Virtue*, xiii.

For some this makes uncomfortable reading, for a critique of liberalism is not to diminish decent liberalism and become populist and shrill. However, failure to confront these problems will only create problems and cede political ground to the reactionary right. Economic and social liberalism do not accord with the instincts of much of the population. Labour needs to be broader in its engagement with conservative traditions and recognize the merits of what Goodhart and others would describe as a postliberal politics.

In some ways, it is in Labour's hands (and within their history) how they choose to respond to these current challenges. I contend that by being more open to faith, less singularly liberal, and less aggressively secular,[16] then the movement could become authentically plural. Furthermore, and more crucially, it would be more open to fresh ways of doing things and enriching conceptions of the good life that are oftentimes overlooked. That really is the nub of my argument.

A truly plural and broad Labour Party would be more amenable to faith. Of course, for Labour, the sense that it owes more to Methodism than to Marx is a relatively well-known statement. However, it can too easily be used to dismiss faith in today's context by a sort of half-hearted acceptance that Labour has a history rooted in ethical but esoteric practices. Yet, looking deeply at Labour history, the religious dimension is not only inspiring, but it also points to a resource that could enrich political life today. A Labour Party that is truly pro-faith would celebrate the achievements of the Salter's, the example of the Lansbury's and the life of Arthur Henderson. Yet, we don't do it that often, in fact, we hardly do it at all. The problem is

---

16. I am mindful that simplistic references to secularism contains limitations. In *Faith and the Public Square* (London: Bloomsbury, 2012), Rowan Williams reflects that "[d]efining secularism isn't easy" (12) and that "in practice, of course, neat secularism is not to be found" (13). In the same book Williams states that "[a] secular society is one in which it is possible to have fair and open argument about how common life should be run because everyone argues on the same basis; the ideal of secularity means that there is no such thing as 'public reason'. Argument that arises from specific commitments of a religious or ideological nature has to be ruled out of court. If arguments of that kind are to be admitted, there is a threat to freedom because assertions are being made which are supposed to be beyond challenge and critique. Behind all this lies the Enlightenment conviction that authority that depends on revelation must always be contested and denied leverage in the public square" (23). It has been pointed out to me that divergent variants of secularism might be constitutional secularism, sociological secularism and ideological secularism. What I am referring to for the purposes of this essay is defining secularism as that tendency to rule out religious convictions from public discourse and deny faith 'leverage in the public square'.

with a party that is too wedded to a modern variant of secularism and hollow outworking of modernity which has no place for the lessons of history, the distinct contribution of faith or the love of place. Nothing is sacred and we lose the breadth and genuine diversity that Labour should contain. The historical stories of Labour's pioneers testify strongly to this rich seam. Yet the party has no memory to reach back to the lessons from past pioneers and in screening out faith it has no desire to reach out to diverse and robust communities of faith today.

The profound tragedy of limiting secular and liberal arrangements means that Labour closes itself off to a rich treasure store of wisdom that the Christian faith provides. For example, I have just finished reading a lively essay collection called *The Crisis of Global Capitalism*.[17] This collection draws reference to Pope Benedict XVI's encyclical *Caritas in Veritate*[18] which is unpacked by theologians and commentators. It is rich in insights and its central observation is that the crisis of global capitalism and secular modernity are concurrent. It infers that a fresh path for political economy might be found which avoids the twin totalitarianisms of neoliberalism and statist socialism. Pope Benedict cites the need for a civil economy rooted in reciprocity and "economies of gift-exchange"[19] rather than the contractual arrangements associated with liberalism. Interestingly, he identifies the interface between secularism and capitalism and liberalism, as follows: "The secular logic at the heart of capitalism is also the mark of the intellectual traditions that have been dominant in the modern age, chief of all political liberalism . . . ."[20]

I have already alluded to the symbiotic relationship between economic and social liberalism. Their orientation would also appear to be part or wholly secular in nature. Thus, these forces that have captured the political elite perhaps also account for the disconnection of ordinary people from participation in mainstream politics who may not share these values or be convinced that they work for them.

I am an evangelical by disposition and believe that Catholic Social Teaching (CST) is streets ahead of evangelical social thinking in many respects.[21]

---

17. Pabst, *The Crisis*.

18. Pabst, *The Crisis*, xi.

19. Pabst, *The Crisis*, 5, 14.

20. Pabst, *The Crisis*, 5.

21. I have recently read Malcolm Brown's book on Anglican Social Theology and that makes a strong argument for this particular contribution. See Malcolm Brown et al.,

A brief survey of the papal *Social Encyclicals*[22] of the last century provide an insight into to the depth and breadth of Catholic Social Teaching. Key themes such as: the dignity of work; just wages; the primacy of labor over capital; human dignity; the promotion of the common good; the legitimacy of trade unions; subsidiarity; and solidarity. They are all elements rich in scope, and social, and political relevance. However, I also observe, more to the point, that certain secular or liberal perspectives would discount such a contribution. Witness the reaction, in some quarters, to the Papal visit to the UK of 2010. If you write off this tradition and ignore applied theology and utterly discount Roman Catholic perspectives, then you overlook oceans of wisdom. This is a profound tragedy and the center-left desperately needs fresh thinking as the traditional orthodoxies are proving to be hollow and empty. Reference to or dialogue with the Catholic Social tradition would be an excellent place to start a renaissance in thinking.[23]

Thus, a pro-faith approach to politics not only recognizes what I would argue is a realistic and true view of the world but it can mean at least public policy can access profound sources of wisdom. I have inferred that a truly plural Labour Party would be pro-faith but moreover it might also on a connected point consider we might be in a postsecular moment in the West. I say this, I hope not out of some narrow—or misplaced—sense of triumphalism but because increasingly observers are inferring that the enlightenment legacy, which was always rather thin is beginning to fragment. As N.T. Wright has said: "The dream of progress and enlightenment has run out of steam."[24] In fact, the fracturing of enlightenment certainties has been linked to the current economic malaise. In a talk focusing on the economic crisis in 2012 Malcolm Brown linked the crash to the philosophical foundations which have underpinned the West for the past few centuries:

> "I would venture so far as to say that what we have on trial here, without any sense of who is to blame in terms of different players in the market now, is quite simply the assumptions of the whole liberal enlightenment project. That may sound overdramatic but I think what we are looking at is a mindset that began with the overall project of the enlightenment itself where it has taken certain

'Anglican Social Theology'

22. Laudato Si' Movement, Social encyclicals

23. There is evidence that there is some awareness of this potential, yet will the center-left only pick and choose those elements of Catholic Social Thinking that fit with its presuppositions? See Matthew Taylor, 'Catholic teaching: The new zeitgeist for Britain's Left'

24. Wright, "Walking to Emmaus in a Postmodern World," Line 34

trajectories from which coming back is going to be extraordinarily difficult, but where in the academy, at any rate in the field of ethics, coming back from that position has been the standard argument of thinkers for the last twenty years or so."[25]

So, if we consider that we are or might be in a postsecular moment—and I cannot venture what that will really mean—then it might be a factor for political parties to ponder. The prospects for all kinds of disciplines and approaches might be radical. As Malcolm Brown alludes to fractures within the enlightenment project having economic ramifications as they have political and social consequences too.

The assertion that secularization theory must be questioned is well substantiated. It was the sociologist Peter Berger who performed a vault face on his original thesis that the world was on an inevitable path towards secularization. Berger has now acknowledged that what we are witnessing is conversely the de-secularization of the world. Has anyone told the left?

"My point is that the assumption that we live in a secularized world is false. The world today, with some exceptions to which I will come presently, is as furiously religious as it ever was, and in some places more so than ever."[26]

Even if we in the UK and Europe are still proving exceptional to the de-secularization process, we should not surely ignore what is happening on other continents. Indeed, if the continent that gave birth to the enlightenment project is now witnessing the fragmentation of that settlement, we should consider we might be in a postsecular era and its implications.

In allowing breadth for the limits of secularism and liberalism (I perceived them as philosophical bedfellows) and acknowledgement of the primacy of faith could heal the disconnect with ordinary people. In many ways, the romantic Labour tradition which I refer to has always found rationalistic Fabianism and liberalism somewhat alien and detached from the concerns of ordinary people:

> "Clement Attlee. He was a man who learned his socialism in the East End. A place where in his words, he said, 'I found there was a different social code. 'Thrift, so dear to the middle classes, was not esteemed so highly as generosity. 'The Christian virtue of charity

25. Brown, "Malcolm Brown asks: what do we value in hard times?," lines 5–13.

26. Berger, *Desecularization*, 2.

was practiced not merely preached' was soon to be alarmed at his first Fabian Society meeting."[27]

Thus, I would contend that Labour is at its best when it is at its broadest and it would be wise to provide space for a postsecular, postliberal and pro-faith narrative. Of course, there is room for other perspectives such ethical socialism, communitarian trade unionism and a *red-green* approach to industrial policy for example. My concern for this chapter is to situate observations about Labour's disconnection within the space opened up by the Blue Labour conversation. That is why I believe it has such a vitally important contribution to make to the UK center-left. The ability to think beyond the parameters that have defined Labour since the 1960s requires negotiation, which is the key theme I have explored. Yet, without recognizing these principal themes Labour risks being bound to a moribund secular and liberal discourse which is a busted flush.

Therefore, I submit that alternative paths need to be found to the stale orthodoxies that characterize Labour and the left. They are empty and hollow. They have run out of road. Blue Labour provides an opportunity to chart a new path, yet one that is rooted in traditions. Labour traditions. From my vantage point the political elites have no compelling answers, the cupboard is bare, and a new approach is needed, paradoxically is not new: it is an ancient path. "The current political and technocratic elites have no answers. Their intellectual capital was informed by the neo-classical tradition of economics . . . This idealized form of human interaction suited the governance model of market choice. But it is devoid of reciprocity, and it leaves individuals with no meaningful relationship to one another."[28]

What then is needed? I do not claim to have the answers. Neither am I seeking a pragmatic shortcut to any Labour Government being elected. I am not claiming Blue Labour is the only show in town, however, it has much to commend it and may well be a vital ingredient in the renewal of Labour. If we want to see the nation renewed, then a transformed Labour Party needs to play a crucial role. Thus, I believe that we, the UK center-left, seriously need to explore the possibilities of building a Labour Party which accepts the limits of secularism, can think and live beyond the liberal straitjacket and that is more skeptical about secularism. I submit that the results would be quite surprising to some. After all, it has been tried before,

27. Byrne, "New Foundations for a New Beveridge: The Right and Responsibility to Work"

28. Cruddas and Rutherford, *Common Life*, 247.

because it was plain common sense, natural to the early Labour pioneers and if revisited and we might just become the Labour Party again:

> "There's a very diverse Christian [tradition] in this country, Catholic and Nonconformist as well as Anglican; and each of them in their different ways speaks of the transformative power of association to resist the domination of the state and the market. The Labour tradition and the Christian tradition are completely linked, and it's about protecting the status of the person from commodification and the idea that our bodies and our natural environment are just to be bought and sold. In the politics of the common good, there has never been a greater need for the gifts that the Christian tradition brings, of which the greatest is love. We have got no love in the system. I have said often that the most important person in the history of the labour movement is Jesus. It's very easy for me as a Jew to take endless inspiration [from him]—and I do. As a carpenter, as a man, he spoke about resistance to the boss and resistance to the king, and he said, you know, that through association you could resist the domination of the worldly powers, the market and the state. And that is his huge gift to Labour. I have spent a lot of time telling people in Labour that it's very, very important that there is not just Christian engagement but Christian engagement in all its diversity. My only fear is that this won't happen."[29]

29. Spencer, *Third Way*, Lines 249–267..

10

Blue Labour and Postliberalism

This article was written at the request of Rev Matt
Bullimore for Crucible—the journal of Christian
Social Ethics in 2014 as it explored postliberalism.

"Blue Labour and its Conservative Party—supporting alter ego, Red
Toryism, signal the end of a liberal ascendancy in British politics."

FRANK BONGIORNO

I am currently thinking very deeply about what it means for me to be a
Christian with an interest in Labour politics and the churches presence
in the public square. A corollary of this reflection has been my involvement
in the Blue Labour movement for the past three-and-a-half years. This is
the closest approximation I have found on the center-left to the values that
I identify with in the twenty years or so that I have been a Labour member.

Blue Labour is a movement situated within the British Labour Party,
which affirms the primacy of: civic society; faith; family; and the honoring
of place. It postulates a political economy that rejects both neoliberalism[1]

---

1. Neoliberalism has been the dominant mode shaping the economies (and societies) of the Western World for the past forty years. George Monbiot describes this system's
chief policy instruments as 'cutting taxes for the rich, privatizing state assets, deregulat-
ing labor, reducing social security' *'If you think we're done with neoliberalism, think again'*,
George Monbiot, The Guardian, 14 January 2013.

and liberal, statist Keynesianism.[2] It is disposed towards a politics of the common good rather than being situated within progressive liberal discourse.

Blue Labour is for good reasons associated with the debate on postliberalism that has attracted some interest in the past couple of years in UK politics. By postliberalism I refer to an intellectual recognition that liberalism is singularly insufficient to explain and establish the good life. It is a disposition broad enough to cover the views of non-liberals (communitarians say who argue that truth is situated within communities rather than abstract values) and those liberals who recognize their creed as a philosophy may have run its course. In unpacking what this term means, David Goodhart refers to.

> " . . . a kind of liberalism (or postliberalism as I would now call it), social democratic in economics but somewhat conservative in culture; reformist towards the continuing wounds of race and class but sympathetic to the rooted communitarianism of middle Britain, and regarding a special attachment to fellow citizens not as a prejudice but as an asset in a more mobile and individualistic society."[3]

It is vitally important to state that this does not mean that everything associated with liberalism is to be rejected. Despite not self-identifying as a liberal, I am willing to concede that liberal principles, as properly understood, are good and can and have contributed to the good life. I am wary of a kind of liberal dominance that can dominate significant sections of public life and ironically become illiberal to other sentiments.

An element of this analysis does indeed entail differentiating forms of liberalism. Some commentators have identified that divergent *liberalisms* have emerged, some are preferable to others:

> " . . . a schism could be detected in liberal ranks long before September 2001. I call the rival camps 'fleshed out' and 'hollowed out' liberalism. The former retains a close resemblance to the ideas of the great liberal thinkers, who were optimistic about human nature and envisaged a society made up of free, rational individuals,

---

2. An economic approach that favors Government intervention in the fiscal cycle to maintain high levels of employment. It proved 'de rigeur' in Western economies until being superseded by Monetarism in the 1970s. For a Blue Labour critique of the Keynesian approach see Maurice Glasman, '*We need to talk about Keynes*', The Guardian.

3. Goodhart, "A 'Liberal Racist'? Me? I Felt Like a Heretic," 37.

respecting themselves and others. The latter, by contrast, satisfies no more than the basic requirements of liberal thought. It reduces the concepts of reason and individual fulfilment to the lowest common denominator, identifying them with the pursuit of material self-interest."[4]

In addition, the conversation has gauged that a proper evaluation of the limits of liberalism is also requisite. The liberalism that I believe has atrophied needs to be clearly identified. As the New Statesman leader reflected in the Spring, " . . . liberalism, at least in some of its guises, does not provide all the answers to Britain's most entrenched problems."[5] Hence, political thinkers have begun to probe and reflect on what is beyond liberalism, hence postliberalism has gained some traction.

I believe that Blue Labour and postliberalism are of more than a passing interest to Christians. However, I would hesitate to describe them as an *opportunity* for the church as that smacks of looking at faith through the wrong end of the telescope.[6] However, in the continuum or tension between the churches prophetic social witness and the necessary pragmatism of political engagement it is a phenomenon to be taken seriously. I hereby explain why this is the case.

Blue Labour is a stimulant[7] to a stale political debate that has proved resistant to orthodox Christian perspectives.

I am fascinated by the interface between faith and politics and this interest has grown in recent years. The challenge of living out an orthodox Christian faith amidst a terrain that presents specific challenges to *serious* Christians has only sharpened my interest and praxis.

These challenges I believe are: an aggressive secularism that resists faith in the public square: a metropolitan liberalism (linked invariably to

4. Garnett, *Snake*, 8.

5. New Statesman "Leader: Liberalism now feels inadequate in this new age of insecurity -The stakes could not be higher,"6

6. I write this article from a reformed evangelical perspective, believing in the primacy of the gospel, the Kingdom of God and the importance of the local church. I perceive politics to be a legitimate expression of public service and missional activity. The distinction needs to be made between this starting point and a totalizing embrace of politics that overlooks faith or seeks to co-opt it.

7. I am indebted to Dr David Landrum for this insight.

secularism) that can border on illiberal tyranny; and the need to forge a common life amidst an atomized society whose foundations are fragmented. I have felt more sensitive to the observation that social and economic liberalism have had their day and secular capitalism is a dehumanizing threat to the planet and society and thus a Christian response is critical. This analysis aligns with the aims of the Blue Labour movement which is situated firmly within postliberal terrain.

These are not the only challenges, but they appear prominent to me and pertinent to the future of center-left politics in the UK. These challenges have shaped the left and proved at odds with public Christian witness. The marginalization of faith denies ordinary people a voice in society. This liberalism is not always malign or conspiring against other contributions, its singular dominance has become the orthodoxy, many who hold to its tenets appear highly uncomfortable or even unwilling to think and act beyond the progressive matrix. As economic and social liberalism have collapsed a vacuum has opened up.

As the nadir of liberal ascendancy is named in some quarters' movements—such as Blue Labour and its conversation partner Red Tory—offer important stimulants to public debate, praxis and the formation of the common life. This is critically important for a number of reasons which I aim to delineate. However, for the purposes of Crucible, I would suggest that they speak to the social and economic challenges that Christians care about, are pro-faith and in part theologically literate, cross-party in nature and crucially affirming of parliamentary democracy. To cite their historical significance, they intentionally are part of a historic mission to restore the place of civic society vis-à-vis the centralizing joint leviathans of market and state.

Maurice Glasman—apparently the "godfather"[8] of Blue Labour—spoke at the Tawney Dialogue of the Christian Socialist Movement in 2011 and cited Jesus as the most formative influence on Labour. He commented that: " . . . the most important person in the history of the labour movement was Jesus."[9] This quote—a surprise perhaps to some—on its own may not mean *a hill of beans*, but if we look at the linkages that Glasman has built with Christian Theologian's John Milbank and Luke Bretherton, both from distinct forms of churchmanship then we can see that the faith element with the Blue Labour wing of postliberalism has substance. The

8. BBC, *Blue Labour*, Line 6.
9. Glasman, *Tawney Dialogue 2011*

liberal center ground has run out of steam and new stimulants are needed to reinvigorate democratic life and strengthen citizenship. It is true that many people engage with Blue Labour from a secular vantage point, yet it is the faith element that could prove one its most enduring features as it underpins and explains many of the substantive themes.

Postliberalism reflects a healthy recognition that economic and social liberalism has had its day:

> "The liberalism that has dominated British politics for a generation is looking battered. The financial crash has eroded confidence in economic liberalism, while the shocking inner city riots have done the same for social liberalism."[10]

Postliberalism acknowledges that the past forty years dominance of the *twin* liberalisms has come to an end. This fragmentation is of course disconcerting, life is now much more unpredictable for many people. For many there is much less money around, wages are being squeezed and foodbanks (thank God for them) are proliferating. Although I allude to the exacting effects of economic malaise and the predicament of the *squeezed middle,* the fragmentation also plays out at the level of culture and identity. The anti-political mood embodied by the not-so *flash in the pan* rise of UK Independence Party (UKIP)[11] and more worrying street activism of EDL are symptoms perhaps of this situation of flux. Sometimes visceral, sometimes more subtle but the challenges of the age are serious. Nature truly abhors a vacuum. The vacuum that opens up requires nothing less than a politics rooted in Christian theology. It recognizes the need to build a generous space that includes others in the construction of a politics of the common good, seeking a more peaceable society and a nation at ease with itself and its neighbors.

Postliberalism does not have a monopoly on the common good but it should have a seat at the table. I write as the Conservative Party conference draws to a close, it could be argued that the modern Conservative agenda is highly liberal. The developing narrative of a reviving economy (not untrue) and the creation of one-and-a-bit million private sector jobs (contestable) sets the scene for a Conservative election campaign that will reflect the

10. Goodhart, *The next big thing?*, lines 1–3.

11. UKIP has now rebranded as Reform UK.

good old years of the 1980s—i.e. Britain is on the road to recovery, don't let Labour ruin it. This to me sounds like a recipe for little real change in our political economy and a rehashed Thatcherism being served up for the British people. Equally, the center-left is still stuck in a progressive matrix. Yet, just like liberalism, the progressive project, despite being well intentioned, has run out of steam, is ill-defined and elitist.

> "The belief in human perfectibility and inevitable moral progress no longer has credibility after Auschwitz and the Gulag Archipelago."[12]

It appears that we have a political class hopelessly distant from the more conservative instincts of British people whether it is on: equal marriage: the UK's role in Europe; family life; or immigration. We seem to be presented with a binary choice that is unsatisfactory. The problem is that the anxiety and uncertainty felt by people, exacerbated by the collapse (almost complete) of trust in public institutions could drive people into the hands of UKIP and even worse the far right. So, postliberalism is not some novel, complacent *back-patting* exercise for social conservatives and fellow travelers. It is an essential project that can, in some manner, connect Christian perspectives and notions of the common good with the complex challenges of our day. We need to be discerning and recognize what is happening. As liberalism has overreached itself and the atomistic society self-evidently creaks, we need 'men of Issachar'[13] who can understand the times and guide the church into its prophetic role of speaking to the nation. Secular voices understand the challenges too "With its emphasis on abstract individualism, liberalism, the great driver of social emancipation and economic prosperity, now feels inadequate to this new age of insecurity."[14]

Postliberalism is a political space that transcends party boundaries but has roots in the traditional party hinterlands

> "Perhaps for the first time in thirty years politics is changing. The old orthodoxy's of left and right are still dominant, but they are no longer hegemonic. Beneath the surface the tectonic plates are

12. Rosenthal, *Niebuhr*, 140.

13. 1 Chronicles 12:32.

14. New Statesman, Leader: Liberalism now feels inadequate in this new age of insecurity -The stakes could not be higher."

shifting, boundaries are blurring, and ideologies are returning to first principles, creating a new terrain that is slowly beginning to emerge."[15]

I am tribally Labour, however tribalism does not equal sectarianism and absence of generosity or refusing to learn from others and their traditions. I am a Christian first and foremost and believe that this nascent postliberalism debate can be fostered in a space that is not crowded out by stultifying machine politics.

Blue Labour—and its opposite—Red Tory, are more than dialogue partners in my book. They share overlapping concerns: a critique of liberalism; an understanding of localism that includes religious institutions (i.e., authentic localism); a promotion of the politics of the common good; the cherishing of civic society; suspicion of unbridled; atavistic capitalism; and an understanding of the limits of secularism. This is not to say that they are the same thing, but I welcome ResPublica's[16] positive work on the social and civic role of the Church of England, a unique contribution for a UK-based think tank and their report on marriage amidst the not very inspiring *debate* on same-sex marriage earlier this year. Equally, I admire much of the work of the Centre for Social Justice and am fascinated by the work of Jesse Norman,[17] who paid tribute to Jon Cruddas and Maurice Glasman. There is a paradox at work here. Just as political parties are essential to a flourishing Parliamentary democracy (and we must will their good health) this is an hour where spaces need to be forged where fellow travelers who sit in different political camps can work, think and agitate together. This means those people of faith, social conservatives and non-liberals who share much in common. They can pursue a politics of the common good and still operate in their party structures. The social and economic problems we face are too great to allow for petty partisanship to halt the development of the common good and a peaceable society. I am not calling for a *new politics*, rather, the development of a mature political space that will allow postliberal insights and activism to emerge.

The new political space that could develop is important. For the political system restrains and marginalizes the harmonization of the instincts that I have referred to. In fact, it appears to mitigate against the privileging of a voice for ordinary people of Britain. Postliberalism is situated in

15. Blond, *Changing the Debate*, 1.

16. Respublica, "Holistic Mission: Social Action and the Church of England"

17. Norman, Tory Rising Star, On Boris, Burke And His Row With Cameron"

a different space to the left-right matrix itself an unnatural product of the enlightenment settlement. If you are postliberal you cannot feel comfortable with the party system however, as I have stated, you don't abandon it either in some utopian search for a *new politics*. Blue Labour is of course situated within the British Labour Party and there it will stay. Yet as it has developed and challenged conventional thinking and Labour-speak, it has disturbed some people—well so be it. We can't go on making the same mistakes. A key challenge for postliberalism will be to find clearer definitions on its substantive themes: to act as a mature agent in the public space and to retain an ability to appeal to, and speak into, the political system.

Postliberalism allows for a reimagining of politics from an ethical perspective

Politics is deeply disenchanted. The dominance of economic and political concerns squeezes out an ethical appeal. I believe that postliberalism can challenge a number of contemporary problems: the cult of youth, a dominance of middle class interests and a general lack of vision and direction in the public square.

Postliberalism opens politics to a community of practitioners who have been doing some theological heavy lifting on politics and *virtue ethics*. I stress we are talking about virtue not moralism, legalism or perfectionism. This is not an abstract academic point. People are clearly yearning for something inspiring, authentic and generous. The liberal and secular frame appears inadequate in building community or even possessing the language from which we can construct the good life. The connection between these theological and ethical sources and public policy could allow for a reimagining of politics around an ethical vision of community that is not dominated by short-term economic and political considerations. Postliberalism stands positioned to articulate a genuinely *new politics* shaped by these insights. It recognizes that liberalism has been complicit in precluding a political conversation that honors the virtues.

> " . . . the predominance of liberal politics has been a key reason why the virtues have received inadequate attention in recent ethical discussion. Liberalism, of course, presupposes and encourages certain kinds of virtues, but that it does so is often insufficiently acknowledged or articulated."[18]

18. Hauerwas and Pinches, *Christians* pxi.

What I posit is no means a given, so much is stacked up against it, but I believe there is a possibility for politics to be reimagined ethically, shaped and sustained by theological resources, that presents a challenge to liberalism without caving into utopianism or nihilism.

The Church has the resources to nourish political debate and praxis.

In my analysis postliberalism must also be postsecular in that I perceive liberalism and secularism to have advanced from or in correspondence to the enlightenment project. As postliberalism allows for a political dialogue that is not confined to a secular straitjacket, it allows for a number of possibilities. The church should possess the resources to shape and nourish a new, distinct political conversation.

It is notable that some politicians are now open to the contribution of Catholic Social Teaching and Anglican Social Thinking. This could be explained by the paucity and hollowness that characterizes much political debate in the UK.[19]

The development of social action and evangelical mission as an integrated whole has been an observable feature of UK church life in the past twenty years. The church, largely, understands the need for a meaningful emotional connection with the poor and marginalized in a manner that political liberals aren't always connected to. Initiatives such as Christians Against Poverty (CAP), Street Pastors, winter night shelters, and foodbanks, all indicate the grassroots engagement that churches engage in to meet social need and demonstrate their commitment to the local place. This was noted in a recent report by the Evangelical Alliance that stated:

> "Faith groups make a vast contribution to their local communities across a range of predictable and surprising activities. Repeatedly local authorities cited the role of food banks, Street Pastors and debt advice centres. Other activities were identified that demonstrate the *cradle to grave* support that faith communities provide, from caring for the young and the elderly to helping with dog training and anger management."[20]

Clearly more can be done, but in many urban areas the church is deeply involved in work with the marginalized. This activity is not undertaken

19. See Anna Rowlands essay 'Postliberal politics and the churches' in the same issue—Crucible—the journal of Christian Social Ethics, January to March 2014.

20. Christians in Parliament, *Faith in the Community*, 7.

for political reasons let alone at the behest of a political party. However, this broad-based work gives the church an authority to speak into difficult issues such as welfare, migration and criminal justice informed by on the ground experience. These insights should be shaping politicians faced with dwindling resources to tackle social problems and concerns about civic participation. If Blue Labour and Red Tory can join the dots the public debate would be enriched and more importantly this work could be embedded and flourish.

Summary

For the first time since perhaps the days of William Temple the Church has not had to conform to some singular secular dominance of public discourse. This is not a cue for triumphalism but perhaps there now exists a distinct space for a robust Christian engagement in politics of a different kind where we truly begin to change the terms of the debate. In that context postliberalism is a small but not insignificant contribution to broader changes that the Church can be alive to speak into lead and serve.

In many ways postliberalism is messy. It defines a spectrum of opinion that accommodates non-liberals, communitarians, ex-liberals, liberals who can see beyond their tradition and others, I am sure. It is one vista amongst many of course. It certainly invites more crisp and robust definition. Nevertheless, it represents a possible opening up of a debate that could be significant for political thought and life in the United Kingdom. As Red Tory and Blue Labour are pro-faith and acknowledge the contribution of Christianity to public life, we need to assess their potential and take them seriously. Postliberalism is indeed messy and so it must be real. Did Christ not engage with mess and reality? This is why an incarnational politics, some might say an "incarnational humanism,"[21] might be a helpful resource.

---

21. See *Zimmermann, Incarnational Humanism.*

11

Compass Challenge

Elephants left in the Room

This short think piece was written for a Compass[1] Challenge, *Elephants in the Room*, a good friend and I wrote two pieces we knew Compass would not accept. I suggested Labour abandon progressivism and embrace the common good.

I would submit that Labour needs to abandon a progressive policy orientation and embrace a disposition rooted in the common good, intentionally aware of Catholic social teaching. This would truly represent a *Bad Godesburg* moment that would make the rewriting of Clause IV[2] look like a momentary pause for thought. It would prove to be an existential moment but one that I believe is urgently required.

I welcome this Compass initiative and concur that there is an elephant in the room, but that is not the only problem. Rather the room itself has shrunk, the door is locked, and the custodians of the dominant progressive worldview have kept the keys, shut the windows and won't let fresh air in. Labour is at its best when at its broadest. The progressive project, despite being well intentioned, has run out of steam, is ill-defined, elitist, inadvertently corrosive and is shaped by a misplaced view of human nature.

1. Compass is a campaigning group on the center-left of UK politics.

2. The Labour Party altered Clause IV of its constitution in 1995; it committed Labour to a policy of nationalization of industry. See 'Clause IV at Twenty'—https://www.theguardian.com/politics/from-the-archive-blog/2015/apr/29/clause-four-labour-party-tony-blair-20–1995.

"The belief in human perfectibility and inevitable moral progress no longer has credibility after Auschwitz and the Gulag
Archipelago."[3]

We should understand the reality of human nature by reference to Augus-
tine and frame our politics around a notion of the common good, informed
by Joseph Ratzinger and *Caritas in Veritate*.[4]

It might feel curious to call for such a fundamental repointing of Labour's values coordinates at such a time. Currently, Labour appears to be
gaining momentum, the Coalition is on the backfoot, and the Tory rank-
and-file appear despondent. However, beyond encouraging opinion polls
and Ed Miliband's sincere approach I would contend that much deeper
work is needed. Profound existential work needs to be undertaken to address Labour's structural problems.

So, what is the problem with *progress*? On the surface it appears harm-
less (it is used with good intent). We want to move forwards, the left desires
to be the agent of change, we are not Tories we don't merely accept and
defend the status quo. We don't refer to Democratic Socialism anymore,
progress is a suitable leftist replacement, so it fits right? In this short time, I
would like to suggest there are three limitations to depending on a progressive mantra:

1. As a concept, it is actually meaningless and is semantically open to
   manipulation. It is warm and attractive and open to being affixed to
   any good cause. So, it elides robust analysis. David Cameron has used
   it, and Nick Clegg coined the phrase "progressive austerity."[5] To me
   this application alone renders it empty and elastic in use.

2. The term is not distinctly Labour, as I mention the Conservative Prime
   Minister uses it and it is a banner for vaguely leftist concerns rather
   than the needs of working people.

3. Progressivism, pushed too far, is actually ultimately dangerous. If, as
   I understand its intent, we frame our politics around the outcomes of
   a utopian, perfect or perfectible goal we can cause damage today and
   achieve no goal at all. We are left with clichés, such as: the ends justify
   the means, pain today is fine, as we are seeking a progressive future.

3. Rosethanl, *Niebuhr*, 140.

4. Benedict XVI, "Caritas in Veritate," https://www.vatican.va/content/benedict-xvi/
en/encyclicals/documents/hf_ben-xvi_enc_20090629_caritas-in-veritate.html

5. "Nick Clegg: I aim to be prime minister," *BBC*

If we impose an elitist, liberal policy prescription seeking a perfect future than hurts today then we are building our politics on fantasy and causing more harm than good.

Instead of shaping a policy narrative suffused in the language of progress we should seek instead the common good. This approach rejects the possibility of a future utopia and humbly acknowledges that genuine differences exist in society. It is an intellectually and philosophically rich concept and derives from a tradition that has been by far the best and lasting influence on British Labour. It has a religious heritage. We find a measure of true progress and social good in reconciling social and economic tensions around building (not theorizing) a common life in the present. It is sought and established through churches, trade unions, small enterprises and co-ops and community groups working for the benefits of others yet seeking their legitimate goals. With reference to this tradition and in the search of the common good Labour can begin to rebuild relationships with associations and communities it needs to relate to. This language and heritage reach beyond the professional liberal bubble.

This *new* approach understands that the public square is multifaceted, fragmented and not univocal. The language of progress has become entwined in elitist and imperial notions, of a liberal persuasion. The goal of the common good is not utilitarianism or about shabby but rather embodies a recognition of the need for desired socioeconomic (and ethical) common outcomes that respect different views and priorities, cognizant that the perfect end is never in sight, yet still hopeful. It is not the cold, brutal logic of the right.

Compass should join the campaign to reject progressivism and seek the common good. In life, tomorrow never comes. As the people-centered Olympics' opening ceremony demonstrates—we have come a long way, there has been much progress of course, but we still face deep problems today. Historically, there has been progress, (we fought for and built the NHS, the US has a Black President), but are we more loving, more wise and happier? I can accept that the search for progress has achieved good ends but as a totalizing goal it is flawed. Labour needs to be postprogressive and search for a deeper language and more authentic values.

I believe that politics must give people hope and allow them the ability to make sense of their lives and to flourish. For me the common good is actually more inclusive and generous than a narrow conception of progress. While progressivism has engendered liberalism-cum-relativism, the common good proposes a genuine moral discourse. It recognizes that other people have different desires and viewpoints, and it allows space to protect the values and aims we cherish. This is real plurality. Progress can be an aim and objective but not an orientation. The left should abandon the progressive project—then we might make some progress.

12

Living in the Love
of the Common People

The following article reflected on Jon Cruddas MP's
prognosis of Labour's 2015 General Election defeat. One
might surmise little has been learned in five years. Yet,
once again faced with inequality and culture wars of
identity and now the depressingly familiar cry of racial
injustice, we need the politics of the common good.

"The opportunity to serve our country—that is all we ask."

—JOHN SMITH

"Our task now is to take note of why we lost and build a future for
the party. This doesn't mean adopting the Conservatives' approach.
It means building a vision of the country based on Labour's values of
family, work, fairness and decency, and rooted in the concerns of the
people we represent."

JON CRUDDAS

This week Jon Cruddas MP published his analysis of last year's election
defeat. The report is based on polling covering the General Election

and the recent local and Mayoral elections across the UK and in London. It deploys typologies to explain the behavior of the electorate as "pioneers, prospectors and settlers."[1] Pioneers are more socially liberal and comfortable with the cosmopolitan world. Crucially, settlers seem to typify once solid Labour voters who now might be attracted to UKIP and are deeply socially conservative. In short, the settlers were not desperate for the formation of a progressive alliance with the SNP.

In general, I agree with much, but not all that Jon Cruddas writes and for that matter the same goes for Maurice Glasman. So, I am not neutral, I hope I am not biased but I am *situated*—to chuck in a word loved by academics. It is a bit like the fact I regard anyone who likes West Brom as having good judgement and bad judgement if they don't: there are prejudices and there are preferences. This is my starting point. I do have a few thoughts of its significance, I hope, from a Christian perspective.

The Church can teach politicians and the Labour Party a thing or two at this current juncture and I know the Church isn't perfect, but it is sui generis. Thus, in essence Labour has got to get *common*. It has got to embrace the common life, get rooted in the common good and learn to love the *common people* and find the common touch. Else it will die. In Scotland—I fear —we have died.

The Common Life

This last Sunday my church in a thankfully uncool part of southeast London cleared away the chairs and for forty-five minutes we had open worship where people could dance and go for it. I didn't embarrass my family with the charismatic two-step (there is still time) but my four-year-old son loved it and entertained on the stage with some confident dance steps, imbibed from Harlem as far as I can tell. It was a wonderful, free and liberating time of worship. I stepped back and noticed Brazilians, old people, young people, professionals, West Africans, Black British, white working class all united in worship. Unrestrained, we had the time of our lives. It was authentic worship. Now, I am not about to say my church is perfect, of course it isn't. However, it is pretty much the most diverse church I have belonged to. Yet, focused on the worship and discipleship of Jesus there is a purpose that transcends all earthly identities that really binds us together

---

1. Cruddas et al., "Labour's Future—Why Labour lost in 2015 and how it can win again—Report of the independent inquiry into why Labour lost in 2015," 12–13.

in community in a common life. This is not just some soppy abstraction about community (which is actually really hard to forge) it is a prophetic statement to a society that finds it hard to live together. A society ravaged by a crisis of identity and inequality.

As the Cruddas report points out, the Labour Party appears to be adrift from the society it is seeking to reach out to and represent. It is becoming *exclusive*! One of the report's key messages reads as follows:

> "The Labour Party is now largely a party of progressive, social liberals who value universalist principles such as equality, sustainability and social justice. It is losing connection with large parts of the voter population who are either pragmatists in their voting habits or social conservatives who value family, work, fairness and their country."[2]

This alarming exclusivity is also the mirror image of another key message that politics is now driven by identity and belonging. (Witness the mass boredom currently with European Union membership being sold as if it were a fridge, get one for £200 less than the other retailer etc.). The report calls for a shift in politics to reflect the dispositions of large sections of the working class.

> " . . . it needs to develop a politics that is radical on the economy and small 'c' conservative—supporting the values of family, work and country."[3]

Maurice Glasman once pointed out the despair that results from an absence of the common life:

> "What you've got is a lot of people who are alone at home watching the telly and having maybe a couple of beers a day. That's no life, but they don't know what to do, where do you go. So that's why relationships are so vital. We flourish with others. Our life is not to live alone outside of relationships, but to find our fulfilment with others in a common purpose."[4]

Flourish, others, relationships and common purpose: does this describe the Labour Party? No, it gets near to describing my church.

2. Cruddas et al., "Labour's Future—Why Labour lost in 2015 and how it can win again—Report of the independent inquiry into why Labour lost in 2015," 9–10.

3. Cruddas et al.," Labour's Future—Why Labour lost in 2015 and how it can win again—Report of the independent inquiry into why Labour lost in 2015," 9.

4. BBC, "Labour's New Jerusalem."

The Labour Party and the word exclusive shouldn't belong in the same sentence but now they do. A political party that once embodied the common life, because it was working class experience that made this a reality in its pain and in its collective joy, now seems unable to generate anything like it. However, the church is a place where it can be lived out. Where we can love our neighbor even if we don't like them. The second chapter of Acts[5]—when goods were *held in common* isn't a blueprint for communism it attests that a mark of the kingdom of God is that the common life occurs.

Once upon a time the church embodied the common life, our life together and this defined working class communities and the Labour Party. It was the journalist Paul Mason who recently and powerfully recognized the critical place of churches as well as trade unions in forging working class life and identity.

> "Without solidarity and knowledge, we are just scum, is the lesson trade unionism and social democracy taught the working class kids of the 1960s; and Methodism and Catholicism taught the same."[6]

Solidarity, the common life, belonging. This idea isn't new either. Centuries ago, John Ball said: "My good friends, things cannot go on well in England, nor ever will until everything shall be in common."[7]

Common Good

The Cruddas Report[8] touches on some issues that make progressives squeamish and that make me squeamish too. Issues of identity, immigration and welfare. Yet, to lower case *c* conservatives who dispositional common sense has been offended these issues matter. Unless they are addressed or listened to, we in Labour don't deserve a hearing. How this is done and worked out is critical. For implicit to the theological approach of the common good is a belief in compassion and a sense of place. The Christian belief in the centrality of incarnation should enable us to work these things

5. See Acts 2v44.

6. Mason, "The problem for poor, white kids is that a part of their culture has been destroyed," Lines 90–92.

7. HOASM, "The Peasant's Revolt in England (1381)," Line 16.

8. Cruddas et al., ""Labour's Future—Why Labour lost in 2015 and how it can win again—Report of the independent inquiry into why Labour lost in 2015."

through with humility: immigration, welfare and Europe can't be left to a binary debate that alienates people and disallows people to tell their story and express their fears.

The common good goes beyond the individual and tribe and allows for a perspective that transcends individual calculation and squaring off different voting interests for an ideal electoral outcome. Our society is fragmented and divided and needs Christian resources. If we leave the debating field to UKIP and a wholly liberal approach don't be surprised that former Labour voters will have left the building.

But what is the common good?

"Public authorities have the common good as their prime responsibility. The common good stands in opposition to the good of rulers or of a ruling (or any other) class. It implies that every individual, no matter how high or low, has a duty to share in promoting the welfare of the community as well as a right to benefit from that welfare. 'Common' implies 'all-inclusive': the common good cannot exclude or exempt any section of the population. If any section of the population is in fact excluded from participation in the life of the community, even at a minimal level, then that is a contradiction to the concept of the common good and calls for rectification."[9]
As Jon Cruddas stated: " . . . the common good concerns the relational."[10]

The common good can help us, indeed must help us as policy makers are lost for the way forward. Old ideas have run out steam, helpful for a while they now have run out of road. Public faith in politics and painfully the Labour Party is low—as this report underlines—and I can't see a resurgence any time soon. The perspective of the common good transcends class divisions—which will get us nowhere—and it embodies a thoroughly Christian approach to public life, a robust and engaged Christian approach to social problems is essential.

The common good is critical if we are to get to the bottom of the painful issues. Does the Labour Party have the will, language or resources to reflect seriously on these issues?

9. Catholic Bishops, "The Common Good and the Catholic Church's Social Teaching: A Statement by the Catholic Bishops Conference of England and Wales," 19.

10. Cruddas, "The Common Good in an Age of Austerity," in *Blue Labour a New Politics,* 90.

Common people/common touch

My Dad told me the story about when as a social worker in Walsall he visited a lady who came to the door crying. My Dad asked her: *whatever is the matter?* She had just heard the news that John Smith had died. I don't mean this in a flippant sense, but can you imagine members of the public crying today at the death of a politician? I also remember my Dad saying that John Smith had *the common touch*, i.e., he could naturally relate to ordinary people. That sense of the common touch of love for the common people, rather than fear, is in short supply. Thus, there is a key point in the Cruddas report which calls for the " . . . building a vision of the country based on Labour's values of family, work, fairness and decency, and rooted in the concerns of the people we represent."[11]

In order to do this, you have got to understand its importance, to want to do it, to love it and love the people whose life embodies this. Now, before we get all proletarian about this, remember John Smith was an Edinburgh QC[12]. People from such backgrounds have a place in the big tent too and rightly so, Labour should always be a broad alliance it's just there is one bit of that tent missing. He had the common touch and was a 'Labour man'. You knew what he stood for. This is another problem identified in the report.

> "Whatever Labour thought its message was, the public was either unclear about it, or saw it as being about protecting public services."[13]

In stark terms the evidence, if it were needed, that Labour has a major problem with its core support is spelt out clearly. It is the socially conservative voters who have left Labour. The common people no longer love Labour and are looking elsewhere for political expression.

> "Labour is losing its working class support and UKIP is reaping the benefits. Since 2005 it has been socially conservative voters who are most likely to have deserted Labour."[14]

11. Cruddas, "Labour's Future—Why Labour lost in 2015 and how it can win again—Report of the independent inquiry into why Labour lost in 2015," 5.

12. QC means Queen's Counsel—is a senior lawyer, by Royal appointment in the UK. Following the coronation of King Charles III it is KC meaning King's Counsel.

13. Cruddas, "Labour's Future—Why Labour lost in 2015 and how it can win again—Report of the independent inquiry into why Labour lost in 2015," 8.

14. Cruddas, "Labour's Future—Why Labour lost in 2015 and how it can win again—Report of the independent inquiry into why Labour lost in 2015," 7

When too many people running and representing Labour don't look, think or sound like the people they claim to represent there is a profound problem. To my mind it was obvious we should have gone into the last election offering a vote for the European Union, even if I am committed to remaining in. Instead, we had a fudge of an offer that was difficult to explain. We did not trust the people.

In addressing this crisis of representation—and there is no immediate, easy fix—the church again potentially speaks to Labour as it does to all parties, though the church is still too suburban and comfortable in location and mindset it has a much closer connection with people and place. Moreover, in many inner city areas, it is the only social institution serving people and giving meaning to their lives.

The report is frank but does offer hope for Labour. I have not done it justice, please have a read. I would submit that it is the Christian faith and church that can speak to this situation. We need to model a common life, champion the common good and not be ashamed of loving the *common people*, the ordinary people. Of course, these values are not the sole preserve of one political party. We need to listen more, much more to ordinary people, it is they who work, raise families and form communities. They or people like them created the Labour Party in the first place and they elect and reject Government's. Labour should listen to and trust the people and be honest about its failings.

Christians believe in truth and hope. We believe in new life, resurrection and a new heaven and a new earth. Having this perspective and conviction must shape our politics.

> "Labour is becoming dangerously out of touch with the electorate, and at the time of writing appears unwilling to acknowledge this growing estrangement. Labour's historical task is to represent the interests of working people in government. That means listening to the people, trusting their judgment, letting them decide the destiny of their country. And it means recognising when we have got it wrong, and learning from our failure."[15]

---

15. Cruddas, "Labour's Future—Why Labour lost in 2015 and how it can win again—Report of the independent inquiry into why Labour lost in 2015," 42.

13

A Labour Party *Rudd*-erless?

Could Labour look to Australia's recent PM for help

This is a blast from the past, I had a keen interest in the Australian Labor Party and for a while was excited at the prospect of Kevin Rudd Prime Minister of Australia as a role model. He had a political philosophy, a faith and made attempts to articulate the important issues of the day in ethical terms. He is well read and admired Bonhoeffer. Say no more.

I was standing at the Tube one Saturday morning during the run-up to the recent General Election, looking forward to a day campaigning for the Labour Party in East London. I noticed a local lad on his way, I presume to a day's training at the relatively local David Beckham football academy. To many, David Beckham, will be a hero, an idol and possibly a role model. Indeed, in the World Cup in South Africa England sorely lacked a Beckham-like figure on the pitch. This reflection made me wonder, if, as Christians in politics can we have role models or heroes without them becoming idols? I am not sure, maybe we can see people as heroes of the faith, but there are certainly people we should take note of. Luther, Calvin, Wesley, Spurgeon would rank in my list.

I believe our involvement in politics is a missional journey. As biblical, spirit-filled, Christians we are fulfilling our calling in the political space that cannot be separated from the building of the church and the extension of God's Kingdom. On this journey, as we travel together, we need many people whom we can learn from and many more to become role models and mentors, rather than heroes per se. I have no doubt that Stephen

Timms has been an inspiration to many on the Christian left, both in his character and his achievements. Someone, whom we should take note of, I believe, in this present time, is the recent Australian, Labor, Prime Minister, Kevin Rudd. Though the Australian Labor Party will have their reasons for swiftly replacing Mr. Rudd with Julia Gillard, there is much the Christian left can learn from the former Aussie premier.

I like Australians, generally, I think they are down-to-earth and have much in common with the British working class. Yes, I admit that some of this is sentimental, I was brought up to be aware of the sacrifice that was made by many young men from Australia and New Zealand in World War One and World War Two. I recently watched the film *Gallipoli* again and it is deeply tragic, but watch the film and get my drift. In 2005 I visited Australia for the first time and like most British men who go there: I went surfing, drank beer, went to Bondi Beach, and . . . read about the Australian Labor Party. Labour was then going through a trauma and the Liberal Party (center-right party) was in full control, led by Prime Minister *Johnny* Howard, who seemed to be popular and had captured large chunks of the working class or *battler* constituency for his own. Labor was not in a good place, and this saddened me.

I once had the privilege of attending a meeting of the Labour Friends of Australia and heard the then leader of the Labour Party, Simon Crean talks about the political situation there. So, the links between the two parties are relatively strong, both have a link to trade unions, there seem to have similar debates about modernization in the past twenty years or so. The former MP Robert Kilfoyle lived in Australia for a while, Jon Cruddas MP worked there, and John Spellar MP enjoys regular visits to Australia that I am sure have a significant political content.

However, my specific interest is what we can learn from, Kevin Rudd, a committed Christian and who, it should not be forgotten, turned things around for the ALP, not the least winning an impressive General Election victory in 2007. In fact, I think there are a few things we can learn from Rudd and these insights I submit are instructive to the Labour Party as it not only seeks to elect a new leader and begins the work of rebuilding within opposition.

Of tremendous importance, I believe, is Rudd's attempt to articulate an ethical critique of capitalism. For example, in an essay entitled *The Global Financial Crisis* in February 2009, he made a thoughtful and erudite case for social democrats to rise to the challenge of arguing for an active state to respond to the failure of the collapse of the financial markets and the limitations of the regulatory system.

> "The current crisis is the culmination of a thirty-year domina-
> tion of economic policy by a free market ideology that has been
> variously called neoliberalism, economic liberalism, economic
> fundamentalism, Thatcherism or the Washington Consensus. The
> central thrust of this ideology has been that government activity
> should be constrained, and ultimately replaced, by market forces."[1]

The essay is a worthwhile read, as it reflects upon the sequence of events that led to the global credit crunch and the self-confidence and contradictions of the neoliberal economic order being exposed. Yet, it is the ability of Rudd to critique this system in ethical terms that pulls no punches that perhaps is refreshing. He states:

> "The time has come, off the back of the current crisis, to proclaim
> that the great neoliberal experiment of the past thirty years has
> failed, that the emperor has no clothes. Neoliberalism, and the free
> market fundamentalism it has produced, has been revealed as little
> more than personal greed dressed up as an economic philosophy.
> And, ironically, it now falls to social democracy to prevent liberal
> capitalism from cannibalising itself."[2]

Rudd locates the global economic failure in its true context, a moral tragedy, for it was greed "wot did it"[3] and he goes on to affirm the fact that the social democratic concept of social justice also to be rooted in an essentially ethical framework. Yet this is not cold, atheistic, materialism it appeals to fundamental beliefs about human moral worth.

> "Expressed more broadly, the pursuit of social justice is founded
> on the argument that all human beings have an intrinsic right to
> human dignity, equality of opportunity and the ability to lead a
> fulfilling life."[4]

This narrative is encouraging and coherent. Perhaps if the British Labour Party had such thinkers and communicators, we would not be in such a malaise now? Rudd proved able to explain the economic crisis from a social

---

1. Rudd, "The Global Financial Crisis," Lines 118–122.

2. Rudd, "The Global Financial Crisis," Lines 314–319.

3. A variation on an infamous headline in the UK from the tabloid newspaper The Sun—Freeman, Open Democracy.

4. Rudd, "The Global Financial Crisis," Lines 347–349.

SECTION TWO | POLITICS

democratic perspective, underpinned by convictions that are social democratic and ethical and not based on statism justified by a cold rationalism.
How can you appeal to the common good without reference to Christian
Socialism? How can you assert that we all have worth and dignity without
appealing to transcendent and absolute truth?[5]

> "Government is not the intrinsic evil that neoliberals have argued
> it is. Government, properly constituted and properly directed, is
> for the common good, embracing both individual freedom and
> fairness, a project designed for the many, not just the few."[6]

In the UK, we need to feel confident in critiquing capitalism from a
Christian Socialist perspective. Perhaps Rudd may show the way. Indeed,
Labour needs to rediscover this appetite, language and ability soon. The
days of managerial accommodation with economic orthodoxy must end.
We will hear a lot about *big* government being bad from the new coalition
administration. Clearly government and governance are good things, as
long as they operate within their legitimate boundaries. In fact, Labour's
Fabian statism surely must be queried, as it at times, runs counter to the
ethical localism of the unions and Christian Socialists who birthed the
party. However, somewhere we must heed Rudd's affirmation of the need
for a just and necessary state intervention, aware that many Labour traditions have been birthed and flourished in spaces apart from or angular to
the state.

Rudd's Christian faith was and still is clearly central to his identity and
politics, indeed he has been described as "the mainstay"[7] of the Parliamentary Prayer fellowship in Canberra. He clearly understands the challenge of
and need to articulate a Christian discourse in the public square. Furthermore, he has evidently thought through what it means to be a Christian
engaged in public life, in the current context where secular humanism and
postmodernism seem to be dominant. He reflects that:

> "A Christian perspective on contemporary policy debates may
> not prevail. It must nonetheless be argued. And once heard, it
> must be weighed, together with other arguments from different
> philosophical traditions, in a fully contestable secular polity. A
> Christian perspective, informed by a social gospel or Christian so-
> cialist tradition, should not be rejected contemptuously by secular

5. Rudd, "The Global Financial Crisis."
6. Rudd, "The Global Financial Crisis," Lines 640–642.
7. Rudd, Wikipedia, Line 689

politicians as if these views are an unwelcome intrusion into the political sphere. If the churches are barred from participating in the great debates about the values that ultimately underpin our society, our economy and our polity, then we have reached a very strange place indeed."[8]

This is an important point, if we are to understand how our engagement does not mirror the aggression and misplaced agenda that seemed to characterize the Christian Right in the USA. It is not about winning arguments or unleashing culture wars. It is about speaking the truth to power and demonstrating a life and community that is commensurate with this high calling.

Importantly, Rudd reminds Christians about the priority the gospel gives to the poor and oppressed[9] I cannot imagine him being intensely relaxed about the grotesque accumulation of wealth or arrival of the superrich in our lexicon. Again, this should stand as a corrective to the UK Labour Party, we are either on the side of the poor or we are not Labour. Again, it is difficult to trace the lineage of the belief that we stand up for those who cannot stand up for themselves, which is beyond a reference to the Christian tradition on the left.

> "I argue that a core, continuing principle shaping this engagement should be that Christianity, consistent with Bonhoeffer's critique in the thirties, must always take the side of the marginalised, the vulnerable and the oppressed."[10]

Rudd did not say sometimes, on occasions, when we feel like it or when it is electorally expedient, he said: ". . .always."[11] This is nonnegotiable. Think about it.

Rudd strikes me as a well-read intellectual who is grounded and rooted and inspired to practical action profoundly informed by what he believes. This could well be why he may be less prone to some of the vacuous, shallow and amoral statements that some politicians make in order to *connect* with the electorate. In another essay he notes his admiration—emphatically—or the moral courage of the German pastor and theologian, Dietrich Bonhoeffer:

8. Rudd, "Faith in Politics.," Lines 240–48.

9. Sheppard, *Bias*, 10

10. Rudd, "Faith in Politics," Lines 134–136.

11. Rudd, "Faith in Politics," Line 135.

"Bonhoeffer is, without doubt, the man I admire most in the history of the twentieth century."[12]

It is telling that Rudd cites Bonhoeffer in this vein. He honors that steadfast man of principle who did not what was right in the face of the monstrosity of the Nazi regime and warned against cheap grace and shallow discipleship. Rudd proceeds to reflect on Bonhoeffer's qualities and message.

> "He was a man of faith. He was a man of reason. He was a man of letters who was as well read in history and literature as he was in the intensely academic Lutheran theology of the German university tradition. He was never a nationalist, always an internationalist. And above all, he was a man of action who wrote prophetically in 1937 that: "when Christ calls a man, he bids him come and die." For Bonhoeffer, whatever the personal cost, there was no moral alternative other than to fight the Nazi state with whatever weapons were at his disposal."[13]

The Labour Party needs to refresh its intellectual traditions, respect for the love of learning, the imperative of an ethical worldview. As Christians on the left, we are not to be bound by the mundane oppression of pragmatism. Bonhoeffer was a man of unquestionable and challenging courage, who pursued Christ and not a career.

Rudd is a rounded politician and thinker. To paraphrase English football fans, he hasn't just got one song. Interestingly, Rudd has[14] been described as a "social conservative."

"I have a pretty basic view on this, as reflected in the position adopted by our party, and that is, that marriage is between a man and a woman."[15]

It might be the social conservatism of Rudd can help us in the UK Labour Party. In a truly plural party, a socially liberal perspective should not be the dominant and solitary voice. We need room for the full breadth of ideas and people who, though economically on the left, are also socially conservative. As a friend commented to me, this category used to be called the working class. Furthermore, I might be so bold to suggest that as Phillip Blond, is arguing for a communitarian Red Tory project on the center-right of British politics we need a comparable narrative expressed and embedded

12. Rudd, "Faith in Politics," Lines 7–8.

13. Rudd, "Faith in Politics," Lines 8–15.

14. Wikipedia, https://en.wikipedia.org/wiki/Kevin_Rudd, line 476

15. ABC News, "Howard, Rudd woo Christians online," August 10, 2007, Lines 63–64.

on the left. Perhaps a good place to start would entail engaging with the Blue Labour thesis, being articulated by Dr Maurice Glasman[16] and elsewhere by John Milbank.[17] This approach affirms the place of faith in public and political life, celebrates the role of family and the primacy of marriage, emphasizes the ethic of hard work and personal responsibility, and recognizes the important of place and community for working people.

Far be it for me to infer that Rudd is Blue Labour, he probably hasn't heard of it, (and he certainly disavows a narrow focus on moral issues in the name of Christian faith), but unless we find a home for such sentiments and the values that many ordinary people hold dear then an overt and oppressive liberalism really could *do* for the Labour Party. We all know of the sinister forces willing to represent working class communities who feel abandoned by the Labour tradition, don't we? One way to begin to work out these themes would be the establishment of a campaigning think tank on the center-left that explores these themes in full, promoting policy and campaigning on the ground in communities. Such an initiative would be, if you like, function as a Labour version of the Centre for Social Justice, distinct in that it would be rooted in social democracy and orientated towards social conservatism. On the left too many think tanks are metropolitan and liberal, I feel increasingly alienated by them, I suspect I am not alone. These issues need to be urgently worked out, indeed, the comments of an ex-Labour Minister and MP sum this insight in a far better style than I can:

> "Labour is best placed to govern because the tradition the times need is ours. We have strong roots in the liberal tradition but we are not a liberal party, our identity is rooted in the interests of working people and an analysis of capital. While there are deep conservative elements in the Labour tradition, and we should honor them—particularly in relation to the ethics of work, loyalty and love of place, family solidarity and a respect for the moral contribution of faith—we do not accept the distribution of assets as they are, we do not accept that inherited mega-wealth is deserved, and we do not accept that our rulers are always other people."[18]

Something in me reckons Rudd, might just agree with that. Rudd appears to be rooted in a thoughtful faith, mindful of the excesses of the Christian right, able to speak with ethical authority on asylum, economics,

---

16. Glasman, in *Blue Labour: Forging a New Politics*

17. Milbank, in *Blue Labour: Forging a New Politics*

18. Purnell, "Where is the vitality and vision to win?," Lines 122–130.

poverty, climate change, internationalism, and also the importance of marriage and family. It is that compassionate, broad, intelligent and ethical approach, that could begin to inform the Christian left as we seek to face the challenges ahead. It is irrelevant to me whether Rudd is—or should be—described as a *hero,* but what is relevant is what he represents and we should certainly note that. I hope this is not the last we hear of Kevin Rudd, but perhaps it is a good a time as any to assess his contribution and political philosophy.

14

National Club March 2016

'Shaping Welfare for the Common Good'

In March 2016 I had the honor of speaking to the National Club,[1] on the subject of welfare. The talk *Shaping Welfare for the Common Good* called for welfare to be renewed on something old, something new, something borrowed, something blue.

" . . . My good friends, things cannot go on well in England, nor ever will until everything shall be in common."

JOHN BALL

I am delighted to have been asked to give this talk this evening. The subjects of welfare and the common good are both close to my heart. I don't claim to be an expert on either matter, however, I do have some thoughts to share.

It is very generous of the National Club to invite me here, thanks to the Chairman and the Programme Committee. It is not often I am invited

1. The National Club is a *'private members club for Christians drawn from a variety of backgrounds, professions and denominations which aims to encourage and support its members in Christian witness in the public square.'* https://www.thenationalclub.org.uk/members

to such prestigious venues as this. I would like to think I am the first trade unionist and West Bromwich Albion fan to have spoken at the Carlton Club but I may be wrong! I am more used to Aldridge Ex-Services Club in my native West Midlands than the Carlton Club. Yet, your heritage and this venue are a useful hook and conversation partner for my humble thoughts.

Perhaps we have more in common, my research suggests that you were founded by the Sixth Duke of Manchester and I lived in Manchester for six years at its university I picked up two degrees. The House of Lords were instrumental in your formation. Believe it or not, I am a big fan of the House of Lords and the idea of an elected second chamber fills me with horror. You celebrated your 150th anniversary at Saint James Chapel. I support the Royal Family and our Queen, wonderful Christian woman that she is. However, you would have found me on Parliament's side in the 1640s, but that is for another day.

I also honor your commitment to the application of Christian principles in public life and in the laws of the nation, I believe—that as Lesslie Newbiggin stated—the gospel is public truth. No subject or institution is out of the bounds for God's Kingdom and the counsel of scripture. You affirm Holy Scripture and the protestant reformation, the power of prayer, and that we all have a public duty to improve our society.

I am an evangelical Christian and am encouraged and challenged by your fundamental principles, I would add that some of the most radical public policy thought being proposed today draws upon Catholic Social Teaching.[2] It is virtually impossible to discuss the notion of the Common Good without referring to this tradition.

Catholic Social Teaching is a valuable resource, it has insights on the dignity of labor, the intrinsic nature of work as vocation, the transformative power of good work, and crucially a stress on seeing humanity in terms of personhood rather than treating people as economic or bureaucratic units. It speaks to a communitarian rather than a liberal/secular approach to the public square, although it is not bound to either left or right on the political spectrum. Crucially it upholds the option for the poor for without the church, what option do the poor have? It is concerned with the scourge of unemployment, and much, much more.

Equally, you draw upon another honorable Christian tradition of Wilberforce and Salisbury—Christian Giants, thank God for them—they are

---

2. Glasman, "The Good Society, Catholic Social Thought and the Politics of the Common Good"

from a tradition of One Nation Conservatism, which I have always found fascinating even though it is not my tradition.

Enough of the preliminary digressions.

Who am I? I am Ian Geary, forty-three years old, I live in southeast London with my wife and three children and worship at an evangelical/charismatic church in Bermondsey. I grew up in Walsall in the Black Country and become a Christian and Labour Party activist at the same time, aged fourteen. Apart from my love for West Brom that is all you need to know about me. I have worked for two Labour MPs, a trade union, various lobbying companies and am on the Executive of *Christians on the Left*. Last year I co-edited an essay collection on the theme of Blue Labour—a stimulant on the center-left which advocates the primacy of relationships in politics, family, place the essential centrality of faith and most importantly asserts the politics of the common good as essential to renewing our civic, political, and social life.

Never has there been a more urgent time to promote the common good: but what is it and how can it *shape* welfare? We live in a time when we face what has been termed a crisis of inequality and identity[3]. The global elite are becoming richer, while poverty—and in-work poverty—are very real and growing problems that, left to their own devices, will wreck our social fabric and the planet. I firmly believe that the gospel applies to every area of public life. Secular approaches of left and right have left people poor, and their potential unfulfilled. We need to focus on human flourishing, and it is the common good that is essential in restoring a strong welfare system. We need a social security system which prevents destitution and that commands the confidence of the people. This requires an analysis of inequality and class while rejecting a narrow class-based agenda.

What is the Common Good?

"Public authorities have the common good as their prime responsibility. The common good stands in opposition to the good of rulers or of a ruling (or any other) class. It implies that every individual, no matter how high or low, has a duty to share in promoting the welfare of the community as well as a right to benefit from that welfare. "Common" implies "all-inclusive": the common good cannot exclude or exempt any section of the population. If any

3. Cruddas, "The Common Good in an Age of Austerity," in *Blue Labour*, 87.

section of the population is in fact excluded from participation in the life of the community, even at a minimal level, then that is a contradiction to the concept of the common good and calls for rectification."[4]

Jon Cruddas has highlighted the contribution of Christianity and other faith traditions to the common good and has emphasized that: "...the common good concerns the relational."[5] I believe it is impossible to discuss this without explicit reference to Christianity. In fact, it is on the concept of relationality that I seek to frame my thoughts this evening. I am taking a risk here, but my view is that the common good is like a marriage. Individualism cannot build a marriage, you have to think, love, and act for the other. You have to see beyond yourself and I fail my own test on a daily basis. There is no detailed five-point plan for a marriage but there are time honored, transcendent principles that help us. And it involves hard work. Equally with the common good there is no prescriptive plan but there is a rich theological and tradition which is rooted in Christianity from which we can draw and apply to the challenges of our day. It involves hard work, which goes against the grain in our shallow, short-termist political culture.

Drawing on marriage or more specifically a wedding ceremony, I will situate my talk with reference to the old adage: "something old, something new, something borrowed and something blue."[6] That is why my talk tonight, aims to be a Christian take of my experience of Labour Politics. Welfare and the common good require *something old, something new, something borrowed and something blue*. I aim to build on this articulating a particular proposition to shape welfare for the common good. It is both concerned for the poor, the working poor and also binding in the rest of the population to the project.

How can the common good help us?

The common good can help us, indeed must help us as policy makers are lost for the way forward. Old ideas have run out steam, helpful for a while they now have run out of road. Public faith in politics and painfully the

4. Catholic Bishops, "The Good Society, Catholic Social Thought and the Politics of the Common Good," 19.

5. Cruddas, "The Common Good in an Age of Austerity," in *Blue Labour*, 90.

6. A traditional English rhyme related to what a bride should wear on her wedding day—see https://danversport.com/weddings/blog/wedding-traditions-explained/.

welfare state is low, and I can't see a resurgence any time soon. The perspective of the common good transcends class divisions which will get us nowhere and it embodies a thoroughly Christian approach to public life—a robust and engaged Christian approach to social problems is essential. We live in a society where:

- More than thirteen million people in the United Kingdom are in low-income households, which is 21 percent of the population, with a million children living in poverty

- Just over half of those in poverty live in working families

- Since 2010, the number of households accepted as homeless has risen, the numbers in temporary accommodation and those placed in temporary accommodation outside their home area have also risen

- " . . . we are one of the richest in the world—and yet some of our communities are among the poorest in all Northern Europe. Even in areas that are recognized as wealthy, there are families or individuals who have fallen behind."[7] These are not my words, the words of a former Prime Minister, Sir John Major.

The common good reminds us that solutions are not all vested with one political party or tradition and that the answers may not dwell within the body politic itself. The common good may not have a crisp definition but we know what it is when we see it in action—for example through the Living Wage campaign—benefitting workers, their families, and companies. Well, it's pretty basic stuff really. And where did the Living Wage come from? An Institute for Public Policy Research (IPPR) away day? No, a Centre for Social Justice (CSJ) report? No, a Treasury Taskforce? No, it came from civil society and was informed by a Catholic Christian commitment to a family wage. It sprung from a tradition and perhaps surprisingly fits the modern context.

We really need the common good, as our society, I believe, faces a paradox. We see the growth in wealth, technology, entrepreneurialism, and bags of social concern, but also debilitating poverty, family breakdown, apathy and indifference, shocking poverty, and the mocking of the poor. If we really want to ensure that *The Hunger Games* remains a dystopian fantasy we need the option for the poor, we need to be radical agitators for the common good.

7. Major, "A nation at ease with itself?," Lines 25–26.

The state we are in

UK society is now not only more pluralistic in its composition, it is much more fragmented and divided. This is a heavily ironic fact when you consider we live in a supposedly more connected society via new media and technology. This is in fact a fantasy. The book of Proverbs states that: "Where there is no revelation, people cast off restraint. . ."[8] This could not be more apposite for the United Kingdom in 2016. We lack a unifying vision and a means and meaning to love one another and to give and support each other. I submit that this is true for the UK and the West, we have lost our moorings. This, I believe, is one of the fundamental challenges to the legitimacy of the welfare state. There is no binding, operative story which gives us an opportunity to address the challenges we face. Well apparently, we lack it, however, I think there is a way that commits to liberating the poor and ensuring working people have more confidence in the system.

I am a passionate believer in the welfare state and the NHS, both gifts from my party to the nation. The welfare state was born following a major world war and the bitter social experience of the 1930s and rooted in pre-World War I liberalism. The desire for social change and support for the post-war Beveridge system was forged in the crucible of the turbulence of these decades. Decades later, although there is still identifiable support for the welfare state, the consensus is just not the same. We would not want to recreate the 1930s and war to regenerate popular support for the welfare state, but we aren't in the same place. This is a major challenge to Christians engaged in public policy, supporters of the common good and those who wish to preserve the welfare state. Public confidence in the system does not exist in the same way it might have done in the post-war context; the reasons for this are complex but I think it is not controversial to say that the welfare system cannot stay the same.

We are not in a good place and although I don't know the answer, I believe a common good approach, rooted in Christian social teaching is the right place to start to begin a new conversation.

How do we get near to the conversation being changed?

8. Prov 29:18.

A way forward

"Something old, something new, something borrowed and something blue."[9] I begin my analogy camping out on something old. Old Labour and its commitment to the poor. I actually found the bifurcation of *old* and *new* Labour to be a false dichotomy, but I will deploy them this evening. *Old* Labour, whatever its faults, was associated as being on the side of the poor. The *Christians on the Left* website explains its approach and identity as follows:

> "Our primary identity is in Christ, not a political ideology, but our reading of scripture inevitably leads us to "speak up for those who cannot speak for themselves," standing against injustice in all its forms, on the side of poor and needy."[10]

Some might think this is old hat and quaint, it is a little patrician, but it is a language I relate to when I recall the reasons I first joined the Labour Party. The Labour Party was born out of the experience of poor people who organized themselves, starting trade unions and cooperative societies and then finding a correlative political voice. Poverty was not abstract to them, for the majority of them, it had been their formative experience. Consider Keir Hardie for example.

> "Keir Hardie later wrote that his upbringing was so hard that he never really knew childhood. First the stigma of being child of single mother in a small nineteenth-century village, then adopted by his mother's new husband who would call him 'a bastard' when drunk. When children today would have been in the first years of primary school, he was working in the shipyards where he saw another boy fall to his death. Later, from the age of ten, he worked in the mines, often alone for hours at a time in the dark."[11]

Think of George Lansbury, a subject that could easily capture twenty-thousand words—as the Labour Mayor of Poplar, East London he and fellow councilors defied the law in the cause of seeking a just rating system in 1921, money was given to the poor rather than the LCC[12] and thirty

9. https://danversport.com/weddings/blog/wedding-traditions-explained/

10. The current *Christians on the Left* website has been updated and does not include this text.

11. "100 Years On—Keir Hardie without a childhood," Lines 2–8

12. LCC means London County Council, the overarching Local Authority body in London at that time

councilors went to jail. I cannot bring myself to call them *rebels* they defied unjust structures and won the day. They were heroes.

Something old, *Old Labour*? Well, I am not sure, but there is a strong tradition of a radical commitment to the poor summed up in the option for the poor of liberation theology that I am sure Lansbury and Hardie would have recognized. Liberation theology is a controversial subject, but it is a corrective to comfortable, dominant theologies. It reminds us of God's passion for the poor. Before we dismiss this out of hand remember John Stott reflected that:

> "[We] may well feel ashamed that we were not in the vanguard of the liberation movement, and that we did not develop an evangelical liberation theology."[13]

So, while Liberation theology may come from a different theological vantage point, we should heed its challenge. It was the response of priests responding to the needs to the poorest of the poor in Latin America which inspired it. We always need loud and *rude* reminders that God is avowedly on the side of the poor. David Sheppard wrote a book entitled *Bias to the Poor* but can God be biased? It makes us think and I hope to act. The title should remind us and challenge us that those human beings who are the last, the least and the lost in society are the most important in God's kingdom.

So, I am talking about different things: an *Old Labour* commitment to address poverty; and the Christian commitment to the poorest. At times these themes have intertwined but they are distinct.

It is clear from the Bible that God is avowedly on the side of the poor and sharing good news with the poor is an absolute priority. It makes demands on us all.

Sharing good news with the poor is not an option for the Christian church. It is a compelling necessity. The poor, like those of us who are not economically poor, are human beings—men and women, uniquely created in the image of God. The difference between the poor and those who are rich is not that some suffer, and others do not. Both rich and poor may be subject to physical pain, emotional stress, and spiritual depression. But the rich have greater control over themselves and their situations. They are free to make choices. Not so with the poor. They have little or no freedom over their bodies or their lifestyle, and little hope for the future. The rich by

---

13. Coffey, "To release the oppressed: Reclaiming a biblical theology of liberation," 1.

definition have power, while the poor are powerless; they are pawns in the hands of others. They are subject to institutionalized structures.

It is worth reflecting on this at length and its pointed reference to powerlessness. We cannot be reminded enough of this fact; as everything that society does or our own instincts lead us is to marginalize the poor, to hoard wealth and power, and to entrench comfort. That is why the poor need a liberation: that is why a God who loves them so much his love can be labeled a bias is so important. Left to our own devices we would shut out the poor.

The poor today are still us and they need the welfare state, but they need much, much more. A common good approach to welfare must put the poorest of the poor first. We fail as Christians, and we fail the basic spirit of the common good if we are not prioritizing the needs of the most vulnerable within the welfare system. Of course, how this is done will be a matter of legitimate debate.

My view is that under this Government too many of the cuts have fallen on the same people: the poor and the working poor. Of course, state benefits alone do not liberate the poor. Welfare dependency and poor lifestyle choices do exist, but I believe that a strong safety net must provide a decent level of material existence. There is concern that the safety net in recent years has been placed under intense pressure. Yet, in this age of genuine compassion and callous indifference the radical option for the poor needs to shape our politics. It is not a left and right thing. It is a concern for Christians and all who seek the common good.

Something New—Welfare Reform

A common good approach would recognize that many people are not content with the UK welfare system. The reasons for this discontent and the policy prescriptions will differ according to one's politics. Yet, I submit this is the case. Lord Maurice Glasman has said:

> " . . . the welfare state has turned out, in many ways to be a brutal, godless and administrative thing that just estranged people and caused people damage."[14]

14. Glasman, "Faith in the Public Square," Missional Practice, 4.

So, I don't believe that welfare can stay in the same place. So, *New Labour* was correct in acknowledging the need for *welfare reform*— a cold and clunky phrase but it captured the need for change.

I believe that Labour in Government did many good things on welfare; the New Deal for the Unemployed and the Disabled, a commitment to end child poverty, raising the employment rate for single parents, and the introduction of tax credits. All couched in the language of rights and responsibilities. Of course, things have moved on from this period: the assertion that work is the best route out of poverty is morally right yet the rise of *in-work poverty* as a phenomenon means this is not so simple. Tax credits have been the subject of recent political debate as they have been pared back. Tax credits give vital support for many on low incomes, but a just wage would be preferable. That is why I would advocate a great shift towards a Living Wage and away from tax credits. Yet if they disappeared entirely, it would leave many families without vital material support. It is a matter of rebalancing people's security away from state sponsored income transfers to revitalized wages at the level of the firm, thus underpinning the intrinsic dignity of paid work.

In fact, some Conservative commentators have acknowledged that at least Tony Blair tried to reform welfare. Well in 2016 people are less generous in their assessment of Labour's record. My point is not to re-live this debate which would get us nowhere but to recognize that the common good approach is not afraid of reform and challenging old ways of doing things. As Nick Spencer said about the future of welfare: "Welfare is always reforming,"[15] to borrow a phrase from the reformation, which I suspect you might appreciate. If we face public concern about welfare, genuine or misplaced, we have to take it seriously and try to address concerns that there is some public confidence restored in the system. Frank Field has gone as far as saying you need to work within the grain of people's instincts. We best serve the poorest of the poor by rebuilding a welfare system which has some measure of public support. This acknowledges that welfare cannot go back to where it was in the post-war period in its totality. I am very proud of what the Attlee Government did to adopt the Beveridge plan, but the challenges today are distinct. Times change but values don't.

15. Spencer, "The future of welfare," 10.

Something Borrowed

In further elucidating the wedding analogy, I feel that a common good approach would entail *something borrowed*, by that I mean my concern is for Labour to learn from the Centre for Social Justice work on child poverty. It would *borrow*—or rather be amenable—to challenge from another tradition. Specifically, I mean the center-left can learn from the center-right on child poverty. I have expressed concern about this Government's welfare cuts and I have concerns that Labour needs to be more imaginative about addressing child poverty. It needs to think of poverty in terms broader than but inclusive of income. Now, I wholly disagree with this Government's redefining child poverty without reference to income; this is just not right. Yet, I would like to see Labour have a broader, relational, family orientated assessment of poverty which also includes or now restored the place of income measurements. Tax credits have been essential to providing vital support to many families across the income scale. Yet, more nuance is needed. Frank Field MP touched upon this in his report on "life chances."[16] It is, at least, one thing I take from my days in the Shadow Department for Work and Pensions (DWP) team. A purely transactional approach will not do.

Which brings me to *Something Blue.*

How can Blue Labour help? Well, it champions the common good; its most crucial contribution and possibly lasting one to public debate. Yet crucially it places a stress on contribution, vocation, and political economy.

Blue Labour stressed the importance of the contributory principle as operatively essential to the welfare state. Indeed, Beveridge intended contribution to be a key foundation of his epochal reforms.

The principle is that those who pay into a social security system need to know when times are hard their contribution is reciprocated. It goes within the grain of working class culture and is essential if we are to gain any confidence in welfare. This is why the Labour Party went into the last General Election with a policy that those who had paid into the system for longer would receive slightly more JSA[17] should they face the misfortune of unemployment. It was a modest but significant policy, it needs to be built upon and adapted in future. It could be added to by increasing payments further to those who find themselves unemployed but have paid into the

16. Field, "The Foundation Years: preventing poor children becoming poor adults"

17. Job Seekers Allowance, a social security payment for those unemployed and seeking work: now replaced by Universal Credit.

system for a period of time. Bursaries for retraining could also be offered to specific groups who have contributed. The definition of contribution should also be broad and generous recognizing cares, voluntary workers, and mothers who have given periods of time to childcare.

Of course: this raises a number of important questions—does this undermine equality? How does it chime with a Christian commitment to help the poor? These are questions I ask myself. Yet, in politics we need to exercise the virtue of pragmatism but not allow pragmatism to be our rigid guide. I would submit that we best serve the poor by redesigning the welfare system so that there is a greater measure of confidence in it. I recall how Nye Bevan secured a deal with the consultants to pave the way for the establishment of the NHS, was this compromise worth it? Absolutely.

The Bible contains both a commitment to the poor and upholds the dignity of work. The same apostle who urged his fellow Christians to " . . . continue to remember the poor. . ."[18] also said: ". . .The one who is unwilling to work shall not eat."[19]

The gospel is free and generous; yet it does not underpin statist liberalism and dependency, it brings and *demands* transformation.

Blue Labour also provides additional insights into the debate. It honors the contribution of civil society to the common good. I passionately believe in the welfare state and a strong system of generous benefits as a sure safety net; without this the outcome is destitution. Yet, I don't believe that the state has all the answers. I believe that civil society should have a more robust role in a broad welfare architecture. I think of the work of *Pecan*[20] helping the unemployed in Peckham or Tom Jackson's *Resurgo Trust*[21] boosting the confidence of young people and making them more employable. I reflect on the work of my friend Russ Rook who put together an attractive offer for the Labour Party to consider as a model where foodbanks could assist individuals with employment and health needs, acting as a springboard to a real future. It is only civil society, predominantly churches, which can provide a relational and spiritual approach to poverty which needs much more than an economistic and statist response. The conception of the dignity of the human person is key; we can't treat people like units to be managed

18. Gal 2:10.

19. 2 Thess 3:10.

20. PECAN is a Christian charity operating in South London, United Kingdom.

21. RESURGO is a non-for-profit in West London focusing on societal change.

and their needs conveniently filed away. The church understands or should understand the worth of all of us.

Furthermore, we need to build an economy rooted in vocation and apprenticeships, along the lines of the Vocational Education and Training (VET) system in Germany. No system is perfect or wholly transferable to the UK but the neglect of vocation until recently has let young people down, damaged the economy and added to social and economic inequality. We need to ensure young people are prepared for work and that employers and schools are engaged and committed to this process. If young people drift through life and end up in low paid jobs the waste is criminal.

Alongside this we need a restoration of the immense contribution that trade unions can make, in fostering partnership like Dr John Lloyd did at the AEEU[22]. I met some great shop stewards in my time at that trade union. They were decent skilled people who loved their members and understood their company's success meant their success. Support for strong unions is not an antibusiness argument. I wonder if we hadn't seen the near decimation of union's we wouldn't have seen the overreliance on tax credits, the endless cycles of low pay and job insecurity and decline of vocation? This is about strong union's gaining respect not through the argument of force but the force of argument. We need workers on the boards of companies and a real balance of power in the workplace. It is possible to be pro-worker and pro-business. The answer to unemployment is don't make people unemployed in the first place or rather don't render them unemployable. I am not suggesting companies never need to let people go, but if we build an economy rooted in high value skill, worker participation and long-term investment maybe we will have a different set of economic problems to deal with, a more balanced economy and lower unemployment. This makes the welfare case different. You really can't talk about welfare without talking about how our economic relationships are structured.

Concluding Remarks

Maurice Glasman has said on the notion of building the common good and the common life that: ". . . there are no books on this, there is no position on this, but this we must understand, and it will take time."[23]

22. AEEU was the Amalgamated Engineering and Electrical Trade Union, for whom I worked from 2000–2003.

23. Glasman, "Faith in the Public Square," Lines 60–61.

These are just a few of my thoughts on a vast but vitally important subject. Just as I am sure a marriage takes time and cannot be secured by a Fabian away day in Hemel Hempstead; the approach of the common good will take time. It will involve learning from different traditions and those with whom we profoundly disagree. I say that renewing welfare will need something old, something new, something borrowed and something blue. Well, the reality is it will need much more.

There are many others who can put it better than me, who really understand the depth and dimensions of the common good. I don't believe in utopia and the politics of a*nother world is possible*, but I see a society where love and sin are realities. I want to see a society where there is a genuine safety net for the poor, where working people have confidence in social security and vocation means something once again because good work transforms lives. But I can't do it on my own or get anywhere near it without the common good and it can't be achieved outside the common life either. So, let's work together and we might discover that after all we really are all in it together.

15

Should Labour oppose individualism?

This essay was written following a contribution I made at a
fringe meeting at the Labour Party conference in Manchester
in 2014 and was organized by the Lincoln Theological
Institute, based at Manchester University. The fringe meeting
was based on the above title and I saw it as a question relating to liberalism or in fact the current variant of liberalism.

"Ever since the Thatcher era, British politics has been defined by
forms of economic and social liberalism. The right won the argument for the former and the left the argument for the latter, or so it
is said. Yet in the post-Crash era, this ideological settlement is beginning to fracture. The right is re-examining its crude economic
liberalism and the left its social liberalism."
". . . With its emphasis on abstract individualism, liberalism,
the great driver of social emancipation and economic prosperity,
now feels inadequate to this new age of insecurity."[1]

In short: yes, I believe that Labour should oppose individualism. Yet opposition alone is insufficient. Labour should propose a positive vision
that transcends the exhausted binary poles of individualism and collectivism. It should propose a view of association and the common life that
respects liberty and personhood but sees individual human flourishing

1. New Statesman, "Leader: Liberalism now feels inadequate in this new age of insecurity—The stakes could not be higher," 6.

contingent on a deeper experience of community. This vision draws on distinctly Christian resources which can avoid the twin tyranny of the individual and the collective. It has an appreciation of the reality of the soul, the example of scripture, an appreciation of society and is situated in a particular expression of socialism. One that is Christian in origin as opposed to a secular, liberal perception of the individual that is atomized and seeing the self as autonomous and sovereign. It is this latter approach that is the root of many of our contemporary problems.

We hardly need any more individualism in the West. Social and economic individualism, rooted in the *revolutions* of the 1960s and the 1980s, have proved empty and disastrous. But a return to state collectivism is neither desirable nor realistic.

Individualism may appeal to part but not all of the electorate. Certainly, parties might win an election with an appeal to individualism, but can a country be transformed by individualism? I don't believe it can or should.

I set out why I believe individualism is inadequate and therefore why Labour should not embrace it.

The Soul

I believe that man has a spiritual dimension. We have a body *and* a soul, the eternal part of our being. This may not be a word heard much in society let alone Labour Party fringe meetings. However, I hold to a Christian worldview, that is my starting point. The late US philosophy professor Dallas Willard said:

> "You are not just a self; you are a soul. You are a soul made by God, made for God, and made to need God made to run on God. Which means you are not made to be self-sufficient."[2]

From the outset, it is clear from that statement—with which I wholly concur—that mere individualism, even situated in a social democratic or communitarian frame, will not do. So, while it is perfectly feasible for political programs to be designed to cultivate individualism or vague abstractions of community, to me they will prove inadequate if rooted in a materialistic and secular view of the person. There is a metaphysical and cosmological framework, which must be considered first.

2. Willard, Review of *Soul Keeping—Caring for the most important part of you*, Lines 24–26.

Scripture

My reference point for interpreting meaning is scripture and theology. This resource tells us that individuals are endowed with dignity and worth, all of mankind is unique irrespective of class, gender, race, economic status or ability. Each creature, made to relate to his or her creator, has inestimable value. But man as the focus of creation is situated in an order of creation and only understands his or her true meaning and orientation when cognizant of that creator. God, revealed through scripture has made clear the worth of everyone, everyone. Nevertheless, the whole counsel of God, does not stop there. God is relational, the mysterious vision of the Trinity, the three in one and one in three gives us a glimpse of this important part of his creative nature was not about an individual but Adam and Eve—partners entrusted with a divine injunction to steward creation. They had responsibility beyond their immediate self-interest and were mandated to flourish and oversee the flourishing of creation. God's plan of redemption is situated in a people, Israel, a community, led by heroic individuals certainly. Jesus' mission is shared by a *collective* of twelve. In Acts 2[3] we see the early church sharing their goods and possessions in an early version of communal living. In the book of Revelation, we see the final triumph of God's people that is corporate in expression."[4]

So, from a biblical perspective the individual is important, but not reified to underpin a creed of individualism. The individual's identity and potential cannot be wholly understood or sufficiently realized without being reconciled to their creator, relating to others for a common purpose or entering a shared story that is larger than the whole. It is here I find it helpful to focus on personhood rather than the individual. A book I read over the summer provides a helpful insight.

> " . . . one person inward-looking, refusing to relate to others, is not a true person. We only become authentic persons when we are able to say with full conviction: I need you in order to be myself. Merton makes use in this context of the distinction between individual and person."[5]

Perhaps personhood is a better starting point than individualism. Scripture and a knowledge of our relation to God provides a sound

3. Acts 2:24–27.
4. Revelation 7:13–17.
5. Ware in, *A Silent Action*, 88.

reference point to appreciate this. Personhood says: "I need you in order to be myself." Individualism alone will fail apart from relationships and the other. It is a nonstarter.

The hunger for liberty and freedom detached from its values base has proved dangerous, as has been pointed out by Phillip Blond. The fundamental problem for liberalism is that it become detached from the Christian roots that fostered it.

Society

One of the most interesting developments in recent years is the reassertion of civic society in political discourse. It is too early to assess where this will go. Clearly, the renewed profile of the primacy of civil society in underpinning the good life renders naked individualism a curious project. Any glimpse at society or its importance must tell us that individualism is insufficient. We all operate in a broader context or space; civic society may have differing forms and may be stronger in certain places than others. Competing visions will seek to define it in different ways. Yet, the aspiration to focus on civic society and its importance tells us perhaps of a hunger for more than we have now. Hyper-individualism has failed us. The evidence of church administered foodbanks, debt advice centers, youth provision, mums and toddlers' groups and host of other activities run for the common good attest to the health of civic society, filling gaps in provision at critical junctures. This is not a complacent analysis, whole areas of society are bereft of community and suffer from the ravages of economic, social and cultural individualism.

This is why—for all its flaws—the *Big Society* should not be too swiftly dismissed. It was not merely a cover for cuts as some on the left initially suggested. It was the recognition that there is more than the state, market and the individual. Given its roots, it should have been the Labour Party making this argument, not the center-right.

Years of market and state dominance have whittled away civic society. But it is because of the potential for civic renewal we should be open to the idea that mere individualism is insufficient. Labour's civic roots should tell us that individualism alone is not a path the party should embrace.

Socialism

"We raise the watchword liberty, we will, we will, we will be free,"[6]
George Loveless, Tolpuddle Martyrs

"The condition upon which God hath given liberty to man is eternal vigilance," John Philpott Curran[7]

The Labour tradition has many streams: secular; socialist; social democratic; Celtic; and Christian Socialist. It should be natural that the socialist, collectivist traditions provide a corrective against individualism per se. In many ways they have; the establishment of free trade unions, the Rochdale pioneers[8], democratic empowerment, the National Health Service, access to national land and beauty were achieved through the strength of common endeavor. Labour has in its DNA a sense of the common life.

However, misty eyed reflection on the achievements of past collectivism is of little use. The corrosive impact of hyper-individualism or social and economic liberalism has wrought deep damage.

"The 2011 riots were signposts to the failure of successive governments to deal with the downsides of two revolutions. A social revolution in the 1960s made us freer, more tolerant and a more vibrant nation. An economic revolution in the 1980s made Britain more prosperous and innovative. But, left unchecked, the combination of the two revolutions has made us more atomized, more unequal and less compassionate. Our culture is more hyper-individualized, and our social fabric is stretched and damaged. The malaise of long-term worklessness, materialism, the inadequacy of the criminal justice system and the lack of positive male role models came together in a perfect storm during August 2011."[9]

As David Lammy points out hyper-individualism and other forces have stretched and damaged us. They render attempts to renew the left's ever-present struggles almost impossible. The challenge is not to give up on a task but to find the resources, traditions, and language, to focus the movement today.

6. "The Story," https://www.tolpuddlemartyrs.org.uk/story.

7. John Philpot Curran, "The speeches of the Right Honourable John Philpot Curran"

8. The Rochdale Pioneers are regarded as the founders of the Co-operative Movement—https://ica.coop/en/rochdale-pioneers.

9. Lammy, *Out of the Ashes,*vii–viii.

It is in the Christian faith and its values and worldview the answer lies. Despite the apparent triumph of unrestrained liberalism many people still yearn for a sense of belonging and association. The desire to cherish relationships, family and place is strong. The discipline and practice of community organizing to mobilize civil society vis-à-vis the market and the state demonstrates association, relationality and mobilized campaigning can still inspire and deliver material change. This is why I believe this debate about individualism in the context of the Labour Party needs as a conversation partner. That partner is Blue Labour and its cognate narrative postliberalism.

As Jon Cruddas has commented: ". . .we face a twin crisis of inequality and identity."[10] The challenge of secular capitalism, environmental degradation and family breakdown cannot be faced by the individual alone. Nor can these challenges be met solely through a political platform designed to win an election. There needs to be a long-term, transformational approach to public life that is pro-faith, postsecular and postliberal. An intention to foster institutional life, allowing individuals to flourish and character to form; honoring liberty but eschewing extreme liberalism and moral relativism, pursuing the common good in the family, locality, workplace, and society. This is not about moralism or utopia. A vision of the common good that is pro-association, pro-person, goes beyond tribe and secures the basis for individual flourishing outwith a liberal frame. This approach can renew society thus shaping politics. Under these conditions, we can see any party, Labour or whoever, not merely opposing individualism but setting out a broader, richer vision of the good life.

10. Cruddas, "Common Good in an age of Austerity," 87.

16

Reflections on Postliberalism and Postliberal Politics

This article was posted on the *Christians on the Left* website on July 22, 2014. It is worth noting UKIP's success in that year's European Elections, registering its existential threat to Labour. Toward the end I try and map out some potential actions for postliberalism.

"Modernity failed our deepest human needs, and comprehensively fouled our physical and spiritual environment in the process; yet the liberalism of modernity, and those other modernists who reacted against it, seem to have exhausted most of what can be said and achieved. There is a sense now of a lack of vision, of aftermath, of epilogue."

PETE LOWMAN

When asked what he thought about the French Revolution, Mao[1] is reputed to have said: "It is too early to judge." My sense with postliberalism is much of it is too early to judge. However, we have more than

---

1. This statement is contested see here for a more detailed explanation: https://www.oxfordreference.com/display/10.1093/acref/9780191826719.001.0001/q-oro-ed4-00018657

sufficient grounds to explore this concept and ponder the potential for a postliberal politics.

Nonetheless, something is happening—albeit uncertain—in UK politics that will not fizzle out. It can either be a moment of fragmentation and stagnation or a re-imagining of the good life; beyond the liberal frame empowered by Christian resources. These are my assumptions as I reflect on postliberalism and prospects for postliberal politics. Thus, it is wholly apposite to reflect on those societal and political changes currently dubbed as postliberalism and assess their political and cultural significance.

We live in a moment of paradox; the dominant liberal paradigm is firmly rooted in the economic, social, and cultural elites but its grip is fragmenting. This may not be enough to break its hegemonic position; perhaps it may not even be desirable; it could be, but something is giving way. I see the evidence as:

1. The economic crash of 2008—neoliberalism has been found out

2. Social liberalism—the 1960s revolution, libertarianism, a view of an atomized society has proved empty and destructive. Social liberalism, in some quarters, is being questioned, more so than ever and more on the center-left.

Postliberalism acknowledges these trends. After the nadir of social and economic liberalism we are left with a dual crisis of inequality and identity.[2] Postliberalism is, to a significant degree, related to the attempt to navigate the way through this crisis.

The United Kingdom has suffered the largest economic shock since the 1930s—a recovery is taking place but is fragile. The gap between the rich and poor is vast; there are now one-hundred-and-four billionaires in the UK with a combined wealth of £301 billion and the highest number on record resorting to foodbanks just to get by.[3] The confident social liberalism of a generation, more liberating to the affluent than the poor, is in question. Increasingly people desire a sense of connection with others, richer identities, tradition and some form of anchoring. The limits of the economic and social liberal revolutions have been reached and we don't know what to do about it.

2. Cruddas, "Common Good in an age of Austerity," in *Blue Labour*, 87.

3. Hargreaves, "Pay inequality is suffocating Britain's economic recovery—and our society," Lines 20–21.

This moment can manifest itself in unpleasant stuff such as the rise of UKIP, perhaps a key signifier of the postliberal moment, who exploit alienation and disconnection. This ethical vacuum needs to be filled by a rich and generous conception of politics rather than dystopia. The elite appear unsighted by UKIP and unsure or even complacent in their response. I would suggest that a more serious analysis is required. Jon Cruddas notes:

> " . . . two forces are driving our politics. The first is people's feelings of powerlessness in the face of rapid social and economic change. The second is the loss of a sense of belonging, a feeling among people that something has been lost from their lives that they will never get back. They feel abandoned, and UKIP is exploiting this mood in Labour's English heartlands, the ex-industrial areas in which decent work and the old culture of the working class have been devastated."[4]

What is postliberalism? In order to scope out the potential for a postliberal politics we need to get a handle on what postliberalism means. However, there is no agreed, coherent definition of postliberalism. As academic Anna Rowlands said:

> "Postliberalism is an intriguingly cacophonous movement, capable of moments of harmony that it is not always able to sustain."[5]

Anna Rowlands was right. We are looking at a disjointed song, as yet unharmonized but until recently the song had not been sung. Liberalism as a force is not on the wane, but the potential for a genuinely plural politics is not a given. Recognizing that the dynamism of the social and economic liberal revolutions is insufficient to nurture the good life is a key feature the postliberal disposition. Uniting Blue Labour and Red Tory streams it does not blithely accept the self-evident goodness of liberalism but advocates a politics of the common good which is communitarian in orientation. It is skeptical in respect to the centralizing forces of the state and the market, seeks to foster a robust civil society, and affirms the primacy of faith, family, attachment to place and the fostering of institutions. It seeks to articulate an alternative political economy and account of the good life to address the challenges of glaring inequality and fractured identity.

---

4. Cruddas, "UKIP isn't a Tory movement. It's a party of the disenfranchised English," Lines 1–7.

5. Rowlands, "Post-liberal Politics and the Churches," in *Crucible*, 25.

My sense is that currently postliberalism represents a broad church of sympathetic perspectives. There are the non-liberal, faith-based communitarians; the liberal skeptics and a broad array of center-left progressives who see that liberalism, in its economic and social expressions has reached its limits. More clarity is required; ten years ago, people weren't having such conversations.

> "The still nascent Blue Labour project does not have any institutional home, nor any text which offers a definition of its principles and objectives, so that it remains rather more of a disposition and a cluster of personal relationships than a fully-fledged project. . . ."[6]

Starting as a disposition is not a bad thing. Certainly, postliberalism requires maturation and a program. Yet, dispositions are natural and strongly rooted, unlike bolt-on ideologies. Speaking personally, as an evangelical Christian, from a lower-middle class background in South Staffordshire and the edge of the Black Country my disposition is a strong moral compass. I am tribally Labour, independent in thinking and find southern, metropolitan liberal progressivism somewhat alienating. However, my roots and formation account for the reason why I don't wholly connect with the political and cultural elite worldview and the dominant groupings on the left.

Is it vitally important to understand that postliberalism is cross-party in nature—Blue Labour and Red Tory—and is not fixed in one camp, it has a strong Christian element. I would argue that this is essential. I can connect to some on the center-right more readily than some on the liberal left on certain issues i.e., family, faith, and ethical matters. This does not mean I am about to leave the Labour Party—I intend to stay.

I do not think everything to do with liberalism is bad. I recognize good things in classical liberalism that may even derive from a Christian worldview.[7] Too often it has become grammatically interchangeable with all that is considered good and generous.[8] This is very shallow and perhaps dangerous and tyrannical if pursued unthinkingly. Liberalism should not be interchangeable with all that is good. In the UK and in the US in certain

6. Sunder Katwala, "Burke, Norman and Glasman—'post-liberalism' in Britain today," 2013, Lines 69–72.

7. While classic liberalism owes a debt to Christianity; it becomes problematic when detached from these moorings becoming a relativistic, shrill form of illiberal tyranny.

8. Philip Blond said at the Blue Labour Midlands Seminar in Nottingham on July 5, 2014 that liberalism has become 'code for all that is good . . .'.

circles to be liberal is self-evidently good. At worst such cheap liberalism morphs into tyranny relativism and ironically *illiberalism*. For example, I would point to the metropolitan tendency to be intolerant of views expressed out with the liberal matrix. Some of the more juvenile responses to the daft comments of UKIP activists is one example of this tendency. Maurice Glasman has referred to the tin ear of the Westminster village. Liberalism is imperialistic, perhaps like any philosophical project. I watched YouTube clip earlier this year enterprisingly constructed by a US student. In a tour de force of Western History from Locke to President Obama anything that was good was attributed to liberalism, anything bad was tyranny! I assert this from the vantage point of Christian faith; all narratives can become totalizing and imperial in nature.[9]

Of course, a measure of nuance is important to this assessment; Mark Garnett has alluded to a "deep and shallow liberalism."[10] Liberal principles, as properly understood, can contribute to the good life. However, this is distinct from liberal dominance in the public square and critiquing liberalism does not mean I am adopting a Conservative tradition as conventionally understood. Alasdair MacIntyre accurately sums this up this position as follows:

> "This critique of Liberalism should not be interpreted as a sign of any sympathy on my part for contemporary Conservatism. That Conservatism is in too many ways a mirror image of the liberalism that it professedly opposes."[11]

In 2011 Phillip Blond introduced an essay collection stating that:

> "Perhaps for the first time in thirty years politics is changing. The old orthodoxies of left and right are still dominant, but they are no longer hegemonic. Beneath the surface the tectonic plates are shifting; boundaries are blurring, and ideologies are returning to

9. Greene and Robinson, *Metavista*, 103–4.

10. '. . . a schism could be detected in liberal ranks long before September 2001. I call the rival camps 'fleshed-out' and 'hollowed-out' liberalism. The former retains a close resemblance to the ideas of the great liberal thinkers, who were optimistic about human nature and envisaged a society made up of free, rational individuals, respecting themselves and others. The latter, by contrast, satisfies no more than the basic requirements of liberal thought. It reduces the concepts of reason and individual fulfilment to the lowest common denominator, identifying them with the pursuit of material self-interest.' Garnett, *The snake that Swallowed its Tail* 8.

11. MacIntyre, *After Virtue*, Xiii.

first principles, creating a new terrain that is slowly beginning to emerge."[12]

So, a new territory is emerging, an undesirable political vacuum perhaps? Within these shifting plates it is postliberalism—in political terms—that seeks to intelligently interpret what is happening. Full definition is required; the challenge is to fill the vacuum with a generous message of hope. I believe this is found in the Christian gospel and that is why postpolitics is a corollary of postliberalism.

In the UK I believe we are now seeing a deep cultural disconnect, perhaps explained by the recent curiosity with UKIP. There is now an almost permanent anti-political element within the UK electorate. In the European and local elections on May 22, we saw UKIP get the largest share of the vote. We need to be wary of rushing to strong conclusions, however, it is folly to write off UKIP as only appealing to disaffected Conservative voters alone. They clearly appeal to the disenchanted white working class in England; for whom Labour voting was once an old-time religion but now feel culturally alienated by the *people's party*. On May 16, 2014, academics Rob Ford and Matthew Goodwin spelled out clearly that UKIP do pose a threat to Labour, as they can tap into this constituency. They wrote:

> "The problem for Labour is that these voters no longer think about politics in general, or Labour in particular, in economic terms. Labour has encouraged this: New Labour played down traditional leftwing ideology in favour of social liberalism and pragmatic centrism. Now many voters with longstanding *old left* economic values associate Labour more with 'new left' social liberalism: feminism, multiculturalism and support for immigration."[13]

This point to me is fundamental, UKIP; not what they stand for, but what they tap into are the flipside of postliberalism. Understanding why people have voted for them is key to realizing why this agenda is important and how we can broker a politics of the common good and renew social democracy.

Our analysis needs to be delicate and nuanced, balancing act; not reading too much into the UKIP surge while not dismissing it either. It may be a complex amalgam of factors: legitimate concern over the European

12. Blond, *Changing the Debate*, 1.

13. Ford and Goodwin, "UKIP has divided the left, not the right, and cut Labour off from its 'old' support—Labour and Ukip voters agree on more economic issues than you might think, presenting a strategic problem for Ed Miliband," Lines 42–48

Union; a visceral anti-political sentiment; collapse in both the British National Party (BNP) and the Liberal Democrats as protest vehicles; or the BBC's interest in conflating the novelty of anti-establishment parties. My instinct is that within the multi-causal account of UKIP they are tapping into the alienation exacerbated by social and economic liberalism and doing so in a negative way. Ford and Goodwin are on the money. This is the context which postliberalism must address.

What is the potential for postliberal politics? and what should be the next or first steps for postliberal politics?

1. There needs to be greater work on defining the concept and space of postliberalism. We should set out the terrain on deepening the politics of the common good, inside and outside of mainstream politics. Informed by a rigorous evaluation of what is happening, connecting Catholic Social Teaching and evangelical energy. Christians can shape postliberal politics; informed by experience in critiquing liberalism and embodying an alternative framework of hope.

2. Honoring and nurturing of institutional life;[14] policy alone is too abstract, too rooted in the intellectual, liberal policy elite and too prone to watering down and compromise to be enough to renew Britain.

3. Seize the postliberal moment within the mainstream political parties. Campaigns and Parliamentary groups could be formed, documents need to be published, conferences could forge ahead with socially conservative and postliberal campaigns. These can respect party boundaries and operate at their margins. There needs to be a reckoning with this agenda; the challenge is far too serious.

4. There needs to be a raising up a new generation of postliberal leaders in public life. Currently, the postliberalism agenda could be vulnerable to opportunistic cherry-picking of ideas in a policy vacuum. This agenda is more likely to be durable when championed by a generation of people who have the values in their blood, are battle hardened, take a long-term view of the challenges ahead and are therefore less prone to being bought off by party machines, becoming bored, distracted or simply give up.

14. In a 'Big Lunch' event on June 1 in South London I saw more common good in action than in reading reports on poverty and social exclusion in just under two years.

There needs to be a distinct engagement between Labour and post-liberalism. It should be the center-left and Labour that stands to benefit from postliberalism, although it should not own this agenda. However, this remains to be seen. Labour should be the natural beneficiaries with its putative link to working class voters and communitarian roots; yet we have a long way to go. There are still variable reactions to Blue Labour; yet for Labour to win again it needs to take this agenda seriously.

> "Blue Labour cannot win Miliband the next election but he surely cannot win without it."[15]

More needs to be done to distinguish a Labour explanation of twenty-first-century Britain from a singularly liberal one. This is why postliberalism provides a space for a distinct Labour story. We came out of the liberal tradition but are not a liberal party.

I believe that postliberalism can play its part in renewing the left. I feel strongly about this agenda. More of the same will lead to more of the same. Yet, the rupture with working class voters runs deep. The people are *conservatives*—note the lower case *c*—the elite is not. Postliberalism lives and breathes outside the M25.

For Labour to be a broad and plural party it needs to be amenable to a pro-faith, postsecular and postliberal. We are facing a crisis of inequality and identity[16]; the economic and cultural apparatus has failed. Postliberalism is a positive response to the failure of economic and social liberalism. However, we know there are alternative responses that present bad choices, for society and politics and the nation's relationship with the outside world. Postliberalism is only a start; much more needs to be done.

In one sentence, I believe postliberalism means that all our gods have failed us. My hope is in the Christian gospel; it can uphold liberty, the common life and provide a politics of servanthood, not domination, it speaks of a tradition that is pre-liberal and transcends all -isms to a life beyond this immanent frame. It is time to start making a much more explicit case for a Christian politics. It can address the sense of exhaustion and lack of vision which characterizes economic and social liberalism as alluded to in the opening Pete Lowman quote.

That is why I believe the challenge presented by the crisis of identity and inequality calls for a robust Christian voice in the public square.

---

15. Darlington, "The strange death and rebirth of Blue Labour," Lines 91–92.
16. Cruddas, Cruddas, "The Common Good in an Age of Austerity," in *Blue Labour*, 87.

Individualism is never enough; it only ever benefited the few and wrought destruction for the many. Liberal modernity has been the big story in the west for 250 years. It will not disappear overnight; yet it has cracks and is contested. Its dominance is over and postliberalism signifies the movement of tectonic plates, and a postliberal politics needs nurturing.

17

Letter to Lachlan

In 2012 when I was working for Stephen Timms MP, I got to meet Lachlan who works for Jenny Macklin, a Labor politician in Australia. At the time she was the Minister for Disability Reform and represented the fantastically sounding district of Jagajaga.

I have an oddball interest in the Australian Labor Party, so this was for me a worthwhile dialogue.

In 2016 Lachlan contacted me via Facebook to ask me what was going on in the UK Labour Party regarding the events of the summer and the European Union vote. I sent an email, dubbed *Letter to Lachlan*.

Hello Lachlan,

I apologize for the delay in me getting back to you. I enclose some thoughts on the political situation here. Please bear in mind they are my thoughts, and I am not neutral but clearly, I hope I am not jaundiced.

Labour Party

So, Labour lost the General Election in 2015. I campaigned in ten constituencies, so perhaps I didn't get a broad view of what was happening. I never expected Labour to win but I didn't think the Conservatives would win either! In the end they won with a small but clear majority. One can guess why Labour didn't win it might be that we were never trusted on the economy, immigration and welfare and people didn't see Ed Miliband as a potential PM. The legacy of the deficit and the Conservative ability to pin the blame on Labour successfully may also have been a major factor. There were also press insinuations that Labour would seek a coalition deal with the Scottish National party (SNP), which to some English working class voters would be unpalatable. I was never sure of how meaningful this was, but it was put out there.

One analysis by Jon Cruddas MP (a Labour MP who is a serious thinker) can be read here:[1] Anyway, there was an election contest within the Labour Party when Ed Miliband stood down as leader. There were calls for a long contest so Labour could have an existential debate, at the time, that was my view. To get on the ballot candidates had to have thirty-five nominations from fellow MPs. Jeremy Corbyn, a London based MP, associated with the left of the Party just made it onto the ballot at the last minute. Moderate MPs lent him their support to ensure there was a broad debate. I doubt any of them expected he would actually win.

Due to new election rules, introduced by Ed Miliband, members of the public could pay £3 and get a vote. This innovation and the fact that Jeremy Corbyn's campaign got early traction meant over the summer of 2015 he seemed to be heading for a clear victory. On September 12—I remember as it was my late father's eightieth birthday—Jeremy Corbyn won, beating three other candidates from the center or center-left of the party. Now, opinion has always been divided on this: most moderates see Jeremy Corbyn and his left-wing policies as unelectable; they remember a comparable period in history (the early 1980s) when Labour lost election after election and suffered from hard left entryism from groups who have little concern for the Labour Party and parliamentary democracy. This is always complicated as Jeremy Corbyn is not an entryist, he is a sincere, principled person but it might be that the movement he represents attracts such groups towards the Labour Party. It is certainly clear that the Corbyn campaign attracted many enthusiastic followers, for many reasons with a sense of energy and idealism.

The past fourteen months have been a period of turmoil and Jeremy Corbyn faced problems as here you had a Labour leader that the members voted for but not the majority of the MPs. It might be that the MPs have not given him a fair run but it was always going to be testy. I felt it was

---

1. Cruddas, "Labour's Future—Why Labour lost in 2015 and how it can win again—Report of the independent inquiry into why Labour lost in 2015."

very unfair to allow people to pay a couple of quid and vote for Labour leader, when other long-standing activists pay much more money and get the same say.

Anyway, after nine months things really came to a head at the European Union Referendum on June 23. I thought it would be close and Remain would win just, I was wrong. The country voted 52 percent in favor of leaving the EU that has added further uncertainty into the British polity. David Cameron stood down as Prime Minister and now Theresa May is Prime Minister. Some within the Labour camp felt that Jeremy Corbyn could have put more into the campaign and there occurred over the weekend after the referendum a sequenced process of front bench Labour MPs resigning in large numbers. I was never sure if it is true that Jeremy Corbyn could have done better in the campaign, I wasn't focusing on his every move. This eventually led to another election over this summer, with twists and turns, new members could join again, this time paying £25 and as the incumbent leader Jeremy Corbyn didn't need to secure MPs backing to get on the ballot. There was even a legal move to try and remove Jeremy Corbyn from being on the ballot! A moderate challenger in Owen Smith MP was found and with little surprise Jeremy Corbyn was re-elected again on the Saturday before Labour Party conference in September. I was at my aunt and uncle's fiftieth wedding anniversary in York, so the golden rule is Labour hold election contests when my family has celebrations. In the end Owen Smith didn't win but all things considered the moderate vote held up well, it will live to fight another day.

So, now I expect Labour MPs and the party need to try as hard as possible to work together and heal the wounds. Jeremy Corbyn has now won twice and in my view on that basis deserves to lead Labour into the General Election. There is a strong suspicion that this will be a bruising election for Labour. My sense is that in the long-term Labour will come good, but people need to be patient. Patience is not a quality that political people are known for. This is part of a historical cycle for Labour, it nearly died in 1931 and again in 1981, but survived. Both these seasons were traumatic so perhaps I am being complacent, but I genuinely believe Labour will come through this, it just will take a long time. We are coming out of thirteen years of Government (1997–2010), prior to this Labour had only ever held power for six years. So, there is a lot to process. More than has been processed before.

The challenge is to keep the party together and maintain a capacity for new ideas and new leaders to come through. I don't think Labour can afford another internal election until the other side of an election when the conversation, hopefully, might be more open. There does need to be, in my view, a moderate offer from Labour but people need to understand the factors that drove many people to vote for Jeremy Corbyn. The challenge is huge for Labour, it needs to win back Scotland (which has been lost to the SNP), appeal to the disaffected working class in the Midlands and North, where it faces a challenge from a populist party called UKIP and still appeal to aspirational voters in the South. It is an enormous task, and is much harder than that faced by Tony Blair, a figure I feel who is unfairly maligned and it is difficult to have a rational conversation about him due to the legacy of Iraq, but he won three elections and was a towering figure. I am not uncritical of him by the way, but the recent period has seen a very unpleasant disregard for Labour's recent past.

This is a potted account and of course it is my view. Some-one else with a different perspective will give you a different account.

Brexit

I touched on this above. The referendum has in many ways rocked the establishment. The areas that voted to leave the European Union in many ways might be the places that feel left behind by London and the big cities, where jobs have been lost and not replaced with decent work and where there has been significant migration. I know this is a difficult subject but the left in the UK needs to find a way to respond to people's anxieties without rejecting migrants and the benefits of migration.

This report[2] appears to explore some of these issues and tensions I have not read it!

One vignette that perhaps sums up the geographical divide is thus: Southwark—the borough where I live in London—voted around 70 percent remain and 30 percent leave. While my hometown of Walsall in the West Midlands, voted by around 68 percent for leave and 32 percent for remain. So, you can almost flip the results! The areas are very different. Almost different worlds.

I don't claim to understand everyone's reason for voting to leave, for some there would be genuine concern at the European Union, an attachment

2. The Centre for Social Justice, "Healing a Divided Britain"

to Parliamentary Sovereignty etc. but also an insular view of the world. For some it might have represented an ideal opportunity to knock the political elite. So many were elated, and many were disappointed. I voted remain and am disappointed, I think it is a bad decision to leave the European Union, but we are where we are.

The new Prime Minister—who supported Remain—is bound to follow the will of the public and pursue the desire to leave the European Union. This is highly complex. Legally the nation needs to trigger Article 50, which triggers a two-year process, the legal means of leaving the EU. I don't think any nation has ever undertaken this. There has been a debate also on what type of Brexit the nation pursues. Do we break free from all regulations and the single market (i.e., hard Brexit) or do we leave but retain some of the environmental and workplace regulations and/or retain access to the single market (i.e., soft Brexit). The context has changed again in the past few days when the High Court has approved a case taken by a group of Remain campaigners which means that Parliament will have to vote on the Article 50 process. Hitherto the Prime Minister had sought to trigger Article 50 without Parliamentary Approval. The Government is expected to appeal to the Supreme Court and may lose. So, there is a high chance of a vote in 2017 and some are floating the possibility of a General Election. These all raise vexed political and constitutional questions.

It will run and run. So, these are my reflections, they are simplistic and my own views, if you asked someone else, on both matters you would get different opinions.

Best wishes, and if you come to the UK again, let me know.

Ian Geary

Politics

Questions for discussion

In the section on *Politics,* I seek to explicate reflections on politics from an explicitly Christian vantage point, you might find the following questions helpful for reflection or discussion:

1. Why is it important that politics is a truly plural space; if so what should this look like?

2. What are the strengths and limitations of liberalism?

3. What is the common good? How can we seek it in the political realm?

4. What does it mean to be 'progressive'? How does this fit with a Christian narrative?

5. How can the common good help us understand what should constitute a modern welfare state?

6. How do we square the fact that Jesus said 'the poor will always be with you' and that the Christian gospel is 'good news to the poor?'

7. Is God 'biased to the poor'? If so, what are the political implications of this statement?

8. Where does individualism belong in politics?

Recommended Reading

Fenner Brockway, *The life of Alfred Salter: Bermondsey Story*, London: George, Allen and Unwin, 1949

Mark Garnett, *The Snake that Swallowed its Tail: Some Contradictions in Modern Liberalism*, London: Imprint Academic, 2004

David Lammy, *Out of the Ashes: Britain after the Riots*, London: Guardian Books, 2011

Adrian Pabst, *The crisis of global capitalism: Pope Benedict XVI's Papal Encyclical and the Future of Political Economy*, Wipf and Stock, 2011

SECTION THREE

Belonging

18

To *Woke* or *Not to Woke?*

That is the question

"Having a form of godliness but denying its power . . . ."[1]

"In a world bereft of the power of revealed religion, we have to face
up to the fact that no-one knows how to live."

BRUNO MACAES

What is the good life? What is human flourishing? One might argue
that at the heart of political debate is a deep, searching existential
question: what is the good life? What are the conditions for human flourishing? I doubt that everyone involved in politics would argue it this way.
They might infer it is left versus right, about abstract notions like fairness
or the sovereignty of the nation or focus on procedure or constitutional
matters. Fair enough. Yet, it is a clear and profound question that if posed
is difficult to provide a glib answer to or if your answer is glib this will be
immediately apparent.

Stanley Hauerwas in summarizing the English shepherd James Rebanks' memoir *The Shepherd's Life* comes accurately close to identifying
the centrality of the debate and more pertinently, the contemporary crisis

---

1. 2 Tim 3:5.

about what is the good life? It is worth quoting extensively to dig down into this powerful vignette.

> "In the last paragraphs Rebanks—who has been a shepherd for many years—reports on a moment in his busy life. It is in the late spring, and he is in the process of returning his flock to the craggy hills. These sheep had been bred to fend for themselves in rocky terrain. He enjoys watching the sheep find their way in the rough fields because they are evidently happy to be *home*. Rebanks imitates his flock's sense that all is as it should be, by lying down in the grass to drink sweet and pure water from the nearby stream. He rolls on his back and watches the clouds racing by. His well-trained sheep dogs Floss and Tan—who had never seen him so relaxed— come and lay next to him. He breathes in the cool mountain air; he listens to the ewes calling to the lambs to follow them through the rocky crags, and he thinks: "This is my life. I want no other."[2]

"This is my life. I want no other" is an extraordinary declaration that one rarely hears today. As odd as it may seem, I want to suggest that the loss of our ability to have such lives, the absence of the conditions that make such a declaration possible in contemporary life, is a clue for understanding our current cultural moment and corresponding politic."[3]

What happens when the culture and its politics loses its roots and telos? When does it becomes divisive, agonistic, and ultimately unproductive? More specifically, what happens when politics becomes a space populated by disparate campaigns and causes that appear well meaning but are disconnected from a deep and rational sense of the good and serve to become a negative phenomenon?

I submit that the *woke* phenomenon is a feature of that seemingly inability to articulate the vision of the good life in an agreeable manner.

Although perhaps deployed as a pejorative term, we are witnessing an increasingly heightened attachment to a shallow form of social justice, that does not result in social betterment or in many cases justice. As Christians we should be discerning about this trend, not fall into reactive name calling but reclaim a robust, deep and gospel rooted advocacy of social justice and renewal.

---

2. Hauerwas, "Is Democracy capable of cultivating a good life? What Liberals should learn from the Shepherds," Lines 27–35.

3. Hauerwas, "Is Democracy capable of cultivating a good life? What Liberals should learn from the
Shepherds," Lines 36–39.

It is highly important and would be remiss not to point out that the term *woke* has an honorable root. In its original use by African Americans, it was associated with resisting racism and oppression. Yet as Abas Mirzaei points out, the meaning, over time, has altered.

> "Being *woke* was originally associated with Black Americans fighting racism but has been appropriated by other activist groups—taking it from awareness and blackness to a colourless and timeless phenomenon."[4]

In his reflection Mirzaei identifies the popularization of the meme "Stay woke" during the growth in salience of the *Black Lives Matter* movement in the mid-2010s. Of note, corporate capitalism stepped in and appropriated or misappropriated it, giving it a wider meaning. The term has now been re-deployed and signifies a kind of maladjusted hyper-liberalism. As former US President Obama—hardly a reactionary—pointed out, it can be reflective of a simplistic, self-righteous politics.[5]

Yet, along with critique must come some measure of corrective. Unfortunately, the word *woke* can be used to silence people—even a prophetic voice—and this is a tendency in contemporary political discourse on the left and the right. It is after all a pejorative term. We would do well to listen to opinions with which we disagree (a practice of community organizing) and learn to disagree in a civil manner.

It is not a healthy or happy situation when anyone who acts with social compassion and sincerity is immediately labeled *woke* as a put down or being placed in a pigeonhole. Just as in the past someone might have been dismissed as a leftie or bleeding heart liberal. I say this out of fairness and balance yet that does not mean I think the *woke* movement is healthy. Rather, juvenile name calling is not good and does not enhance our public discourse. Yet being *woke* is inseparable from the name-calling culture and collectively this negative dialogue is harmful to the common good and search for a peaceful politics.

To some, the term is indicative of the latest phase of the cultural left's attempt to assert itself. As former Australian Labor leader, now a re-elected MP, Mark Latham said in his maiden speech:

---

4. Mirzaei, "Where 'woke' came from and why marketers should think twice before jumping on the
social activism bandwagon," Lines 10–13.

5. BBC, "Barack Obama Challenges Woke Culture."

"The Leftist project, then and now, is about control. Having, with the fall of the Berlin Wall, lost the struggle for economic control, the Left got smarter. It shifted from the Cold War to a culture war. It moved from pursuing economic Marxism to pushing cultural Marxism."[6]

There may be warnings from recent history. In the 1960s, a moderate trade union leader Bill Sirs, warned the movement what would happen if good virtuous standards were replaced by aggressive and self-referential orientations.

"Somehow, we must capture the imagination of the British People all over again . . . We have to let the public see the better side of trade unionism—all the millions of man-hours of voluntary work that trade unionists do up and down the country, week-in, week-out. The way in which we care for our sick and elderly workers, our pensioners; the way in which we support communities, welfare centres, social clubs and all the sort of facilities for young people; the way in which we help to run our town councils, sit on the bench of the nation's [England and Wales] magistrates' courts, and play a part in the cultural, artistic and religious life of the nation."
"The vast majority of trade unionists, like the rest of the British people are hard-working, loyal and patriotic. Yet this is not the image the public has of a trade unionist. They only see the bawling, yelling, sloganizing ranter, the work-shy, idle card-playing shop floor worker or striker."
"The false images have to be removed before it is too late, and we must use every technique in the book to bring about a change in the public's perception of who we are and what we do . . . to see the day when Britain's trade unionists are more influential than before—not because of the power they employ—but because of the contribution they make to the life of the nation."[7]

Although specific to the trade union movement it shows a difference between a politics of quiet service that accords with the common good and an unappealing politics located in the same institutional form. How you do something is as important was what you do.

A certain approach to politics can in the long run achieve the aims you seek; another is more limiting. It is more fruitful to advocate a politics that meets people's needs than one of purely posturing positions.

---

6. Hon. Mark Latham's Maiden Speech, Lines 61–64.

7. Sirs, *Hard Labour*, 142.

All this suggests that in our politics, we need greater civility, reflection, depth and not shallow name-calling. We can do much better.

A Matter of Debate

It is a delicate and complicated issue, but Christians need to be humbly engaged as our faith has a social dimension but not a social dimension alone. There seems to be some conflict or even confusion amongst Christians as to how to respond to *woke*. To call it out or have more empathy, witness the concerns of US Roman Catholic Archbishop Gomez,[8] conveyed in a speech in November 2021 likening the *woke* movement to a form of religion and saying:

> "With the breakdown of the Judeo-Christian worldview and the rise of secularism, political belief systems based on social justice or personal identity have come to fill the space that Christian belief and practice once occupied."
>
> "Whatever we call these movements—'social justice', 'wokeness', 'identity politics', 'intersectionality', 'successor ideology'—they claim to offer what religion provides."

However, in contrast another US Roman Catholic voice suggests there needs to be more thought and empathy.

> "Issues like climate change and systemic racism are labeled pejoratively by the political right as part of a 'woke' agenda, but those concerned about such things have identified real and present threats. There is overwhelming evidence that climate change is human-induced and must be curtailed. Huge majorities of Black and Indigenous Americans tell us that systemic racism corrupts our institutions, and statistical data reflects this. If the 'woke' are overly concerned with perception, the 'unwoke' have failed to perceive at all."[9]

It's a complex and contested space. Yet so much attached to the *woke* agenda is opposed to Christian faith and practice and where not targeting faith, freedom of speech, which we should all be concerned about, I offer up the following examples:

8. Gomez, "Reflections on the Church and America's New Religions," Lines 52–55.

9. Bonnette, "Catholics: Embrace being 'woke'. It's part of our faith tradition.," America—The Jesuit
Review. Lines 24–29.

- The slow and steady watering down of Christmas[10]

- Cancel Culture. There are many examples[11] of people and institutions being barred from the public square, notionally in the name of tolerance but ironically proving intolerant. It is not uncommon for them to entail elite reactions to orthodox Christianity.

- The harassment of UK academic Kathleen Stock[12] for expressing feminist views on gender and the fixed nature of biological sex.

Deep social justice and social responsibility and shallow social justice—a distinction

It is a reasonably well attested truism that if something is counterfeit, fake or a forgery then that indicates the existence of something authentic, true and genuine. There are alternatives.

A reflective response to the *woke* movement would at least require an objective thinker not to tar all good work for the common good and social justice with the same brush. I passionately believe in social justice and there seems to be a tendency for some, notably the political right to dismiss this term and deride it by deploying the *woke* label.[13] This is to be challenged. Social justice needs to be re-claimed not jettisoned.

However, I would submit that the key point to make is that this phenomenon is a wake-up call that the world needs to authentic manifestation of the love, power and justice of the Kingdom of God.

In my view there is deep, true, liberating compassion in the Christian gospel exemplified in the Old Testament prophets (Amos, Micah and Isaiah), Matt 25:31–46, Jas 2, and in Catholic Social Teaching—in particular the preferential option for the poor. This is a central aspect of the Christian faith, it is historic and stands the test of time, by a significant margin.

---

10. Neil Oliver, "The relentless erosion of Christmas, and Christianity itself, is essential for those whose mission it is to unmake Britain, says Neil Oliver," GB News

11. Christian Concern, "The cancel culture: the intolerance of the tolerance agenda"

12. Hinsliff, "Kathleen Stock: 'On social media, the important thing is to show your tribe that you have the right morals," The Observer

13. I simply ask the reader to undertake a YouTube search on woke it is not uncommon to see disparaging critiques of social justice.

In fact, the term social justice was coined by Roman Catholics[14] in the nineteenth century. Deep social justice gives glory to God, witnesses to the gospel, is a fruit of its word and is a corollary of the kingdom—but not an end in itself.

It is fundamentally important to balance Christian compassion and correlative programs of action with equally Christian sensibilities of the limits of human capacity and our proclivity to folly and debasement. We need to remember we live in a sin filled world, not utopia, any good achievement can be corrupted by the power of sin and turned into an idol.

In contrast, the *woke* movement, associated with the cultural left, latched onto authentic themes such as racial justice, human rights, and environmentalism, and turns them into a shallow creed. Associated with a shrill politics, Twitter mobs, self-righteous posturing, and rigid positions this is unappealing and counterproductive. It can be adopted by people who disdain Christianity and demonizes opponents rather than seeking to broker a politics of the common good. We are called to be radical but not extreme.

It is the sundering of social concerns from a Christian spirituality, then set into orbit that is the root of the problem. In fact, is this humanism devoid of a spiritual root what Solzhenitsyn[15] warned the West about?

"If the world has not come to its end, it has approached a major turn in history, equal in importance to the turn from the Middle Ages to the Renaissance. It will exact from us a spiritual upsurge: We shall have to rise to a new height of vision, to a new level of life where our physical nature will not be cursed as in the Middle Ages, but, even more importantly, our spiritual being will not be trampled upon as in the modern era."

In fact, it might be the case that as G.K. Chesterton reflected that:

"The modern world is full of the old Christian virtues gone mad."[16]

Woke seeks to assert a position and does so stridently and publicly, not quietly and not letting the left hand know what the right hand is doing. We witness a lot of noise with no human betterment achieved at all, rather and ironically an act of dominance achieved.

As N.T. Wright suggests in response to criticisms that the Church of England had adopted a woke agenda on race:

14. Novak, "Social Justice: Not what you think it is," The Heritage Foundation.
15. Solzhenitsyn, "A world split apart," Lines 514–519.
16. Beale, "The 'Mad Virtues' of a secular society," Lines 8–9.

" . . . but the truth . . . is that the 'anti-racist' agenda is a secular attempt to plug a long-standing gap in Western Christianity. The answer is to recover the full message, not to bolt on new ideologies."[17]

So, if gaps in the Church's witness are filled with secular energies, then the answer is the full gospel, not sitting back and judging society's attempts to establish justice.

Woke as anti-tradition

As Christian history attests the long history of social concern is embedded within Church history, the Old Testament prophets, the early church,[18] Saint Francis, the social concern of early Methodism, Wilberforce, the early non-conformist trade unionists, Martin Luther King Jr. and, more recently, Jubilee 2000.[19] I name but a few, but these examples have a genealogy. Yet—to my mind—contemporary *wokeism* doesn't fit in this tradition nor even respect it.

Make no mistake, to critique *woke* is not to be reactionary, defend the status quo or disavow a passion for justice. I would submit that the key is to articulate and to contextualize for each generation gospel rooted Christian social concern in a clear and embodied way. In fact, Karl Barth was emphatic:

"The Church must stand for social justice in the political sphere."[20]

Indeed, in her classic or what will be a classic *The Crucifixion: Understanding the Death of Jesus Christ*, Fleming Rutledge underlines how dynamic conceptions of God's righteousness have powerful implications for justice.

" . . . The righteousness of God is God's powerful activity of making right what is wrong in the world. When we read in both Old and New Testaments, that God is righteous, we are to understand that God is at work in his creation doing right. He is overcoming

17. Packiam, "Is the Church Too "Woke?," Lines 17–21.

18. Acts 2:42–47—although not relating to 'social justice' per se infers a community life of the early church where there was a dynamic spiritual life embodied in a loving community and a radical social ethic.

19. Jubilee 2000 was a global campaign to eliminate the debt of developing nations— https://en.wikipedia.org/wiki/Jubilee_2000.

20. Barth, *Community*,173.

evil, delivering the oppressed, raising the poor from the dust, vindicating the voiceless victims who have no one to defend them."[21]

Justice is from God and Godward, *woke* is, too often, bound up in man's agenda and man's ways. Yet, we have no option to participate with God in his righteous quest for justice. However, this affirmation of the church's social role needs gently and unequivocal delineation from other social trends that articulate in a different register.

As Christians we need to beware the latest fad and trend that grips society and can impinge on the church. Liberal idealism and progressive Christianity and the now less mentioned emerging church movement spring to mind. What can be *the* issue today and feel immanent and all-consuming may appear different in ten years' time. Hence the security of a living tradition.

The Human Redemptive Priority

For Christians there is a clear danger to the *woke* trend that has nothing to do with the issues being championed or the way they are addressed. I refer to the potential danger that *woke* as a form of religion can be an alternative to the church (a false empty one for sure) and if it infects the church, it can displace the gospel.

J. M. Comer, the US church leader and voice of reason has reflected that: "Progressive Christianity,"[22] which is not too far from *wokeism,* can inhibit discipleship and is in effect a means of people exiting the Church. As someone said to me, you go from the gospel to social gospel to no gospel. This is a tragically observable trend. Or as another friend reflected: "If it isn't the gospel, then it is ghastly."

If Churches adopt political and social stances imported from the world it becomes another gospel and distracts from the primary focus of the church. Christians need to keep the main thing the main thing—a Christological and ecclesiological funded hierarchy of priorities.

Please don't hear what I am not saying. This is not a plea for no social action or no political advocacy; rather it is a gentle reminder that social action is rooted in the gospel and subservient to the gospel. The best articulation of this important distinction I have read is this paper *The Human*

---

21. Rutledge, *Crucifixion*, 328.
22. Comer, "Where can Progressive Christianity Lead?"

Redemptive Priority.[23] The gospel must come first, and then other acts of advocacy and service can follow, but never replace the central message.

Summary

I fear I have trod where angels fear to tread. The scope for caricature and misunderstanding on this matter is significant. For Christians, we need to be focused on Christ not culture, yes, we need to engage in culture intelligently yet when Paul engaged with the Athenian intellectuals[24], he was cognizant of their culture, yet he did so to point to the living God and the resurrected Christ who will judge one day.

For sure, *woke* is perhaps a rebuke to Christians, when we don't engage, we get liberalism on steroids. Perhaps. If so, we have to ask ourselves, has it emerged in a vacuum in the public square we created?

As Peter Leithart has reflected on Rod Dreher's warnings about the anticipated trajectory of progressivism:

> "Dreher warns that progressivism will become a global ideology, leaving Christians and other moral conservatives with no place to go. If he turns out to be right, we Americans have only ourselves to blame."[25]

After all, if we had done our job properly on justice, racial justice, the environment, and care for the marginalized, there would be no need for *woke*, nor any space for it. In one sense we should honor a passion for justice but not abandon discernment.

> We have a better story to tell. That is the point. Not to judge the *woke* movement outright, but with empathy and discernment to narrate and embody the true gospel. This requires the ". . .whole will of God" as Paul refers to in Acts.[26]

Yet, there is hope, Australian Christian leader and cultural observer, Mark Sayers,[27] brilliantly diagnoses the times we live in and calls for a reliance on the word of God and the Holy Spirit to navigate these times.

---

23. Novo. "The Human Redemptive Priority."

24. Acts 17:16–34.

25. Leithart, "Global Wokenes?," Lines 61–63.

26. Acts 20:27.

27. Sayers, "We do not have a plan, but we have the person of Jesus."

As Christians our call is not to mirror the latest show in town. It is to love God, seek his Kingdom, fulfill the Great Commission, make disciples, and plant churches, serve society in Christ's name, and speak truth to power. When we lose this focus and fail to be regulated by our true vocation, we become dominated by other agendas. The Bible calls them idols. When we focus on things other than the Kingdom and the Church we might get trapped in unhealthy pre-occupations and causes that are less than God's best. If this happens on a mass scale—seemingly from a blank page, where there is no Christian root—you get *woke*.

If on the other hand we model biblically rooted, prayer fueled, loving political engagement and activism for the common good we can hold onto the good and model beautiful alternatives to foster divisive approaches to politics. There is a difference. This is not about *throwing the baby out with the bath water* and rejecting justice and transformation in favor of reactionary modes. As the previous article I referred to earlier within the US Catholic context states:

> "Issues like climate change and systemic racism are labelled pejoratively by the political right as part of a 'woke' agenda, but those concerned about such things have identified real and present threats."[28]

I revisit the quote as there is a required corrective to underline. It is about connecting *justification* and *justice*. This is a challenge to reflect upon and not outrightly dismiss what we see in the world, informed by our faith and seeking the common good. This is about empathy and confidence in our faith, not withdrawal from the world and name calling. In respect of this issue, it calls for discernment. If you like a *deep* rather than a *shallow* liberalism, a distinction set out by Mark Garnett.[29]

The twin dangers of not engaging and/or engaging in line with the world's agenda are both equally perilous. After all, we were warned of the

28. Bonnette, "Catholics: Embrace being 'woke.' It's part of our faith tradition.,," Lines 24–26.

29. '. . .a schism could be detected in liberal ranks long before September 2001. I call the rival camps 'fleshed-out' and 'hollowed-out' liberalism. The former retains a close resemblance to the ideas of the great liberal thinkers, who were optimistic about human nature and envisaged a society made up of free, rational individuals, respecting themselves and others. The latter, by contrast, satisfies no more than the basic requirements of liberal thought. It reduces the concepts of reason and individual fulfilment to the lowest common denominator, identifying them with the pursuit of material self-interest.' Mark Garnett, *The snake that Swallowed its Tail.*

current scenario by a zealous courageous British, Christian leader of the nineteenth century who lived for the gospel and the poor, in a real full-blooded sense not in a shallow world of twitter protest, name calling and strident dogmas. In a speech he said:

> "The chief danger that confronts the coming century will be religion without the Holy Ghost, Christianity without Christ, forgiveness without repentance, salvation without regeneration, politics without God, heaven without hell."[30]

One possible take on the *woke* phenomenon might be that liberal modernity simply cannot sustain the common good or a consensus on the good. You end up with a shallow, rigid, posturing liberalism and a name calling, reactionary response. Indeed, we might well be entering the end game of liberalism.

Will we ever be able to say: "This is my life, I want no other?" Nevertheless, God will have and has had the final word. Ultimately, it is not about being *woke* or *anti-woke*, rather, the Christian hope, now and in the future gives us all the hope and vision we need to serve the God of justice in this world, in the name of his Kingdom, not an earthly utopia.

> "But I know that God's new world of justice and joy, of hope for the whole earth, was launched when Jesus came out of the tomb on Easter morning; and I know that he calls his followers to live in him and by the power of his spirit, and so to be new-creation people here and now, bringing signs and symbols of the kingdom to birth on earth as in heaven. The resurrection of Jesus and the gift of the Spirit mean that we are called to bring real and effective signs of God's renewed creation to birth even amid the present age. Not to bring works and signs of renewal to birth within God's creation is ultimately to collude, as Gnosticism always does, with the forces of sin and death themselves. But don't focus on the negative. Think of the positive: of the calling, in the present, to share in the surprising hope of God's whole new creation."[31]

---

30. Booth, "New York World," 8–9.
31. Wright, *Surprised*, 220.

19

Place—personal, prophetic and political

Belonging can find many attachments, good and bad, as it appears in a rootless world people are increasingly seeking an anchor, this might simply be manifest in a sense of *place*: a special and meaningful association with a recognized geography and location. I explore what this means in Christian terms and naturally it has political implications.

In my earlier speech to the National Club in London in 2016, I said:

> "Who am I? I am Ian Geary, forty-three years old, I live in southeast London with my wife and three children and worship at an evangelical/charismatic church in Bermondsey. I grew up in Walsall in the Black Country and become a Christian and Labour Party activist at the same time aged fourteen. Apart from my love for West Brom that is all you need to know about me. I have worked for two Labour MPs, a trade union, various lobbying companies and am on the Executive of Christians on the Left. Last year I co-edited an essay collection on the theme of Blue Labour—a stimulant on the center-left that advocates the primacy of relationships in politics, family, place the essential centrality of faith and also most importantly asserts the politics of the common good as essential to renewing our civic, political and social life."

Perhaps this is overwrought, yet in this essay I seek to unpack the theological and political importance of the concept of place. It is a vast mine to tap, and I can barely do it justice. It is difficult to talk about belonging without reference to place as for many people it constitutes part of their sense of belonging.

> "Listen to me, you who pursue righteousness and who seek the LORD: Look to the rock from which you were cut and to the quarry from which you were hewn."[1]

In 2017, I had the privilege of being allowed to attend the Catherine Programme Summer School in the Netherlands. This is a Salvation Army training program based on theology and social work and is named after the formidable Salvation Army pioneer Catherine Booth. I gained many insights while at the Catherine Programme Summer School, yet there is one that stands out.

A talk given by a Welsh Salvationist, Major Steve Dutfield, focused on Salvationist Doctrine, this is a fascinating subject matter, but it is what preceded the talk that encouraged me. He spent a good ten minutes talking about his upbringing, the town he grew up in and how his story impacted on his formation.

His story of people, place and social justice was influenced by the Salvation Army but also the environment in which he grew up. He had a sense of place and was able to articulate it in a meaningful way in a Christian context.

I personally relate to this, as I grew up in a postindustrial small town and inherited from my family a sense of political history and faith. I have developed in many ways since then but have not lost this attachment.

While at the course this sense of place was further unpacked when me and Joshua Herbert, the only other British person on the course, talked about our work in the UK to the assembled summer school attendees. Joshua was to be spending the following year in Goldthorpe Salvation Army Corps, South Yorkshire. By coincidence I had organized a visit by the local MP, Rt. Hon. John Healey MP, to the Corps in July 2016. The MP opened a new kitchen, where the Territorial Envoy and staff had overseen feeding many local people—from toddlers to the elderly. I recall meeting

---

1. Isa 51:1–2—'These were the Israelites who sincerely wanted to trust and obey God but found it difficult to do so because impending captivity seemed to contradict God's promises. The Lord called them to consider their history, their origin'. *https://net-bible.org/bible/Isaiah+52*, Constables Notes.

individuals with learning disabilities volunteering at Goldthorpe Corps who felt valued. At the kitchen launch, the officer said a few words about the love of God and read a portion of scripture. It was moving and powerful to see a church modeling what I understand "the common life" as accounted for in Acts[2], which is a sign of the Kingdom of God. Goldthorpe was once a mining town and was significant in the Miner's Strike of 1984–5. I reflected that context is important, but the Bible, tradition, experience and Doctrine are crucial too. This visit made a strong impression on me.

Oxford Reference defines *place* as: "Either the intrinsic character of a place, or the meaning people give to it, but, more often, a mixture of both."[3]

I would submit that place is a biblical and theological category, it has personal and human significance and in this age of fluidity and identity crisis it has political importance. Furthermore, it is my view that the importance of place has been overlooked in a world of globalization and allegedly *open borders*.

By place I mean, an attachment to a particular area and community and I grant it emphasis as it has a particular resonance in theology and politics. Like any category it can have good and bad aspects if pushed too far. For the Christian it is a penultimate rather than an ultimate category, nevertheless, it has received insufficient attention and that needs a corrective.

Place as a Category in the Christian Faith

The article starts with a reference to the start of Isa 51. In a deeply challenging time for Israel, they are asked to consider their history and heritage as a guide and source of strength. Similarly, in our discipleship we need to be aware of our own background, history and formation both good and bad.

The theologian of the Old Testament, Walter Brueggemann states that:

> "The Bible itself is primarily concerned with the issue of being displaced and yearning for a place. Indeed, the Bible promises precisely what the modern world denies."[4]

This sums up pithily what I seek to convey. In pondering the failure of modernity's offer of mobility and endless choice he submits that:

2. Acts 2:44.

3. OxfordReference.com, Line 1.

4. Brueggemann, *The Land*, 2.

"It is now clear that a sense of place is a human hunger that the urban promise has not met. And a fresh look at the Bible suggests that a sense of place is a primary category of faith."[5]

I believe that place is an increasingly important biblical category. For example, Anglican Bishop, John Inge,[6] has written on the subject and he has sought to properly affirm the scriptural and theological importance of place where it has been largely overlooked.

An emphasis on place, particularly a geographical commitment at first glance seems at odds with elements of the Christian tradition. Certainly, the Christian faith centers on themes of journey and mobility that appear to be the dialectical opposite of place. God calls people from places to other places i.e., Abraham journeys at great lengths to fulfill his calling. The growth of the church naturally entailed geographical movement and displacement. Christians are called into a unique *community* that binds us to people of other places and nations in a covenantal relationship. Furthermore, our belief is that one day this earth—temporary and contingent—is temporary and contingent, shall be renewed with a ". . .new heavens and a new earth."[7] It cannot be over emphasized that place is penultimate, to over stress it is to disavow other important Christian themes and even to lapse into a pale mimicking of nationalism. However, while it needs to be held in tension with other truths my concern is it has been actually neglected and left unpacked. Within a theopolitical framework some attention needs to be given to the particular so the whole story is told and fulfilled. Place needs to be put into its *place* i.e., where it fits within a broader theological context, but it needs to be spelt out and affirmed to be appreciated in its fullness.

Place is paradoxical and dialectical, Christians are part of a universal church and within that polity there is mobility, fluidity and attachment to and love of place. This needs to be set in context.

A good example of this is the work undertaken recently by a group of institutions to locate the importance of the church in the current COVID-19 pandemic, *The Plague and the Parish*.[8] wonderfully situates the importance of the church amidst the challenge taking place globally, nationally and locally with an emphasis on the particular.

5. Brueggemann, *The Land*, 4.
6. Inge, *Theology of Place*.
7. Isa 65:17.
8. Together, "The Plague and the Parish—An invitation to the Churches"

Within the meta-narrative of this pilgrimage, there is attachment to place. I would suggest, from my observation, that for working class communities' place is highly important, yes there are exceptions. In my experience it is more common for working class communities to strongly identify with an area, its history, institutions and football teams relatively more than for middle class professionals who have moved to areas because of work and social mobility. Of course, there are many, many examples of middle class professionals moving to areas and developing a commitment to the place and giving something back, yet sociologically there can be a distinction drawn. This is what David Goodhart was seeking to unpack in his work *The Road to Somewhere.*[9] As perhaps evidenced by the 2016 referendum on European Union membership, there is a section of population who have strong attachments to communities and geographies and another who are less attached to a fixed local or national identity. To a large degree these reflect class patterns. Although we can all be a mixture as life is complex.

I remember being at the Oval, the Cricket Ground in London, watching a test match when I heard someone behind me saying: "Guardian journalists don't get identity" and he said with certainty: "I was born in Southampton General Hospital and I support the Saints." So, a strong identification with an area can evoke a sense of rootedness, stability and commitment to the places well-being, its institutions, its environment, families and businesses.

Place is linked to personal spirituality

For me, it is something I feel strongly about, even I cannot help myself when I explain what is important, I refer to place. For example, in my earlier essay on reflections on postliberalism I draw on my roots to make a point.

> "Speaking personally, as an evangelical Christian, from a lower middle class background in South Staffordshire and the edge of the Black Country my disposition is a strong moral compass. I am tribally Labour, independent in thinking and find southern, metropolitan liberal progressivism somewhat alienating. However, my roots and formation account for the reason why I don't wholly connect with the political and cultural elite worldview and the dominant groupings on the left."[10]

9. Goodhart, *The Road.*
10. Geary, "Reflections on Post-Liberalism and Post-Liberal Politics," Lines 70–77.

I always enjoyed walking and praying in my hometown of Aldridge past the cricket field and down country lanes on the border with Staffordshire. For me this was for many years a special place. The Celts talked of "thin places"[11] where the presence of the Kingdom of God might be experienced more tangibly.

Recently The Salvation Army has reopened the iconic Strawberry Fields, Liverpool, with a new purpose. Obviously made famous by the Beatles Song, the original home was a special place for John Lennon who, used to play in its grounds as a child. We may all have special places that might have a spiritual significance for us. People talk about locations or places being their *happy place*.

There has been much talk about cultural relevance in the UK church in the past twenty years, but only a small portion—perhaps—on place and class. There are exceptions. This is an insight yet to be further developed. It could help with mission. For example, my church in Bermondsey in recent years has held a special church service in line with Remembrance Sunday. It is gospel centered and has involved serious reflection on the experiences of the First and Second World Wars. This is an example of sensitive and contextual outreach in an area which experienced the Blitz and whose working class community will identify with the armed forces.

Place as a Political Category

Place is political and has a class component, it is bound up strongly with identity. The failure to appreciate this has meant politicians on the left have missed a trick in recent years. MPs represent distinct geographical areas so in some ways place is an understood part of the political process. Some people vote for the MP who best represents their local area rather than having an affinity with a political tribe.

A sense of place as a political category can be the lens, we understand various political developments. As communities have witnessed huge and constant changes people have felt their place has been impacted upon, not always with their consent. Rapid change from residential development, the impact of immigration, the closure of industries, and the reconfiguration of public services, have been some of the factors that have brought change. As the pressures on place and belonging have intensified, they severed generations long links to established political parties, particularly the Labour

11. Sacred Journey, Thin Places.

Party. In particular, elements of the Labour Party seemed unable to understand working class support for leaving the European Union and worst still how people would feel if their vote was undermined by another referendum. A multiplicity of factors has been at play, but it is not difficult to draw the dots between a failure to appreciate a sense of place and therefore a misunderstanding of a healthy patriotism.

For a period, political scientists showed some awareness of place. There was some attention paid to the changing values of the UK through the lens of "values modes"[12] i.e., some people are *pioneers* and more socially liberal and optimistic and some are *settlers* are more socially conservative and less optimistic. At the time this was applied to some degree to explain Labour voters transferring their vote to UKIP.[13] I tend to think people do not easily fall into these neat categories—identity is complex—but at least this work tried to understand but it was perhaps for instrumental reasons and had little purchase.

I feel in the years ahead respect for place is going to become an increasingly important political factor, although it interacts with other factors too. I would say it we can get the theology right, we can speak into the political discourse.

So why is this important?

In many ways, the story of the *Prodigal Son*[14]—the epitome of the gospel— is a story of place. The socially mobile younger brother leaving home for the *far* country, blowing everything and coming *home* to a place and a family and a father. It is a summary of the gospel message, and the homecoming is a deep, moving act of reconciliation with the Father.

Apparently, nostalgia—often deployed in a dismissive way—can mean to yearn for *home*, and to be away from current pain (in its Greek root).[15] As King David expressed when he cried:

---

12. A methodology developed in 1973 by Cultural Dynamics to aid political and marketing campaigns—https://en.wikipedia.org/wiki/Values_Modes#:~:text=The%20 Values%20Modes%20model%20was,%3A%20Settlers%2C%20Prospectors%20 and%20Pioneers.

13. Peccorelli, "The new electorate—why understanding values is the key to electoral success"

14. Luke 15:11–32.

15. Wick, "Homecoming and Pain:On the Etymology of Nostalgia"

". . . Oh, that someone would get me a drink of water from the well near the gate of Bethlehem!"[16]

Thus, perhaps to the modern mind, a sense of place linked to a perceived preferred past is prone to being classified as nostalgia and therefore being dismissed.

However, place properly understood is a corrective to the liberal assumption that we all need to move on and out of where we were born and that there is some global, free *good life* waiting out there for us all to discover.

By a reappraisal of place, we can discover an awareness of the importance of Christian commitment to places as mission, understanding areas, their history, its places and pain and how the gospel story applies.

As Mary Glenn reflected, this commitment to place takes time but it is part of our calling to be peacemakers.

> "God calls us to live in places (i.e., cities, rural communities, neighborhoods), to invest our lives, to build relationships, and to share the journey. A theology of place shapes our beliefs and behavior in and with the land and our neighbors. As we develop a theology of place, we become more deeply committed to the community that we have been called to live in and to seek it's shalom. Shalom is a comprehensive concept that expresses society as God intended it to be, including a sense of wholeness, harmony, and justice. The church is called to be reconcilers and peacemakers in the world, in our specific location and context."[17]

This reference to Jer 29 and the call for God's people to work for the common good in the alien environment in which they found themselves embodies the prophetic importance of place and its political outworking. It can lead to a more informed, just and contextual politics that is related to a real understanding of local communities. It can lead to a more generous conversation where people's sense of place is not dismissed at the first instance. Furthermore, it can be more open to broader forms of political activity such as community organizing[18] that facilitate a space for churches and faith groups and local institutions to work together for the common good.

---

16. 1 Chr 11:17.

17. Glenn, "Jeremiah 29 a biblical framework for place," Lines 16–21.

18. The Centre for Theology and Community, "Community Organising"

It can lead to a re-evaluation of someone's commitment to an area as something to applaud and celebrate and not just deride people who never move on.

The era of globalization may be in crisis, and much is up in the air, now more than ever with the pandemic. However, in spite of this and also as a consequence of the challenges we face a reassessment of place is vital for a Christian sense of mission and politics in this disorientating era.

In referring to James Rebanks' book *The Shepherd's Life*,[19] about shepherding in the Lake District, Stanley Hauerwas points out that the contentment gained in a traditional vocation in a stable location defies the aspirations of liberal modernity.

Toward the end of the memoir in which Rebanks describes the hard life and work of being a shepherd, he is lying on his back watching the sheep he has let loose in the fells, and he thinks: "This is my life. I want no other."[20] An extraordinary claim I suspect few in our social orders can make. So let me give you the advice I think you need if you hope to one day be able to say: "This is my life. I want no other."[21]

Contentment, perhaps elusive to many in this crazy world may come in many forms but we should not lose sight of the life that can be rooted in customs and places that secular modernity overlooks or has sought to crush. The Christian faith has the resources to revisit the riches of these dispositions and attachments and place them in the context of an expansive generous story that makes sense of them and does not belittle them. The reaffirmation of place has the potential to be a gift, if only it is given its proper due or indeed proper place.

19. Rebanks, *The Shepherd's Life*.

20. Rebanks, *The Shepherd's Life*, 287 in Hauerwas, "Stanley Hauerwas: Don't Lie," Lines 23–28.

21. Rebanks, *The Shepherd's Life*, 287 in Hauerwas, "Stanley Hauerwas: Don't Lie," Lines 23–28..

20

Tradition and Identity

This following reflection deals with my concerns about the desire for a second referendum on the decision made by the UK to leave the European Union. I did not vote to leave the UK but felt that the vote to leave should be respected; the efforts to seek another referendum where instructive about the state of UK politics and the maladies of the left. We are now the other side of Brexit.

"We will cope, whatever is thrown at us."
—Lady at public house, Suffolk, England. Easter Sunday 2019

I camped in Suffolk with my family over Easter. After attending a Vineyard church service (in a motor components factory social club that reminded me of my trade union days) we went for a pub lunch. It was a traditional Sunday lunch, and I went large on the roast beef and Yorkshire pudding. The children played in the play area, and it was searingly hot. I got talking to a middle-aged man who had grown up in London and then moved to Suffolk. He was a lorry driver. We talked about football and how much Ipswich had changed, in particular the impact that immigration had had on the area. His mother joined us and when we said goodbye she said: "We will cope, whatever is thrown at us." She was talking about the UK and Brexit. Now she didn't refer to either Brexit and the UK, but I am sure she was.

We will cope—that is the attitude of a good majority of English working class opinion, and it shapes their gritty optimism to leaving the European Union and also their anger that there is an elite resistance to doing so. This faith in being able to withstand whatever life presents is not just based on optimism with no root, it is based on the fact that the country has at times coped whatever has been thrown at it and the lion's share of pain and sacrifice has been born by the working class, be it through austerity or in the wars. I am not asserting an exceptional view of the unique character of the *great* British people I am referring to a social disposition forged in history. It explains why millions of people, previously Conservative and Labour voters, have backed the new Brexit Party and I am afraid liberals just don't understand this perspective. If they did more Labour MPs would have the decency and political nous to take this seriously.

I ask comrades who are Christian and on *the left* to consider the case why the aspirations of many people, whom we should care about—by dint of faith and then politics—could abandon Labour forever (and many of them had said cheerio long before the referendum, but let's hope it was au revoir).

Thus, my assertion is that Labour must accept Brexit and move on. A compassionate pro-working class vote, and Christian voice needs to be robustly made into this possibility.

I say this as I am of the view that the gospel has a bias to the poor and more importantly God does. as Bishop David Sheppard asserted. So, we should at least listen to the voices of the working class and poorer communities that have voted to leave and again expressed their frustration at the inertia and arrogance of the political class—via the decisive vote for the Brexit Party in the European Elections.

I am not given to quoting Latin, I was relegated from the Latin class to Classical Studies at an early stage of secondary school but there is an old saying: *Vox Populi, Vox Dei*, which is Latin for: "the voice of the people is the voice of God."[1] Please think about this for a minute in the light of my key ask. It might fall apart if you applied it to every public policy position, but it is a good starting place.

Now, I am not asserting that there is a Christian monopoly on the Leave or indeed the Remain side of the debate, that would be erroneous and simplistic, idolatrous even. However, given what has happened in the past three years. A humble, prayerful and Christian perspective should at

---

1. A Latin phrase: https://en.wikipedia.org/wiki/Vox_populi#Vox_populi,_vox_Dei.

least consider the merits of this possibility. And this voice needs to be heard within the Labour Party, given the overt dominance of the middle class, liberal and progressive groupthink that is determined, apparently to resist a democratic vote.

As Jonathon Rutherford has recently said Labour is " . . . is losing its traditions and becoming the Whig party"[2] and we know what happened to them.

I never considered writing this article, I voted Remain in 2016 and I was disappointed by the result for a long time. I prayed about it and after a long period came to acceptance. Others will have different conclusions but that is where eventually I landed. For human and political reasons. These are as follows:

The need to reeducate myself. Having voted remain but now accepting the result, after a long time I became more aware of the flaws of the European Union that I will be honest I was unaware of before. So when people accuse leave voters of *not knowing what they voted for*, I am afraid that also applies to Remain voters. In fact, I would say there is a disconnect between an emotional/identity fueled, mainly well-meaning and principled internationalism and the occasional, brutal reality of the European Union. Look at the way Greece and Italy have been treated for one example.

The rationale for a second referendum. Moreover, I am unconvinced by the wisdom of a second referendum for the country and actually for the Labour Party to be contemplating it. For a long time, I had an *alarm bell* ringing about the *People's Vote* even when I was struggling with the result. Basically, it makes the remain side look like sore losers and if there is one thing people don't like it is that inability to accept loss. It is something the working class cannot abide either! I don't like the fact that West Brom lost to Aston Villa in the playoffs, but they did, and I don't think there should be a *People's Playoff* to revisit or confirm the result. It is what happened.

The imperative of democracy. There is a serious and precious democratic principle at stake. You hold an election and accept the result, win or lose. Without that approach there is no trust, and nothing is binding. The system doesn't work without an underlying acceptance to accept and work within the grain of the result and its consequences. If a dictatorship in a developing country kept calling elections until it secured the desired result, then liberals would decry it. That is unless we are discussing the 2016

---

2. Rutherford, "Nigel Farage and Our Democratic Nation," Lines 53–54.

referendum! On this point, Chris Bickerton an academic, leave supporter and Breton by identity reflects:

> "A second referendum would be a blow to the heart of our parlia-
> mentary democracy. It would introduce the principle—elitist to
> the core—that the legitimacy of a political decision rests upon a
> judgment about the knowledge that informed it. And it would rely
> on a dirty plebiscitarians as a way out of the political impasse in
> Westminster. Those arguing for a second referendum should be
> careful what they wish for. Chaos is rarely a harbinger of good
> outcomes."[3]

If there is another referendum and of course the result would more than possibly be the same where does that leave us? Is it worth it? Those sections of the nation that voted Leave would be effectively told their vote was worthless and ergo they are worthless, no matter how it would be presented. If remain won the sense of betrayal would be profound and scarring and justified, for a generation. I live in Southwark which was roughly 70/30 Remain/Leave but am from Walsall which was roughly 70/30—Leave/Remain. I would not wish to go back home and tell everyone: *oh that vote didn't count, we need another go*. No thanks. The potential problem is well summarized in the words of Larry Elliot, of *the Guardian*:

> "If the Remainers get their way, the votes of all those people will be
> proved to be completely worthless, and nothing will really change.
> The people who run this country don't give two hoots about people
> in Stoke-on-Trent and Hartlepool and all those places that voted
> heavily for Leave. But if the vote is reversed, what sort of backlash
> are we going to get in four- or five-years' time? I think we could
> see a really aggressive form of right-wing politics. There is going
> to be a massive alienation in those parts of Britain, who will feel,
> rightly, let down."[4]

Furthermore, there is an existential need and historical commitment galvanizing Labour's need to represent working class opinion. Not accepting the result of the referendum means Labour seems incapable of articulating the voice of significant sections of its historical support base. This is a point of principle not electoral triangulation, but actually—and paradoxically—in the long term it would benefit Labour. The fact that the party has

3. Bickerton, "Arrogant Remainers Want a Second Vote: That Would Be a Bad Day For Democracy,," Lines 86–92.

4. Larry Elliott, "The establishment is trying to keep us in the EU," Lines 98–105.

edged towards a Remain position of sorts reflects how little working class leverage there is in the Labour Party. It is sobering.

To be frank I do not blame people for voting for the Brexit Party; they have been pushed into this by the mainstream parties. Talk of racism and Nigel Farage being in favor of privatization —maybe true—but they are a singularly inadequate criticism in this context when voters have been left with little option. When I receive Labour's emails spelling out their analysis of the Brexit Party all I see is the usual hollowness that is rooted in a lack of vision.

In the recent and unexpected European Elections—that should not have been taking place—I searched my heart about voting Labour like never before. Voting Labour, which I have done in every election, is part and parcel of being a member. I hold myself to account that if I cannot vote Labour anymore, I cannot be a member. I contemplated abstaining and contemplated voting for the Brexit Party. In the end I voted Labour and but I do not blame voters for not voting Labour this time.

I ask myself, is this challenge (i.e., Brexit) Labour's last chance to re-connect with the working class? I am dismayed that we have come to this. We have enough problems—proved by elections since 2010—of securing working class electoral confidence without allowing this unnecessary dilemma to happen. It could be a real tragedy and is avoidable.

And as for the elections, lo and behold every region in England—apart from London—voted for the Brexit Party, with the West Midlands and East Midlands doing so decisively. If people really want to diminish Nigel Farage's surge and outflank the Brexit Party, it is simple, accept Brexit. Yes, in the short-term we lose some voters to the Liberal Democrat's and the Green Party, but common sense and history points the other way. Accept Brexit and the Brexit Party no longer has a rationale to exist. For whatever *messaging* is thrown at the people, they have made their minds up. So where do we go now?

UK and Europe—The future—Christian and Socialist

There is a future path to follow, that is internationalist, pro-European and social democratic, but it needs to be built based on an acceptance of leaving the European Union. Also, it must be Christian, Sacramental, Evangelical and Catholic, Social and therefore democratic, rooted in Solidarity and resisting liberal capitalism in its rawest form. It needs to be local and communitarian and not tied to transnational, technocratic elites.

We can debate the options and the debate can be healthy and fertile. Yet we need to fight for a vision of a new future, not fight a losing battle. *Remain and Reform* is not possible. The European Union is incapable of reform. My preference would be a Labour led UK that forges a Democratic Socialist Commonwealth as part of a *world Christendom*. Ok, but at least that generates a debate.

I admit that for me it has been a long journey, my initial hope had been wishful thinking and illusory. I understand all the arguments against this view, as I held them. I understand the social Christian roots of Europe, and they are noble, but they have been corrupted.

I understand the argument for peace—I grew up with my Grandmother telling me about the two world wars. I have taken my family to Ypres and the Somme. We have been to Normandy too. And yet, now the European Union and the issue of Brexit is disturbing our civic peace.

I, too, understand, the argument around workers' rights, but many of the legislative benefits could be enshrined in UK law through our own impetus. A social Europe is not a potent reality. The trade union argument is not a one-way street.

We held a referendum as a binary choice, this forces a yes and no, fault lines ran through both arguments. Yet, that was the challenge, and these were the rules; it is too late to reinvent what has happened. Whatever has been thrown at us we need to get on with it.

The Christian USP is we don't see this question or indeed any question as ultimate or shouldn't and that liberates us to be reconcilers. We believe in the gospel and building the church. Part of our Kingdom work is seeing the common good. Leave or Remain I would suggest that it is our top priority to work for peace and pray for resolution. Man's efforts have floundered.

Yet, we live between ". . .the time between the times."[5] and as Richard B. Hays says, we walk a fine line between caring for this broken world and truly being involved and engaged and yet looking for the world to come. As he carefully reflects:

> "To live faithfully in the time between the times is to walk a tight-rope of moral discernment, claiming neither too much nor too little for God's transforming power within the community of faith."[6]

5. Hays, *Moral Vision*, 27.
6. Hays, *Moral Vision*, 27.

We will cope, whatever is thrown at us, because we will have to. Whatever step we take, the path is hard: Brexit or a second vote. Whatever your views and response to this article, think who the *we* is in your life? Who are the *us*? Are you connecting to and respecting the people whose views may well be in line with the mother from Suffolk and I suspect many people? For it starts with relating and praying and being human and loving our neighbor. Also, we can model how to disagree agreeably. I am better at *well disagreeing than disagreeing well* so you can help me with this.

Given the scale of the voted in June 2016, there are probably thirty-three million opinions on Brexit; not the binary variants we see dominating public discourse. My view is that we should leave, preferably with a deal. I do not agree with the manner that the current Prime Minister has approached matters, it has been gung ho and ironically undermined Parliament. Yet, despite this galvanizing my opposition to no deal, we must leave nonetheless, the votes must be respected. People are tired of this process, and it must be brought to closure.

Let's make sure whatever is thrown at us, we are not *throwing* it too and that we identify with those on the receiving end of economic and political decisions, usually at the sharp end. Historically, they made the Labour Party their party, the regions of England that voted for Brexit also were some of the handmaidens of the Labour movement. So, whatever was thrown at them was transformed into something bearable and beautiful and if Labour aligns itself with the people in the end, we will more than cope.

Maybe there is hope, after we leave the European Union, Labour might face reality, accept what has happened and be reconciled to voters in the so called *left behind* communities. The position adopted at the party conference in September 2019 sort of leaves room for that option. However, it would have been preferable to have accepted Brexit more consistently rather than the complex and unprincipled maneuverings we have witnessed.

We need to remind ourselves of the big picture and the primacy of the gospel. The future is uncertain, and the challenge is ginormous, but the stakes are high. We either have a Christian Europe or a dying, decaying liberalism in the West that sees anything beyond its purview as bigoted and is blind to its own folly. It really is "back to the Bible or back to the jungle"[7] as Luis Palau said. Or expressed differently but making a comparable point John Milbank has submitted that:

---

7. Bewes, "A Nation at the Crossroads," Lines 45–56.

"My faith would certainly be that the Church will never be destroyed even if it's reduced to a minority. Other than that I think the situation we're in at the moment is that there is a strongly emerging Christianity many parts of the world, in China for example. And that there are some signs of a reviving Christian culture and intellectual tradition in Europe. In the face of an otherwise increasingly superficial and vacuous culture. If those two factors can coalesce, then I think there is a possibility of the emergence eventually of something like a global Christian order. It is not impossible. But I think unless a kind of world Christendom, then the future will be dark beyond our wildest expectations."[8]

8. Goldsmiths, "Interview with John Milbank.", Lines 341–42.

21

The New Class War,
But Not as We Know It

This essay is a review of *The New Class War: Saving Democracy
from the Metropolitan Elite*[1] by Michael Lind, the American
conservative. This book was written not to foment class war,
rather, it shines a light on the new dynamics of class conflict
in the West; and it suggests how a revived working class sense
of agency and association can bring about social peace in a
world where elite, corporate and technocratic power is total.

"But now in Christ Jesus you who once were far away have been
brought near through the blood of Christ. For he himself is our peace,
who has made the two one and has destroyed the barrier, the dividing
wall of hostility, by abolishing in his flesh the law with its command-
ments and regulations. His purpose was to create in himself one
new man out of the two, thus making peace, and in this one body to
reconcile both of them to God through the cross, by which he put to
death their hostility."

EPH 2:13–16

---

1. Lind, *The New Class War.*

"Class conflict, born out of asymmetries of power, is a paradigmatic challenge that corrodes a common life over time."

LUKE BRETHERTON

The phrase *class war* makes me a little nervous: it evokes emotions of divisive connotations of *them* and *us*, violent revolution, negativity and the controversy it can generate. From a Christian perspective it seems antithetical to God's Kingdom: values of peace, love for all and working for the common good. Class can sometimes evoke notions of *us versus them* rather than the harmonious common life to which Christians are called.

All the above is true: yet what if by ignoring class issues and the pain and domination people feel we are failing to allow for a biblically rooted response to social fracture? Furthermore, is this failing in our gospel duties and meaning we are living in denial of society's brokenness? Even worse, if we leave the *devil to take the hindmost* as a society doesn't that actually generate resentment and conflict?

Is there a vision of a good society—distinct from revolutionary theory and utopian platitudes—that can meaningfully address class issues? Can we reflect on class problems—not to exploit them for political ends—but to seek to address them to create a plural society built on empowerment and respect that engenders peace?

Certainly, this is a complex matter, notwithstanding the connotations of conflict class is a contested term. As Christians, we cannot support an anthropological account of our meaning and existence that is purely economic and deterministic. We do need to proceed with discernment.

The US conservative thinker Michael Lind's book *The New Class War*[2] is short and compelling. Focused on the experience of the USA and to some extent Europe, it provides an explanation for the recent rise in populist politics. In short, he notes that the rise of a professional, managerial class in the West: liberal, tech-savvy, based in hip, affluent urban areas and more often than not secular has come at the expense of working class communities in small towns: who have seen manufacturing decline, immigration rise in a manner that has undercut wages and that this all has the appearance of a *class war*. Certainly, when you reflect—and we saw this in the Brexit debate—that the professional "overclass" as Lind calls it does not

2. Lind, *Class War.*

appear to understand or actually like the values of the working class it has the appearance of . . . class war.

> The government, economics and culture are all foci of a new class war.[3] In all these spheres the working classes have lost power to a new *managerial elite* and this in turn has causes a "populist backlash."[4]

This is played out in the US and the UK and in some Western European nations. It is not per se the *old class war* of the industrialists or landowners versus the working classes. The new professional managerial class is now dominant, and this disenfranchises the working class in the realm of politics, economics and culture; crucially including religion.

Lind is not suggesting the required response is revolution, but an intentional rebalancing of social equilibrium in the name of peace:

> "Achieving a genuine class peace in the democracies of the West will require uniting and empowering both native and immigrant workers while restoring genuine decision-making power to the non-university educated majority in all three realms of social power—the economy, politics and culture."[5]

In a short book, Michael Lind accounts for the rise of populism and a peaceful solution that is a far cry from the uninspiring liberal knee-jerk response of assuming all populists are simply "bigots."[6] Yet, to build the case for a positive solution we need an honest analysis of the socioeconomic dynamics at play.

If we reflect on contemporary issues, class has not gone away; there is the impact of the brutal cuts to social security[7] and the ongoing failure to address chronic housing conditions as evidenced by Grenfell highlights this in the most stark and tragic manner. As Owen Jones correctly pointed out:

> "The Grenfell disaster should have provoked a national debate about Britain's housing crisis. That it did not is indicative of a macabre hierarchy that everyone knows exists. After all, those most

3. Lind, *Class War*, xxi.

4. Lind, *Class War*,.;xii–xiii.

5. Lind, *Class War;* xiv–xv.

6. Lind, *Class War*, 103.

7. Butler, "Cutting benefits harms mental health and hits most vulnerable hardest, says study"

likely to suffer the consequences of Britain's social crises are the poor and people of colour."[8]

I remember talking to a Labour MP saying I understood class was an issue but feeling a little squeamish about the matter. He looked at me as if I had lost marbles commenting: "It is obvious," i.e., the UK is significantly characterized by class inequality.

There was a time when such issues could not be discussed. In his speech to the Labour Party Conference in 1999, Tony Blair[9] confidently asserted that: "the class war is over," admittedly with the aim of promoting equality and aspiration. Well, the old one employer versus employees may be over in one sense but a new one has emerged. As Michael Lind shows, previous class conflicts have been addressed temporarily. This is not through revolution but through legitimate, orchestrated working class organization to achieve an equilibrium in society and some relative peace.

However, that the professional over-class seem densely populated in the US Democrat and Labour Parties throws our perception of class war on its head? It is those associated with the parties of the left who have in part being caught up in this new dynamic.

We should consider Lind's insight: that support for UKIP and Donald Trump was not in every case powered by bigotry but structural forces have been at work and—by and large—working class communities have felt left behind, misunderstood and left with little economic, educational and cultural capital. Therefore, when the demagogues do their work, they are exploiting a situation that should not have been allowed to fester. The language of class may make us feel uncomfortable and recoil but if we can reflect on these issues and work for the common good and not be in denial then, against all the odds, a plural society might be constructed. If we don't the outcome could be scary. *The Hunger Games* might actually be coming sooner than we think.

The links between the Trump phenomenon and Brexit have been well rehearsed. They were distinct events in distinct nations yet there are structural correlatives at play. Both were electoral disruptions in protest at a seemingly out of touch elite. Both capitalized on a long-term social trend that has been in play perhaps for decades.[10]

8. Jones, "The cladding scandal reveals how Britain treats its poorest people," Lines 37–40.

9. Blair, "Leaders Speech," Labour Party Conference Bournemouth 1999, Line 27.

10. Lind, *Class War*, 68.

It is not easy to accept if you have political commitments like mine, Michael Lind details how Donald Trump was able to connect with the alienated working class who were shut out of political debate:

> "Alone among Republican candidates in the 2016 presidential primaries, Donald Trump both denounced the Iraq War as a mistake and opposed cuts to Social Security and Medicare. This combination of views was the exact opposite of the orthodox conservative party line."[11]

In making this point Michael Lind is not endorsing Trump here but trying to get underneath the bonnet of what happened. I like many people were aghast at the fascistic events at the Capitol Building on January 6.[12] This should be condemned and rightly was. However, there is a distinction between Trump supporters and the majority of his voters. In November 2020[13], more than seventy-two million voters backed Trump (an increase of nine million from 2016). Are they all crazy, right wing conspiracy theorists? I suspect not.

Equally, just as some of the Leave campaign messages in the referendum campaign were tasteless that does not mean the millions of people voting to the leave the European Union shared those views or motivations. Simply dismissing the voters backing populist projects betrays a complacent unwillingness to dispassionately discern what is happening and develop a positive alternative.

Interestingly, Michael Lind seems to understand also where religion plays into this equation, although he looks at religion with a very broad definition. That the professional *overclass* has a tendency to look down on the religious disposition of the working class is telling. The professional managerial class has a tendency to see working class citizens as bigoted in an ironic and well bigoted, shortsighted way.[14]

I am afraid that in recent years the Labour Party has become less amenable to the Christian faith. It is deeply tragic when you reflect for a moment on the party's roots. Labour owes more to Methodism than to Marx,

11. Lind, *Class War,* 74–75.

12. See this insightful article by Peter Leithart, https://theopolisinstitute.com/leithart _post/carnival-in-the-capitol/.

13. BBC, "US Election 2020: Results and exit poll in maps and charts."

14. See Michael Lind, *The New Class War,* 111 for a nuanced distinction between socially conservative dispositions of religious people and genuine bigotry.

more to Moses then Momentum and more to the Apostle Paul than progress and yet it is largely and functionally sundered from its religious roots.

In fact, when you consider the treatment of the former Shadow Minister for Faith, Janet Daby MP for a comment that appeared to my mind wholly reasonable it makes one reflect does the Labour Party really have space for orthodox Christians? Labour's capture by the professional managerial class has left it, at points, deeply averse to public religion.

This is a crucial point, for religious freedom is the key to human flourishing and Labour should be a party of liberty not liberalism as George Loveless,[15] of the Tolpuddle Martyrs reminded us it is liberty that is the watchword of the very movements that birthed Labour, in prison he wrote these words: "We raise the watchword Liberty, we will, we will, we will be free."[16]

The denigration of trade unions and marginalization of Christianity have been two unappealing features of recent years in the UK. In many ways Lind's analysis has stark lessons for the left in the UK.

As we consider this question it is worth posing the broader existential question: is there a great realignment taking place in politics? Is this a blip or can the Labour and Democrat parties truly prove themselves plural and embrace working class social conservatism and people of faith and their convictions? If not, maybe over time new parties could emerge. I actually think this is unlikely and would suggest as Michael Lind has argued that re alignments take place but within the existing party structures i.e. like when the US working class moved their support in part from the Democrat's to the Republicans under Nixon and Reagan. The reasons may not have been positive, but they did occur.[17]

If we are in the midst of a realignment, such as the *Red Wall*[18] infers does the Labour Party have the sense and skill to respond appropriately? What will Labour do? When a party has under half of its members based in London and the southeast and 77 percent of its members[19] belong to the ABC1 class[20] then radical action is required now.

15. "The Story," The Tolpuddle Martyrs, https://www.tolpuddlemartyrs.org.uk/story.

16. "The Story," The Tolpuddle Martyrs, https://www.tolpuddlemartyrs.org.uk/story, Line 15.

17. See Mark Stricherz, *Why the Democrats are Blue*.

18. The name given to UK parliamentary constituencies long held by Labour MPs that voted Conservative in the 2019 General Election. See Mattinson, *Beyond the Red Wall*, 17–29.

19. Bale, "Inside Labour's massive membership base," Line 23.

20. A social scientific approach to categorizing social class—https://en.wikipedia.

The question of realignment makes the questions posed by Michael Lind more pertinent and the challenge harder.

So, what is the way ahead? For Michael Lind, the way forward entails establishing a more balanced 'democratic pluralism.'[21] By actually rebuilding trade unions, restoring practices like collective bargaining and allowing space for religious organizations in the civic square can there be greater empowerment for working people? This is a constructive proposition, yet, given the turbulence of recent years the stakes are high.

More importantly, what can Christians do? The gospel is one of reconciliation and this applies to every sphere of life: economic, social and cultural. We can pray, have a mode of peacemaking and an intrinsic belief in a rich, deep equality that means all sections of society are included. I would infer this means in the polity all social classes have a place at the table. This requires action and a political program that can deliver the necessary transformation: a belief in the politics of the common good that genuinely seeks to resolve conflict by recognizing the socioeconomic reality of our common life.[22]

Can our civic and political structures model a mode of empowerment and representation that in some way mirrors the Kingdom of God?

There are some signs within the Labour tradition. My undergraduate Thesis looked at the influence of nonconformity on the Labour movement and focused in particular on Arthur Henderson MP, a Labour MP who rose to become Foreign Secretary after the Great War. He had a genuine conversion experience as a boy and made his way through the trade unions to parliament to the cabinet. Known affectionately as *Uncle Arthur*, he was key when the Labour Party nearly collapsed in the late 1920s and early 1930s.[23] To date, he is the only member of the industrial working class to have led a British political party.[24] His involvement in trade unions saw him place an emphasis upon conciliation rather than dispute. Although you could debate the tactics of such an approach carte blanche, I would suggest that

org/wiki/NRS_social_grade.

21. Lind, Class War, xv & chapter nine,"Making the World Safe for Democratic Pluralism," 146–165.

22. For a rigorous and theologically informed account of class, that takes it seriously yet delineates its limitations while reflecting on how Christian worship might subvert its detrimental impact see Luke Bretherton "Communion and Class," 201–226 in *Christ and the Common Life.*

23. Wrigley in *British Labour Leaders* eds Clarke and James.

24. McKibbin, *Arthur Henderson*, 79.

jaw, jaw, is better than war, war[25] backed upon by strong working class representation. I would submit that we need a few more *Uncle Arthurs*.

In fact, do we need to reinvent the wheel? It was institutional life, largely religious that provided the British working class with dignity and agency. Paul Mason has written an excellent article on working class culture, and education: he underlines how historically the church was a powerful social institution which strengthened working class communities.

> "Without solidarity and knowledge, we are just scum, is the lesson trade unionism and social democracy taught the working class kids of the 1960s; and Methodism and Catholicism taught the same."[26]

We believe not in class war but peace and harmony; we believe in the common life not atomization and class dominance. Yet this does not mean a disavowal of serious analysis of the inequalities and conflicts already taking place. No one would seriously—I hope—suggest that the path to racial justice does not first take stock of the deep, historical and virulent injustices experienced by African Americans and Black Britons and the class injustices that also have an impact here! Therefore, to bring about a positive Christian influence on a peaceful and plural society we need to recognize and see what has been taking place and its woeful consequences. We are not here to bless the establishment in its changing forms nor to inaugurate utopia.

If we don't act and redress this social imbalances Michael Lind suggests the outcome could be awful . . .

To be precise this needs an intentional and robust Christian approach that engages in these crucial social and political questions, to quote John Milbank: " . . . I think unless a kind of world Christendom, then the future will be dark beyond our wildest expectations."[27]

The place of churches, trade unions, housing associations and community organizing with a dynamic and constructive role in the public square is vital. However, this is not enough: these institutions need to be championing a narrative that reflects the religious, cultural, economic and

25. A quote attributed, perhaps inaccurately to Prime Minister Winston Churchill—https://winstonchurchill.org/resources/quotes/quotes-falsely-attributed/.

26. Mason, "The problem for poor, white kids is that a part of their culture has been destroyed," Lines
90–92.

27. Goldsmiths, "Interview with John Milbank," Lines 341–2.

political aspirations of the working class; in its true diversity. It requires a richer theopolitical imagination, informed by the Church as *polis*.[28]

As a friend told me simply unless you have the gospel you end up with what is grotesque. This is a sensitive topic that requires a gospel lens and a hermeneutic of reconciliation. It is time for Christians to be involved in all aspects of society and attend thoughtfully and prayerfully to ending the new class war on behalf of those at the sharp end; not through denying the felt reality of class but finding an intentional, creative and peaceful way through division and political, cultural and economic inequality. It is a message that has particular relevance on the left, given its historic mission that seems to have gone off track. Lind's insights—although focused across the pond, in significant measure—have resonance and are worth some consideration.

---

28. Hauerwas, *Good Company*, 6.

22

Blue Labour

Stories of the Common Good

This article was written to situate the *Blue Labour: Forging a New Politics* book in a specifically theological context, drawing on is critical resource, the common good. Stanley Hauerwas seemed as good a conversation partner as any to engage with for some help. I attempt to posit the theological and political power of story (narrative) as a legitimate contribution to political life.

Narratives of place and identity need stories to explicate and assert their legitimacy. In many ways Blue Labour allows these stories to find their place in political conversation, for example, consider how hard it has been for the left to afford validity to a sense of English identity as a political category.

The American theologian Stanley Hauerwas cited the Richard Adams' novel *Watership Down* to demonstrate the " . . . oral significance of narrative for construing the Christian life."[1] In an essay in which he thoughtfully unpacks this point we are instructed that: " . . . Watership Down is meant to teach us the importance of stories for social and political life."

Blue Labour: Forging a New Politics published in February 2015 is a collection of essays or stories, situated as the title suggests, in the broader story known as Blue Labour. Blue Labour offers a social and political narrative that speaks of the primacy of faith and family life, as well as those

---

1. Stanley Hauerwas, "A Story formed community" in *The Hauerwas Reader,* 172.

anchors that give working people meaning and belonging, including the value and dignity of good and meaningful work. It also honors a sense of *place* in undergirding the attachment ordinary people have to their local community. A disposition that has been degraded and tested in the modern world but still holds true for many people. It is these stories and traditions which constitute Blue Labour. Blue Labour allows these stories to be articulated and therefore offers a real opportunity for Labour to reconnect with ordinary people. Allowing those stories which secular modernity resists or disowns to be fully expressed implicitly recognizes the importance of the people who can articulate and identify with these stories.

One practical means to allow these stories to be voiced is through the discipline of community organizing. An approach central to the formation of Blue Labour. This point is well made in an essay by Arnie Graf, the American community organizer who has worked with the Labour Party in recent years. He recounts the powerful story of Marian Dixon, an African American Roman Catholic woman from Maryland who as a young girl insisted on sitting on the front row of her church much to the chagrin of local elders. After months of persistence Marian Dixon triumphed. Graf reflects:

> "She had never been involved in anything outside of her family, her parish, and the school where she taught, but her story told me all that I needed to know about her."[2]

To draw upon Hauerwas's literary device, what stories have been constituting UK political life? What has been their impact? Have these stories been truly diverse in nature? Political discourse has for too long been characterized by a secular *illiberal* variant of liberalism crowding out the narratives that constitute the lives of working people. The marginalization of faith denies many ordinary people a voice in society and a sense of agency. Liberalism's singular dominance has become *the* orthodoxy. Some who hold to their tenets appear highly uncomfortable or even unwilling to think and act beyond the progressive matrix. However, as economic and social liberalism has fragmented a vacuum has opened up. In the light of the crisis, we face new stimulants that are needed to reinvigorate democratic life and strengthen citizenship. The vacuum that opens up requires nothing less than a politics rooted in Christian theology. In fact, the alternatives are far worse. Blue Labour recognizes the need to build a generous space that includes others in the construction of a politics of the common good, seeking

---

2. Graf, "Community Organising and Blue Labour," in *Blue Labour*, 75.

a more peaceable society and fostering a nation at ease with itself and its neighbors. Many people engage with Blue Labour from a secular vantage point. Yet it is the element of faith that could prove one its most enduring features as it underpins many of the substantive themes.

Blue Labour has stimulated a debate about a range of themes, policies, practices, and institutional forms, that constitute this essay collection. These themes are rooted in the politics of the common good—an approach to politics informed by Catholic Social Teaching which resists the dominance of sectional interests in public life. For example, Jon Cruddas in reflecting on the profound challenges facing Britain writes " . . . we need to look to an idea deeply rooted in Christian life and thought. The idea of the common good."[3]

Maurice Glasman draws upon Catholic Social Teaching—a program with practical import—that can offer:

> " . . . durable materials, appropriate practices and profound insights in a synthesis which can challenge and defeat the combination of economic and political liberalism that has subordinated diversity to homogeneity, institutional mediation to individualized care packages, vocational training to transferrable skills and neglected entirely the conditions for flourishing markets and democracy."[4]
> Blue Labour is essentially about rendering life more meaningful, peaceable, and bearable for working people, without offering them false utopian dreams. Allowing people to express their stories unmediated must surely be a healthy part of democratic life and associational spaces can facilitate this process. Thus, Luke Bretherton asserts that practice comes before theory and a good apprenticeship in the craft of politics comes through the immersion in associational forms of " . . . self-organized institutions and mutual associations such as unions, churches, residents' associations, small businesses and disability support groups."[5]

These vignettes attest that Blue Labour is very much a postpolitical approach. Indeed, the UK center-left, seriously needs to explore the possibilities of building a Labour Party which accepts the limits of secularism, agile enough to think and practice its politics beyond the liberal straitjacket.

---

3. Cruddas, "The Common Good in an Age of Austerity," in *Blue Labour,*87.

4. Glasman, "The Good Society, Catholic Social Thought and the Politics of the Common Good," in *Blue Labour,*17.

5. Bretherton, "Vision, Virtue and Vocation:Notes on Blue Labour as a Practice of Politics," in *Blue Labour,* 219.

A particular Blue Labour story speaks of the future of political life in the UK reckoning with a pro-faith, postsecular and postliberal narrative. Its explicit reference to a politics of the common good, rooted in Catholic Social Teaching means it is of profound interest to genuinely orthodox Christians. It is a story rooted in a particular tradition, as Maurice Glasman has commented:

> "The Labour tradition and the Christian tradition are completely linked, and it's about protecting the status of the person from commodification and the idea that our bodies and our natural environment are just to be bought and sold. In the politics of the common good, there has never been a greater need for the gifts that the Christian tradition brings, of which the greatest is love."[6]

The General Election will see many stories being narrated. Perhaps Blue Labour will allow in time the stories to change and a different social and political conversation to emerge.

6. "Labour Pains," *Third Way,* Lines 253–259.

23

The *Underdog*

It's a Wonderful Life

In the final contribution, I include a short article about my favorite film *It's a Wonderful Life* I try and use this film as a metaphor for faith and politics. Of course, it is a story about the painful triumph of the *small man* and for football fans everywhere we love the *underdog* and perhaps this is why the film is and will always be a classic.

Whether we are celebrating Christmas for reasons of faith or otherwise we could all do a lot worse that watch the Frank Capra classic *It's a Wonderful Life*. While some see a saccharine indeed unapologetically sentimental story, it contains themes that are relevant and inspirational. As a Christian Socialist I see the story as powerful and inspiring.

The film focuses on a particular man, George Bailey, who gets to see what life would be like in his hometown had he not been born. Through supernatural help, God sends an angel, Clarence, to show him what life would have been like in Bedford Falls, had he never lived.

In essence, we see that without Bailey, a virtuous family man and communitarian owner of a building and loan company, Bedford Falls becomes corrupted at the hands of a nihilistic, cynical tyrant called Potter whose dominant desire is to make money. Many other negative things happen in Bedford Falls simply because Bailey wasn't there to prevent them or exert his influence. It's a lovely story, but is it just a lovely story? For me, at this time, when we can be more open to reflection it contains some powerful messages.

Firstly, the film reminds me that no life is worthless, Capra intentionally wanted to communicate this. We see that one life can, overtime have immense impact, without the impact of that life, who knows what can happen? What would life be like in the UK had Keir Hardie, Clem Attlee, Barbara Castle or Nye Bevan never been born?

Furthermore, we are to hold onto hope and reject cynicism. George Bailey is a hopeful person, but he is perhaps not hugely successful. Yet, he is a man of character, a man of virtue, who loves his family and is respected in the community. He is hopeful, he is a dreamer, he is a romantic rather than a rationalist and I believe Labour needs its romantics.

This is not about wishful thinking. I heard a senior colleague give a recent talk to our department at work. He said: "We face the brutal facts, but have hope." We are today surrounded by many brutal facts, but there is hope.

In addition, the Capra classic reminds us of what success really is. Our hero is not a careerist, in the film, Bailey never quite achieves all he wants to do. He is forced to stay at home and tend the family business when he would rather travel the world. He faces personal disappointment and has broken dreams. Through this painful process his real success is born, but it is not apparent. What is success for Labour? What is success for us? Is it winning or achievement or is it more than that but less perhaps obvious? Similarly, if our political purpose becomes only orientated towards winning and achievement at all costs then we lose something of value. As the film ends Clarence sends Bailey a note saying: "No man is a failure, who has friends." This reminds me that relationships should trump achievements.

The business and community ethos of Bailey is one of compassion and communitarianism. It is not one of naked individualism, or a nihilistic, predatory capitalism. His business provides people with decent homes so they can remain decent citizens. You get the impression that the business makes a surplus and values its employees, but it is not subsumed towards generating grotesque profits.

The opportunity Bailey is given; of seeing what life would have been like had he not lived is something none of us will get. He sees his town become a soulless, chaotic, dog-eat-dog place of disenchantment. Compared to a decent town with some semblance of community and where he is held in high regard. This powerfully reinforces the truth that no life is worthless, no one should be overlooked or put down. Politics can too often focus on the big picture and the abstract and ignore or crush the individual and his or her worth.

We see that in the end, there is no wealth, but life, family and friends. At Christmas time, I like to be reminded that my worth is not defined by my economic utility or achievement but has been forever changed because an extraordinary event occurred to very ordinary people two-thousand years ago—and that has changed my life.

Happy Christmas and best wishes for 2018—it really is a wonderful life.

Belonging

Questions for discussion

In the section on Belonging, I seek to explicate reflections on politics from an explicitly Christian vantage point, you might find the following questions helpful for reflection or discussion:

1. From a biblical and theological vantage point what do you make of the 'woke' phenomenon?

2. Is there a new 'class war'? If so what should be the Christian response?

3. Is 'place' an important category for Christians?

4. How should: a) the local Church engage with a sense of place? b) political parties engage with a sense of place?

5. In what ways is narrative important for politics?

6. What is your story and how does it define your political outlook?

7. What impact can community organizing have for faith communities and local politics?

Recommended Reading

John Inge, *A Christian Theology of Place: Explorations in Practical, Pastoral and Empirical Theology*, Ashgate, 2003

Michael Lind, *The New Class War: Saving Democracy from the Metropolitan Elite*, London: Atlantic Books, 2020

Luke Bretherton, *Christ and the Common Life: Political Theology and the Case for Democracy*, Grand Rapids: Eerdmans, 2019

Stanley Hauerwas, *In Good Company: The Church as Polis*, Indiana: Notre Dame, 1995

Conclusion

Towards Christian Humanism:
Seeking a more humane politics

"Christ came to heal and unify humanity, not to break it into private faith and public reason. The Christian lives in the eschatological age. In this era the secular derives its full value and relative autonomy from the same God who will eventually renew it completely. Neither radically denying the world in the light of the eschaton nor living as if this world were our only context of meaning corresponds to a properly Christian life. The Christian ethos does not dissolve the eschatological (ultimate-penultimate) tension into either fundamentalism or complacency. Christian ethics, to use Bonhoeffer's terms, should breed neither radicals nor compromisers."[1]

I offer these essays as my reflections that weave a common thread yet stretch back over a decade, rooted in faith, politics and belonging—or a blend of them—where appropriate.

As I reflect on justifiable concern with the overreach of liberalism, I am increasingly convinced this does not equate to or warrant illiberalism and an ungenerous politics. As the previous quote from Jens Zimmermann infers: Christians are called to the vision to "heal and unify humanity"[2] and it may be that an incarnational Christian, humanism can provide the resources for a fresh and hopeful political future and avoid the *scylla* and *charybdis* of extreme liberalism and extreme illiberalism. By this I mean a politics that is generous and transformative that coheres with the grain of people's experience, not imposing alien ideologies on them.

1. Zimmerman, *Incarnational Humanism*, 271.
2. Zimmerman, *Incarnational Humanism*, 271.

As a Christian I see my faith as fundamental, yet within the immanent frame I have political orientations, human interests, and feel I am outworking my faith—dialectically—in the context of these passions and attachments. Thus, this summarizes my vocation. I am grateful for a church, family and friends who remind me where my true identity lies, a "new creation,"[3] and as Stanley Hauerwas and Will Willimon would say: "a resident alien." Yet, as James K. A. Smith infers, those who are "resident" and "alien"[4] are bound to a common life, the choice is how do we live in the light of this truth. In reflecting on how I have journeyed as a *resident alien*, I have offered up some imperfect thoughts, I hope you enjoy them.

"You have searched me, Lord, and you know me. You know when I sit and when I rise; you perceive my thoughts from afar.

You discern my going out and my lying down; you are familiar with all my ways. Before a word is on my tongue you, Lord, know it completely.

You hem me in behind and before, and you lay your hand upon me. Such knowledge is too wonderful for me, too lofty for me to attain.

Where can I go from your Spirit? Where can I flee from your presence? If I go up to the heavens, you are there; if I make my bed in the depths, you are there.

If I rise on the wings of the dawn, if I settle on the far side of the sea, even there your hand will guide me, your right hand will hold me fast.

If I say: "Surely the darkness will hide me and the light become night around me, even the darkness will not be dark to you; the night will shine like the day, for darkness is as light to you.

For you created my inmost being, you knit me together in my mother's womb.

I praise you because I am fearfully and wonderfully made; your works are wonderful; I know that full well.

My frame was not hidden from you when I was made in the secret place, when I was woven together in the depths of the earth.

Your eyes saw my unformed body; all the days ordained for me were written in your book before one of them came to be."[5]

---

3. 2 Cor 5:17.

4. Smith, *Awaiting the King*, 54

5. Ps 139:1–16.

Afterword

At first glance *Faith, Politics and Belonging* appears an idiosyncratic book. It ranges across deeply unfashionable terrain, ground which remains detached from much of our modern political conversation. Where, for instance, do you hear discussion of: theology and Labour politics; and Christianity and the meaning of socialism?

Having known Ian for many years—his journey is very similar to my own—I can confirm that the book is a very personal text. His true personality and his vocation, his calling, is revealed in these pages. Such as when he writes:

"I became a Christian when I was fourteen, not too long after I had become politically aware. Essentially, my Christian and political journeys occurred during the same period . . . Over the past twenty-four-years that I have lived and explored the Christian life while being involved and active in center-left politics. On the basis of the past twenty-four-years, I expect to be on this journey for the rest of my natural life."

Ian is a supporter of Blue Labour, a movement which is much misunderstood. It is worth reminding ourselves of what this tradition actually stands for, rather than how it has been caricatured by ill-informed opponents. The term was first outlined by Maurice Glasman in 2009 to identify an exiled Labour politics that retained a "fundamental commitment to work, faith, family, and country."[1] Throughout the emphasis within this movement is on that forgotten word, fraternity, and on human relationships. Rather than focus on the traditional progressive territory of liberty

1. Rhodes, "The architect of Blue Labour: an interview with Lord Glasman," Lines 48–49.

and freedom or distributional justice and economic equality, this alternative reasserts the desire for roots—and nurturing the local and national community—and is concerned with ethics rather than questions of economic utility.

Of course, this approach did not simply emerge in 2009 with the insights of Maurice Glasman. It can be traced back much further, to figures such as: Thomas Carlyle; John Ruskin; William Morris; and—more recently—with the philosopher Alasdair MacIntyre, to name just a few.

Within the history of the British Left—and the prehistory of the Labour Party—this type of political disposition is best associated with, what is sometimes described as, the early *religion of socialism* of the late nineteenth century. Influences included dissident, *non-conformist* protestant voices—including Methodists, Baptists, Congregationalists, Quakers, and Unitarians. It also included assorted churches such as the: Brotherhood Church; the Labour Church, later renamed the Socialist Church; the Ethical Church; the Salvation Army; and Temperance Church; as well as catholic voices. It also included groups such as the Fellowship of the New Life—alongside visions of *socialist fellowship*—and the moral economy associated in particular with Ruskin and Morris. These largely forgotten pioneers of ethical socialism sought to challenge the scientific status of economics, and the separation of economic value and utility from questions of human life, and deterministic assumptions regarding modernity and the evolution of socialist society found within much early socialist economic thought.

In the critical last decades of the nineteenth century the *religion of socialism* was for many a way of life and often their work took the form of a *crusade*. The historian Stephen Yeo[2] has explained the way such advocacy often involved forms of conversion, with socialism akin to religious vocations, with activists often termed *apostles* or *evangelists* for the cause. Ian's journey always reminds me of these early political and religious activists.

Such spiritual or ethical socialist traditions are embedded within ancient traditions of thought regarding the promotion of the common good and human virtue.

Despite playing a vital role in Labour's prehistory, the significance of this ethical tradition diminished over time. It is clearly visible in the leadership of Labour under Keir Hardie, Ramsay MacDonald and George Lansbury, and the early history of the Independent Labour Party. We can locate postwar leaders—such as Clem Attlee, and John Smith—within this

---

2. Yeo, "The Religion of Socialism in Britain," 5–56.

tradition, as well as the early approach adopted by Tony Blair. In addition, as I mentioned, it has most recently reappeared in the *Blue Labour* movement that seeks to advance associational forms of life beyond the state.

A home for such a mixture of political and spiritual sentiment has over the years been the Christian Socialist Movement (CSM). Launched in 1960, CSM brought together the Socialist Christian League and the Society of Socialist Clergy and Ministers under the leadership of Donald Soper. It affiliated to Labour in 1998 and renamed as *Christians on the Left* in 2013. Throughout, it sought to uphold the early tradition of ethical socialism and questions of human virtue in Labour's debates about purpose and justice.

We can detect this ethical approach in the work of many key Labour intellectuals, such as Tawney, who figures throughout this book.

Overall, although often imprecise, these ethical or virtue based traditions of justice originate in the sphere of interpersonal and spiritual relationships and extend into the wider social realm shaping understanding of both community and economy. It offers a politics of the individual rooted in the social goods that give meaning to people's lives: home; family; friendships; good work; locality; and communities of belonging.

This tradition is Ian's political and spiritual home and this book is a vital intervention to help re-establish the ethical foundations of the British Labour Party. It is an immensely important re-statement of a belief system that historically formed the cornerstone of much British socialist thought. It could once again reanimate our political life at a time when people are crying out for a renewed sense of meaning and purpose in their lives.

I am proud of Ian for putting together this very personal collection. His contribution will endure, just as the *religion of socialism* has endured.

Jon Cruddas MP, November 2023

Glossary of terms

Blue Labour—a movement relating to the UK Labour Party that promotes the common good, the primacy of faith, relationships, vocation and a sense of place.

Catholic Social Teaching—A corpus of teaching informed by Papal encylicals that affirms the dignity of labor, a moderate approach to wealth creation, concern for the environment and sanctity of life in its fullest expression

Centre for Social Justice—a Thinktank in the UK that seeks conservative solutions to problems of social justice

Christian Socialism—a political movement in the United Kingdom that recognizes that a fundamental element of the gospel relates to social justice and equality

Christians on the Left—A Christian body affiliated to the UK Labour Party

Common Good—Hard to define precisely, this is an approach to politics that seeks to find outcomes in political and economic life that avoid the dominance of one class or group. It has its roots in Christian teaching.

Liberalism—the political, cultural, economic, political and theological movement that sees freedom as primary in all matters. It has its roots in Christianity, Renaissance Humanism and the Enlightenment

Liberation Theology—a theological approach that prioritises the voice and preference of the poor

Living Wage—a wage that is intentionally designed to support and feed a family; informed by Christian teaching it has become a feature of UK political decision making

One nation conservative—the center-right of the UK Conservative Party that seeks to cherish social harmony

Postliberalism—the political movement that recognizes that liberalism is not the singular means of securing the good life but does not support illiberalism either (not to be confused with postliberal theology associated with the Yale school).

Progressivism—the approach to politics and other aspects of culture that articulates and acts as if moving toward a perfect utopia is both desirable and possible; it is a secularized form of the Kingdom of God

'Red Wall'—In the main working-class, constituencies in England that having long voted for the Labour Party voted Conservative in the 2019 UK General Election out of deep disenchantment

Respublica—a postliberal thinktank in the UK

Social Conservatism—a disposition that values family, marriage, place and tradition and is sceptical towards overt progressivism.

Bibliography

Alliance Evangelical, "What kind of society?" https://www.eauk.org/resources/what-we-offer/reports/what-kind-of-society. 2017.

Attlee, Clement. "Leader's speech." Scarbrough, Labour Party conference 1951. http://www.britishpoliticalspeech.org/speech-archive.htm?speech=161.

BBC Radio Four. "Labour's New Jerusalem." 27 May 2013.

BBC Website. "Barack Obama Challenges Woke Culture." 30 October 2019.

———. "US Election 2020: Results and exit poll in maps and charts." 13 November 2020.

———. "Blue Labour: Party's radical answer to the Big Society?" 21 March 2011.

———. "Nick Clegg: I aim to be prime minister." 23 September 2009.

Bale, Tim. "Inside Labour's massive membership base." Labour List, 6 October 217.

Barth Karl. Editors Preface, *Church Dogmatics The Doctrine of God.* Volume 2, Part 1: "The Knowledge of God." London: T&T Clark, 1957.

Barth, Karl. *Community, State and Church—Three Essays.* Eugene, OR: Wipf & Stock, 1960.

Beale, Stephen. "The 'Mad Virtues' of a Secular Society." Catholic Exchange, 9 August 2016. https://catholicexchange.com/mad-virtues-secular-society/.

Benedict XVI. *Caritas in Veritate.* https://www.vatican.va/content/benedict-xvi/en/encyclicals/documents/hf_ben-xvi_enc_20090629_caritas-in-veritate.html.

Bentley-Hart, David. *The New Testament: A Translation.* New Haven, CT: Yale University Press, 2017.

Berger, Peter L. "The Desecularization of the World: A Global Overview." in *The Desecularization of the World: Resurgent Religion and World Politics*, edited by Peter L. Berger, 1–18. Grand Rapids, MI: Eerdmans, 1999.

Beck, Richard. "Democracy and the Demonization of the Good." Experimental Theology, 23 February 2017. http://experimentaltheology.blogspot.com/2017/02/democracy-and-demonization-of-good.html.

Bewes, Richard. "A Nation at the Crossroads." *Decision Magazine*, 20 January 2017.

Bickerton, Chris. "Arrogant Remainers Want a Second Vote: That Would Be a Bad Day For Democracy." *The Guardian*, 16 January 2019. https://www.theguardian.com/global/commentisfree/2019/jan/16/second-brexit-referendum-mps-democracy-peoples-vote.

Bickley, Paul. *Building Jerusalem: Christianity and the Labour Party*. The British and Foreign Bible Society, UK, 2010. https://ccfe.uk/wp-content/uploads/2020/01/partisan-lab.pdf.

Blair, Tony. "Speech by UK Prime Minister at the Meeting of the NATO-Russia Council." 28 May 2002. https://www.nato.int/cps/en/natolive/opinions_19840.htm.

Bonhoeffer, Dietrich. *London: 1933-1935*. Edited by Hans Goedeking et al., trans. Isabel Best and Douglas W. Stott, 284–285. Vol. 13, *Dietrich Bonhoeffer Works*. Minneapolis, MN: Fortress, 2007.

Bono. Quotemaster. https://www.quotemaster.org/q0de01a6102b14da73d0a8063f18dd176.

Booth, William. "New York World." 30 December 1900.

Bradley, Anthony. "'The new legalism." World. https://world.wng.org/2013/05/the_new_legalism/? in "What Is Flourishing?" Hugh Whelchel, May 20, 2013. https://tifwe.org/what-is-flourishing/.

Blair, Tony. "Leaders Speech." Labour Party Conference Bournemouth 1999, British Political Speech Archive. 1999. http://www.britishpoliticalspeech.org/speech-archive.htm?speech=205.

———. "Labour Party Conference Speech." Labour Party Conference Blackpool 2002, British Political Speech Archive, 2002.

Blond, Phillip. "Foreword." In *Changing the Debate: The Ideas Redefining Britain*. Respublica, July 2011.

Bongiorno, Frank. *Blue Labour: Lessons for Australia*. School of History, Research School of Social Sciences Australian National University, Australian Fabian Society, ACT Branch, Smiths Alternative Bookshop, Canberra 19 April 2012.

Bonnette, Kathleen. "Catholics: Embrace being 'woke.' It's part of our faith tradition." *America: The Jesuit Review*, 26 May 2021. https://www.americamagazine.org/politics-society/2021/05/26/wokeness-pastoral-cycle-see-judge-act-240639?utm_source=piano&utm_medium=email&utm_campaign=9886&pnespid=6_c4ViobZ f8EwqnHpjrlGImF5kKjCsUqNPajz.Rj8xZmi7WiEUki2MIEAdozcWyQ5ovlDhrW.

Bretherton, Luke. *Christ and the Common Life—Political Theology and the Case for Democracy*. Grand Rapids, MI: Eerdmans, 2019.

———. "Vision, Virtue and Vocation: Notes on Blue Labour as a Practice of Politics." In *Blue Labour: Forging a New Politics*, edited by Ian Geary and Adrian Pabst, 217–233. London: IB Tauris, 2015.

Brockway, Fenner. *The life of Alfred Salter—Bermondsey Story*. London: George, Allen and Unwin, 1949.

Butler, Patrick. "Cutting benefits harms mental health and hits most vulnerable hardest, says study." *The Guardian*, 2 February 2021.

Brown, Malcolm et al. *Anglican Social Theology—Renewing the vision today*. London: Church House, 2014.

Brown, Malcolm. "Malcolm Brown asks: what do we value in hard times?" *Bishop's Blog*, 23rd March 2012. https://bpdt.wordpress.com/2012/03/23/malcolm-brown-asks-what-do-we-value-in-hard-times/.

Brueggemann, Walter. *The Land: Place as gift, promise and challenge in the Bible*. 2nd ed. Minneapolis: Fortress, 2002.

———. *Truth Speaks to Power—The Countercultural Nature of Scripture*. Kentucky: Westminster John Knox, 2013.

Byrne, Liam. "New Foundations for a New Beveridge: The Right and Responsibility to Work." 9th March 2012.

Centre for Social Justice. "Healing a Divided Britain." October 2016. https://www.centreforsocialjustice.org.uk/library/4852-healing-a-divided-britain.

"The Common Good and the Catholic Church's Social Teaching: A Statement by the Catholic Bishops Conference of England and Wales." London: The Catholic Churches Bishops Conference, of England and Wales, 1996. https://cbcew.org.uk/plain/wp-content/uploads/sites/3/2018/11/common-good-1996.pdf.

Christian Concern. "The cancel culture: the intolerance of the tolerance agenda." 10 July 2021. https://christianconcern.com/comment/the-cancel-culture-the-intolerance-of-the-tolerance-agenda/.

Christians in Parliament. "Faith in the Community:strengthening ties between faith groups and local authorities." June 2013, http://2019.christiansinparliament.org.uk/wp-content/uploads/2019/02/Faith-in-the-community-FINAL.pdf

Christians on the Left. "We need to talk about relationships." 29 August 2017.https://www.youtube.com/watch?v=CeiiS62ckZo&t=6s.

The Centre for Theology and Community, "What is Community Organising?" http://www.theology-centre.org.uk/what-is-community-organising/.

Coffey, John. "To release the oppressed: Reclaiming a biblical theology of liberation." Cambridge Papers, Jubilee Centre, Volume 18, Number 4, December 2009.

Comer, John Mark. "Where can Progressive Christianity Lead?" Q Ideas, December 1, 2020.

Connolly, William E. "Why I am not a Secularist." University of Minnesota, 2000.

Cruddas, Jon. "George Lansbury:The unsung Father of Blue Labour." Labour Uncut, 8 May 2011.

———. "The Common Good in an Age of Austerity." in *Blue Labour: Forging a New Politics*, 87- 95, eds Ian Geary and Adrian Pabst, I.B. Tauris, London, 2015.

———. "The Common Good in an Age of Austerity." Ebor Lecture York St John, 9 July 2014.

———. "UKIP isn't a Tory movement. It's a party of the disenfranchised English." The Guardian, 8 May 2014.

Cruddas et al. "Labour's Future—Why Labour lost in 2015 and how it can win again—Report of the independent inquiry into why Labour lost in 2015." https://www.scribd.com/doc/313245238/Labour-s-Future-19-05-16, May 2015.

Cruddas, Jon, and Jonathan Rutherford. "Common Life: Ethics, Class, Community." In *The crisis of Global Capitalism: Pope Benedict XVI's Social Encyclical and the future of political economy*, edited by Adrian Pabst. Eugene, OR: Wipf & Stock, 2011.

Curran, John Philpot. "The speeches of the Right Honourable John Philpot Curran" Speech upon the Right of Election for Lord Mayor of Dublin, 1790, as quoted in Bartlett's Familiar Quotations

Darlington, Richard. "The strange death and rebirth of Blue Labour." Progress Online, 27 September 2012.

Davensport, Weddings. "Wedding traditions explained: something old, something new, something borrowed, something blue." https://danversport.com/weddings/blog/wedding-traditions-explained/, 11 April 2018.

Davis, Rowenna. "Labour needs to rediscover its conservatism." The New Statesman, 20th April 2012.

Donald Peta, Iggulden Tom and staff reporters. ABC News, "Howard, Rudd woo Christians online." 10 August 2007.

Dreher, Rod. *The Benedict Option—A Strategy for Christians in a Post-Christian Nation*, Penguin Random House LLC, New York, 2017.

Ekblad, Bob. *Pledging Allegiance to the Kingdom of God: A New Christian Manifesto.*, Westminster John Knox,:Louiseville, Kentucky, 2008.

Elliott, Larry. "The establishment is trying to keep us in the EU." Spiked Online, https://www.spiked-online.com/2018/10/19/the-establishment-is-trying-to-keep-us-in-the-eu/amp/. 19 October 2019.

Field, Frank. "The Foundation Years: Preventing Poor Children Becoming Poor Adults." Independent Review of Poverty and Life Chance, Final Report, December 2010.

Ford, Robert, and Goodwin Matthew. "Ukip has divided the left, not the right, and cut Labour off from its 'old' support." *The Guardian*, 16 May 2014.

Freeman, Des. "Was it 'the Sun wot won it'? Lessons from the 1992 and 2015 elections." Open Democracy, https://www.opendemocracy.net/en/opendemocracyuk/was-it-sun-wot-won-it-press-influence-in-1992-and-2015-elections/. 12 May 2015.

Garnett, Mark. *The Snake that Swallowed its Tail:Some Contradictions in Modern Liberalism*, London: Imprint Academic, 2004.

Geary, Ian. "Blue Labour And Post-Liberalism." Together for the Common Good, https://togetherforthecommongood.co.uk/leading-thinkers/blue-labour-and-post-liberalism, 17 February 2014.

———., "Reflections on Post-Liberalism and Post-Liberal Politics." COTL website, http://www.christiansontheleft.org.uk/reflections_on_post. 22 July 2014.

Glasman, Maurice. "The Good Society, Catholic Social Thought and the Politics of the Common Good." In *Blue Labour: Forging a New Politics*, 13- 26, eds Ian Geary and Adrian Pabst, IB Tauris: London, 2015.

———. "Catholic Social Thought and the Economics of the Common Good." 10 October 2019. https://www.commongoodfoundation.org.uk/our-work/catholic-social-thought-and-the-economics-of-the-common-good.

———. Chelmsford Cathedral, The Keene Lectures 2010, Re-inventing the Weal, Lecture 1: "In the Rich Man's World." 3 November 2010.

———. CSM's Annual Tawney Dialogue, "Creating the Good Society: How Then Shall We Live?" 30 March 2011.

———. "Faith in the Public Square." Journal of Missional Practice, Issue Four, Spring 2013.

———. "We need to talk about Keynes—and his Viagra economics." The Guardian, 8 July 2012.

———. "Labour Pains." interview by Nick Spencer, Third Way, March 2012.

———. "My Blue Labour vision can defeat the coalition." The Observer, 24 April 2011.

Glenn, Mary. "Jeremiah 29 a Biblical Framework for Place." Fuller Studio, https://fullerstudio.fuller.edu/sidebar/jeremiah-29-a-biblical-framework-for-place/.

Gomez, Archbishop. "Reflections on the Church and America's New Religions." address to the Congress of Catholics and Public Life in Madrid, National Catholic Register, https://www.ncregister.com/commentaries/archbishop-gomez-reflections-on-the-church-and-america-s-new-religions. 4 November 2021.

Goodhart, David. "A 'liberal racist'? Me? I felt like a heretic." Standpoint, September 2013.

———., "The next big thing? Blue Labour and Red Tory: the age of post-liberalism." Prospect Magazine, 21st September 2011.

———., *The road to somewhere—The New Tribes Shaping British Politics*, Penguin: United Kingdom, 2017.

———., "Welcome to the post-Liberal majority." The Financial Times, 11th May 2012.

Gumbel, Nicky. "Bible in One Year." 15 November 2016.

Graf, Arnie. "Community Organising and Blue Labour." in *Blue Labour: Forging a New Politics*, 71–78, eds Ian Geary and Adrian Pabst, IB Tauris: London 2015.

Greene Colin and Robinson Martin. *Metavista: Bible, Church and Mission in an Age of Imagination*, Authentic Media, 2008.

Groody, Daniel. "Crossing the Divide: Foundations of a Theology of Migration and Refugees." *Theological Studies* 70 (2009) 638–667.

The Guardian. "Clause IV at Twenty: Tony Blair changes the Labour Party constitution." https://www.theguardian.com/politics/from-the-archive-blog/2015/apr/29/clause-four-labour-party-tony-blair-20-1995 29 April 2015.

Hauerwas, Stanley. "A Story formed community: Reflections on Watership Down." In *The Hauerwas Reader*, edited by John Berkman and Michael Cartwright. Durham, NC: Duke University Press, 2001.

———. Commencement Lecture, University of Aberdeen, "Stanley Hauerwas: Don't Lie." 2017.

———. *In Good Company: The Church as Polis*, Indiana: Notre Dame, 1995.

———. "Is Democracy Capable Of Cultivating A Good Life? What Liberals Should Learn From The Shepherds." Stanley Hauerwas website, https://stanleyhauerwas.org/is-democracy-capable-of-cultivating-a-good-life-what-liberals-should-learn-from-shepherds/. 2 November 2016.

———. "The politics of the church and the humanity of God." *ABC Religion & Ethics*, 18 June 2012. https://www.abc.net.au/religion/the-politics-of-the-church-and-the-humanity-of-god/10100464.

Hauerwas, Stanley, and Richard Bondi. "Memory, Community, and the Reasons for Living:Reflections on Suicide and Euthanasia." In *The Hauerwas Reader*, edited by John Berkman and Michael Cartwright. Durham, NC: Duke University Press, 2001.

Hauerwas, Stanley, and Pinches Charles. *Christians among the Virtues: Theological Conversations with Ancient and Modern ethics*, University of Notre Dame Press, 1997.

Hauerwas, Stanley, and William H. Willimon. *Resident Aliens: Life in the Christian Colony*. Nashville: Abingdon, 1989.

Hargreaves, Deborah. "Pay inequality is suffocating Britain's economic recovery—and our society." *The Guardian*, 13 May 2014.

Harris, John. "These horror stories offer the left home truths." *The Guardian*, 15 March 2010.

Hattersley, Roy. *Blood and Fire: William and Catherine Booth and their Salvation Army*. London: Abacus, 2000.

Hays, Richard B. *The moral vision of the New Testament: Community, Cross, New Creation: A contemporary introduction to New Testament Ethics*. Edinburgh: T&T Clark, 1997.

Hinsliff, Gaby. "Kathleen Stock: 'On social media, the important thing is to show your tribe that you have the right morals.'" *The Observer*, 5 December 2021. https://www.theguardian.com/uk-news/2021/dec/05/kathleen-stock-interview-university-sussex-transgender-headlines-2021.

House of Bishops' Pastoral Letter on the 2015 General Election. The Church of England, 17 February 2015.

Hunter, Paul. "Labour's Missing Millions." *Shifting Grounds*, 11 April 2012.

HOASM. "The Peasant's Revolt in England (1381)."

Inge, John. *A Christian Theology of Place: Explorations in Practical, Pastoral and Empirical Theology*. Ashgate, 2003.

International Churchill Society. "Quotes Falsely Attributed to Winston Churchill." https://winstonchurchill.org/resources/quotes/quotes-falsely-attributed/.

International Co-operative Alliance. "The Rochdale Pioneers." https://ica.coop/en/rochdale-pioneers.

Fraser, Giles. "Assisted Dying is the equivalent of a zero- hours contract with life." 28 August 2015. https://www.theguardian.com/commentisfree/belief/2015/aug/28/assisted-dying-is-the-equivalent-of-a-zero-hours-contract-with-life.

Goldsmiths: University of London. "Interview: John Milbank." https://www.gold.ac.uk/faithsunit/current-projects/reimaginingreligion/landmark-interviews/john-milbank/.

Jones, Owen. "The cladding scandal reveals how Britain treats its poorest people." *The Guardian*, 2 February 2021. https://www.theguardian.com/commentisfree/2021/feb/02/cladding-scandal-britain-treats-poorest-people-grenfell-tower.

Jubilee 2000. Wikipedia. https://en.wikipedia.org/wiki/Jubilee_2000.

Katwala, Sunder. "Burke, Norman and Glasman—'post-liberalism' in Britain today." Open Democracy, 18 July 2013.

Keller, Tim. *Generous Justice—How God's Grace Makes us Just*. London: Hodder and Stoughton, 2010.

Kuhrt, Jon. "The Unpredicted Tinderbox3 factors which fuelled the riots." Resistance and Renewal, 9 August 2011. http://jonkuhrt.wordpress.com/.

Labour List, Corbyn, Jeremy. Jeremy Corbyn Speech to Labour Party Conference, "Corbyn praised for slamming online abuse in conference speech." September 29, 2015.

Labour List. "100 Years On—Keir Hardie without a childhood." 26 September 2015.

Lammy, David. *Out of the Ashes—Britain after the Riots*. London: Guardian, 2011.

Laudato Si' Movement. "Social encyclicals: Catholic lens on the world's social issues." 11 May 2022. https://laudatosimovement.org/news/social-encyclicals-catholic-lens-on-the-worlds-social-issues/.

Leech, Kenneth. *Through our Long Exile*. London: Darton, Longman and Todd, 2001.

Leithart, Peter. "Global Wokeness?" Theopolis Institute, October 14, 2020. https://theopolisinstitute.com/leithart_post/global-wokeness/.

Latham, Mark Hon. "Inaugural Speech." Legislative Council Hansard, 8 May 2019. www.parliament.nsw.gov.au.

Leithart, Peter. "Carnival in the Capitol." President's Essay, Theopolis, January 11, 2021.

Lind, Michael. *The New Class War: Saving Democracy from the Metropolitan Elite*. London: Atlantic, 2020.

Lowman, Pet., *A long way east of Eden—could God explain the mess we're in*. Milton Keynes: Paternoster, 2002.

Major, John. "A nation at ease with itself?" 11 November 2015, NCVO.

Macaes, Bruno. *The Dawn of Eurasia: On the Trail of the New World Order*. London: Penguin, 2019.

MacIntyre, Alasdair. *After Virtue: A Study in Moral Theory*. 3rd ed. London: Duckworth, 1985.

Mason, Paul. "The problem for poor, white kids is that a part of their culture has been destroyed." *The Guardian*, 4 April 2016. https://www.theguardian.com/commentisfree/2016/apr/04/the-problem-for-poor-white-kids-is-that-a-part-of-their-culture-has-been-destroyed.

Mattingly, Terry. "After 70 years, It's (still) a Wonderful (Catholic) Life in Frank Capra's epic." December 6, 2016, https://www.tmatt.net/columns/2016/11/30/after-70-years-its-still-a-wonderful-catholic-life-in-frank-capras-epic.

Mattinson, Deborah. *Beyond the Red Wall—Why Labour lost, How the Conservatives Won and What Will Happen Next?* London: Biteback, 2020.

Mayor of London. "London Living Wage." https://www.london.gov.uk/programmes-strategies/business-and-economy/london-living-wage.

McGuinness, Feargal. "Social Background of MPs." House of Commons Library Paper, 14th December 2010.

McKibbin, R. "Arthur Henderson as Labour Leader." *International Review of Social History*, 23.1 (1978) 79–101. doi:10.1017/S0020859000005708.

Meilaender, Gilbert. "Keeping Company." First Things, October 1996. https://www.firstthings.com/article/1996/10/002-keeping-company.

Merton, Thomas. *Conjectures of a Guilty Bystander*, Garden City, NY: Doubleday, 1966.

Meyer, F.B. *The Secret of Guidance*. Fleming H.Revell Company, New York, Chicago, Toronto, 1896. https://www.ccel.org/m/meyer/guidance/guidance.htm.

Metcalf, Samuel F. and Prince, Darren. "People First: The Human Redemptive Priority." Novo Mission Org, Anaheim, California, 2018.

Mirzaei, Abas. "Where 'woke' came from and why marketers should think twice before jumping on the social activism bandwagon." *The Conversation*, 8 September 2019. ://theconversation.com/where-woke-came-from-and-why-marketers-should-think-twice-before-jumping-on-the-social-activism-bandwagon-122713.

Monbiot, George. "If you think we're done with neoliberalism, think again." *The Guardian*, 14 January 2013.

Morgan, Kenneth O. "Labour's Greatest Hero." *The Guardian*, 19 September 2008.

Norman, Jesse. "Tory Rising Star, On Boris, Burke and His Row With Cameron." *Huffington Post*, 8 August 2013. http://www.huffingtonpost.co.uk/2013/08/08/jesse-norman_n_3726375.html.

Novak, Michael. "Social Justice: Not what you think it is." The Heritage Foundation, 29 December 2009. https://www.heritage.org/poverty-and-inequality/report/social-justice-not-what-you-think-it,

NRS Social Grade. https://en.wikipedia.org/wiki/NRS_social_grade.

Oliver, Neil. "The relentless erosion of Christmas, and Christianity itself, is essential for those whose mission it is to unmake Britain, says Neil Oliver." *GB News*, 3 December 2022. https://www.gbnews.com/opinion/the-relentless-erosion-of-christmas-and-christianity-itself-is-essential-for-those-whose-mission-it-is-to-unmake-britain-says-neil-oliver/400670.

Ortberg, John. Review of *Soul Keeping—Caring for the most important part of you*, Zondervan, April 2014, quote by Dallas Willard, *Soul Keeping*, dwillard.org.

Oxford Reference. Overview: sense of place. https://www.oxfordreference.com/display/10.1093/oi/authority.20110803100454793#:~:text=%27Sense%20of%20place%E2%80%A6is%20an,)%20GeoForum%2022%2C203).

Oxford Reference: Zhou Enlai (Chou En Lai) 1898–1976, Chinese Communist statesman, Prime Minister 1949–76. https://www.oxfordreference.com/display/10.1093/acref/9780191826719.001.0001/q-oro-ed4–00018657.

Oxfam Report. "Richest 1% bagged 82% of the wealth created last year." 22 January 2018.

Pabst, Adrian. "Christianity ended the cold war peacefully." *The Guardian*, 11 November 2009.

———. "Introduction: The Future of Political Economy." In *The Crisis of Global Capitalism: Pope Benedict XVI's Social Encyclical and the Future of Political Economy*, by Adrian Pabst. Eugene, OR: Wipf & Stock, 2011.

Packiam, Glenn. "Is the Church Too "Woke?" A Letter from N. T. Wright, 27 March 2021. https://www.glennpackiam.com/post/is-the-church-too-woke-a-letter-from-n-t-wright.

Paytner, Neil. *The Still Small Voice: A Book for Busy People*. Glasgow: Wild Goose, 2012.

Peccorelli, Nick. "The New Electorate: Why Understanding Values Is The Key To Electoral success." Institute for Public Policy Research, October 2013. http://www.cultdyn.co.uk/ART067736u/new-electorate-voter-values_Oct2013_11359.pdf.

Perkins, Anne. Barbara Castle, Obituary, 4 May 2002. https://www.theguardian.com/politics/2002/may/03/obituaries.anneperkins.

Polyani, Karl. *The Great Transformation: the political and economic origins of our time*. Boston: Beacon Press, 2002.

"Vox populi, vox Dei." https://en.wikipedia.org/wiki/Vox_populi#Vox_populi,_vox_Dei.

Purnell, James. "Where is the vitality and vision to win?" *The Guardian*, 10 January 2010.

Rebanks, James. *The Shepherd's Life: A Tale of the Lake District*. United Kingdom: Penguin, 2016.

Reimer, Johannes. *Missio Politica: The Mission of Church and Politics*. Langham Global Library, 2017.

Respublica. "Holistic Mission: Social action and the Church of England." 10 July 2013, https://www.respublica.org.uk/our-work/publications/holistic-mission-social-action-church-england/.

Rhodes, Mandy. "The architect of Blue Labour: an interview with Lord Glasman." 4 February 2015. www.holyrood.com.

Roosevelt, Theodore. "Citizenship in a Republic," Speech at the Sorbonne, Paris, April 23, 1910. https://www.presidency.ucsb.edu/node/346006.

Rosenthal, Alexander. "Reinhold Niebuhr and the Crisis of Liberalism: Augustinian Realism and Democratic Politics in the Post-Enlightenment." In *From Political Theory to Political Theology—Religious Challenges and the Prospects of Democracy*, edited by Peter Losonczi and Aakash Singh. London: Continuum, 2010.

Rowlands, Anna. "Post-liberal Politics and the Churches." *Crucible: The Christian Journal of Social Ethics* (Jan–Mar 2014).

Rudd, Kevin. "The Global Financial Crisis." *The Monthly*, February 2009.

———. "Faith in Politics." *The Monthly*, October 2006.

———. Wikipedia. https://en.wikipedia.org/wiki/Kevin_Rudd.

Russell, Bertrand. "Why I am not a Christian." Touchstone, 1967.

Rutherford, Jonathon. "Nigel Farage and Our Democratic Nation." 9 July 2019. https://www.bluelabour.org/2019/05/18/nigel-farage-and-our-democratic-nation/.

Rutledge, Fleming. *The Crucifixion—Understanding the Death of Jesus Christ*. Grand Rapids: Eerdmans, 2015.

"Thin Places, Holy Spaces: Where Do You Encounter God?" A Sacred Journey: practicing pilgrimage at home and abroad. https://www.asacredjourney.net/thin-places/.

Sayers, Mark. "We do not have a plan, but we have the person of Jesus." Global 2020, Kings Church London, 26 November 2020. https://vimeo.com/483965583.

Schluter, Michael. "Is Capitalism morally bankrupt? Five moral flaws and their social consequences." *Cambridge Papers* 18.3 (Sep 2009).

Shelter launches new social housing commission, 23 January 2018. https://england.shelter.org.uk/media/press_release/shelter_launches_new_social_housing_commission.

Sheppard, David. *Bias to the Poor*. London: Hodder and Stoughton, 1984.

Sirs, Bill. *Hard Labour*. London: Sidgwick and Jackson, 1985.

Smith, James K. A. *Desiring the Kingdom: Worship, Worldview and Cultural Formation (Cultural Liturgies)*. Ada, MI: Baker Academic, 2009.

The Social Mobility Commission. "The State of the Nation." 2017.

Solzhenitsyn, Alexandr. "A World Split Apart." Harvard University, American Rhetoric—Online Speech Bank. 8 June 1978. https://www.americanrhetoric.com/speeches/alexandersolzhenitsynharvard.htm.

Spencer, Nick. "The future of welfare: a Theos Collection." 2014.

Statesman New. "Leader: Liberalism now feels inadequate in this new age of insecurity: The stakes could not be higher." 27 March 2013.

Stott, John. *Issues Facing Christians Today*. 4th Edition., Grand Rapids, MI: Zondervan, 2006.

Stricherz, Mark. *Why the Democrats are Blue: How Secular Liberals Hijacked The People's Party*. New York: Encounter, 2007.

Suriano, Ben. "Three Questions on Modern Atheism: An Interview with John Milbank." In *God is Dead" and I Don't Feel So Good Myself: Theological Engagements with the New Atheism*, by Andrew David et al. Eugene, OR: Wipf and Stock, 2010. https://view.officeapps.live.com/op/view.aspx?src=http%3A%2F%2Ftheologyphilosophycentre.co.uk%2Fpapers%2FMilbank_SurianoInterview.doc&wdOrigin=BROWSELINK.

Tawney, R. H. "Commonplace Book." In *The British Political Tradition Volume Two: The Ideological Heritage*, by W.H. Greenleaf. New York: Methuen, 1983.

Taylor, Matthew. "Catholic teaching: The new zeitgeist for Britain's Left." BBC Radio 4 Analysis, 5th November 2012.

Together for the Common Good. "The Plague and the Parish: An Invitation To The Churches." 29 May 2020. https://togetherforthecommongood.co.uk/news/an-invitation-to-the-churches.

"Tolpuddle Martyrs: The Story." https://www.tolpuddlemartyrs.org.uk/story.

The Trussell Trust. "UK Foodbank Use Continues to Rise." 25 April 2017. https://www.trusselltrust.org/2017/04/25/uk-foodbank-use-continues-rise/#:~:text=UK%20foodbank%20use%20continues%20to%20rise%20as%20new%20report%20highlights,past%20year%20%E2%80%93%20436%2C000%20to%20children.

Wallis, Jim,=. "What Is The Circle Of Protection?" *Sojourners*, 28 April 2011. https://sojo.net/articles/what-circle-protection.

Walker, Andrew G., and Robin A. Parry. *'Deep Church Rising: Recovering the Roots of Christian Orthodoxy."* LondonI Society for Promoting Christian Knowledge, 2014.

Ware, Kallistos. "Afterword." in *A silent action: engagements with Thomas Merton*, by Rowan Williams. London SPCK, 2013.

Wick, Julia. "Homecoming and Pain: On the Etymology of Nostalgia." Longreads, 14 August 2014. https://longreads.com/2014/08/14/homecoming-and-pain-on-the-etymology-of-nostalgia.

Williams, Rowan. *Faith in the Public Square*. London: Bloomsbury, 2012.

———. "Knowing our Limits." In *Crisis and Recovery: Ethics, Economics and Justice*, by Williams and Elliot, 19–34. Basingstoke: Palgrave Macmillan, 2010.

Wright, N.T. "Walking to Emmaus in a Postmodern World." In *The Challenge of Jesus: Rediscovering Who Jesus Was and Is*. Downers Grove, IL: InterVarsity, 1999. from 'Walking to Emmaus' worldviewpublications.org, Prequel 2000.7, copyright 2000.

Wright, Tom. *Surprised by Hope*. London: SPCK, 2007.

Wrigley, Chris. In *British Labour Leaders*, edited by Charles Clarke and Toby S. James. Westminster: Biteback, 2015.

Values Modes. Wikipedia. https://en.wikipedia.org/wiki/Values_Modes#:~:text=The%20 Values%20Modes%20model%20was,%3A%20Settlers%2C%20Prospectors%20 and%20Pioneers.

Yeo, Stephen. "The Religion of Socialism in Britain." 1883–1896.' *History Workshop Journal* 4.1 (1977).

Zimmermann, Jens. *Incarnational Humanism: A Philosophy of Culture for the Church in the World*. Downers Grove, IL: InterVarsity, 2012.

Author Index

Subject Index